INTO THE EAST
Three Journeys Through India & Nepal

Christopher M. Ochs

KITSAP
PUBLISHING

Into the East: Three Journeys Through India & Nepal
First edition, published 2018

Copyright © 2018, Christopher M. Ochs

Paperback ISBN-13: 978-1-942661-98-6

All rights reserved. No part of this book may be reproduced or transmitted in any form or by any means, electronic or mechanical, including photocopying, recording or by any information storage and retrieval system, without written permission from the author, except for the inclusion of brief quotations in a review.

Published by Kitsap Publishing
P.O. Box 572
Poulsbo, WA 98370
www.KitsapPublishing.com

To Parkash

My dear friend, knight in shining tuk-tuk, brother from another land, and the perfect embodiment of the warmth and welcome of India and Nepal.

Preface

This book did not begin as a book; rather, it originated as articles (what is now *An Introduction to India* and *A Return to India: Culture, Inclusion & the Trek to Agra*) for my blog. By the time I realised both were too long to be traditional articles, I was planning my third trip to India (with the possibility of going to Nepal). While the first two parts were written from memory and photographic notes, I took very seriously the intention of writing at length about this third journey given I was on holiday on my own dime and free to explore. I had more time to revisit a small piece of a country I had seen before and allow my journalistic curiosity shape a broader, richer experience to memorialise. That's when I decided to take what I had written before and add what would later become *There Is No Time Like the Present*—what is an account of living like an honourary citizen to balance the former two journeys written as an amateur tourist.

The purpose of this book is to impart my experiences as a Westerner visiting the aptly regarded *exotic* East. This book is not intended as a travel guide, though many of my experiences may serve as tips and wisdom for first-time travellers to India and Nepal, specifically Delhi and Kathmandu, respectively. The book was written in the spirit of discovery from a Westerner's point of view and in what I hope is sufficient detail to allow readers to live vicariously, finding inspiration and piqued curiosity about the culture, daily life, people, and traditions I encountered. And perhaps, if I did my job well, you will want to travel to these places yourself.

Both *An Introduction to India* and *A Return to India* were written after I returned from business trips to India. The nature of the business that brought me to the country was related to, as of this writing, the last four years working as a patent paralegal (though, my Legal experience goes back another eight years). I am grateful and thrilled that working in this industry led me to travel overseas for the first time, but writing about the time abroad was of utmost importance to me. On weekends of my arrivals and after each workday on both trips, I had to get out and immerse myself in the foreign surroundings. The five-star lodging was only useful to me for sleeping and personal care while the decadence was only inauthentic sanctuary for visitors. Beyond the walls of hotels was where I preferred to be.

Aside from a love of descriptive writing, I also wanted to share with readers a few of my many interests, namely fibre arts, journalism, and typewriters—all of which were part of my travels. I found myself fascinated with fibre arts in 2009, beginning with crochet, then spinning yarn, knitting, and finally, weaving. Journalism, hand-in-hand with my love of writing, may have evolved from attentive journalling since my teens and an innate compulsion to document the world around me. Introduced to foreign travel, it was natural to write about the experiences. Typewriters—in my mind, perfect machines for journalistic writing with a tactile experience akin to fibre arts— provide a great deal of fascination for me. My exposure to and use of these mechanical wonders began well before my interest in fibre arts and journalism. There was Mom's electric Brother as a child, then buying my first manual typewriter at a neighbour's garage sale for 50 cents (a Remington Standard from the 1950s), then, as an adult, buying my first manual portable typewriter (a 1945 Smith-Corona Clipper) in mint condition. After four years of only mild fascination with and use of the Clipper, 'typewriter fever' inexplicably and unexpectedly took hold in March 2016 and has been an obsession since.

Typewriters, in fact, were instrumental in the writing of the third part of this book, *There Is No Time Like the Present*. By the time I started to write this section, I was already heavily into collecting typewriters, so it made sense to put my machines to use to write the rest of the book. Aside from using my typewriter collection for letters and notes, they are wonderful machines for creative writing and set a pace that requires me to slow down and write contemplatively instead of carelessly speed-writing. There was no one machine I used for this section's manuscript either. I used a great number of my typewriters for composition, selecting each one depending on which I gravitated to before every writing session, and whether I was typing indoors at my desk or out on my deck. Aside from their nostalgic charm, I prefer drafting on typewriters for the following reasons: 1) I don't have to worry about losing data (I just have to make sure hardcopies aren't destroyed by fire or flood), 2) I feel that they inspire and draw *from me* where as one *feeds* data into a computer, 3) the tactile ink-on-paper process makes me feel more connected to my writing in a visceral way, 4) they force you to separate the editor-you from the writer-you so that you aren't interrupted by prompts to edit while you're just trying to get the words out, and 5) with proper care, typewriters will last generations (as many already have) and *out*last our digital devices.

Aside from writing the book, the biggest challenge I faced was converting the typewritten manuscript into digital format…*manually.* While *An Introduction to India* and *A Return to India* were initially drafted in *Word*, the typewritten draft of *There Is No Time Like the Present* amounted to 200 double-spaced pages. Followed by handwritten edits, notes, and scribbles between the lines, the hardcopy was ready for transcription into *Word*. The reasons I didn't first scan the hardcopy through optical character recognition (OCR) were that the manuscript already had copious X-overs, but more importantly, the manual transcription process was another intentional layer of editing; it was the last intimate editing phase between paper and pixels before everything was in digital format. After the entirety of *Into the East* was in *Word*, it was sent out for final edits. What I also love about having a wildly-marked-up hardcopy of my rough draft is that I have all my initial changes in one place as a record of my thought process. *Word* has 'Track Changes' and other editing software has similar features, but there is a story in an author's handwritten notes and revisions that preserves the human element of the writing process.

Since setting foot in Delhi for the first time on May 30, 2015, *Into the East* has been over a three-year-long project. Each of the three journeys has left me profoundly changed—humbled, grateful, and with incurable wanderlust. I am also changed as a writer. Having travelled to two extraordinary countries with the intention to write has given me a comfortable foundation to continue travel writing. I wish to keep the momentum and travel somewhere new in the world after each project. As differently as I feel now compared to before I took my first journey overseas, I look forward to further enlightenment, inspiration, and stories to share of the world. India and Nepal were a splendid beginning.

Namaste.

An Introduction to India

*"Live as if you were to die tomorrow.
Learn as if you were to live forever."*
-Mahatma Gandhi

The day I learned I was being sent to India for work, I wasn't sure what to do with all the excitement. It was an ordinary day when my boss sent me an instant message notifying me of the decision. It was so unexpected that I felt like a bottle of champagne that was just shaken, but I didn't know where to aim the cork. At 31, I had not yet travelled overseas, so to *finally* have the opportunity to do so without having to consider preparation of my own finances was beyond my wildest dreams. I always *wanted* to travel overseas, but I thought I would start by visiting somewhere like England or Ireland, so I never thought my overseas travel would begin in a place as far away and exotic as India. Hailing from San Diego and having lived in the Pacific Northwest for three years at the time, I've been to Mexico and Canada, but intracontinental travel didn't have nearly the same allure.

Once I was able to harness my enthusiasm, I realised there were still a lot of things to do. The next step was to get my passport, Indian visa, and vaccinations. Depending on where you go in India, I learned that at least some inoculations are recommended. Since I was going to be staying in Delhi and working in nearby Noida, I only needed hepatitis A and B, typhoid, and malaria vaccinations. Yellow fever is also recommended but only if travelling to more rural areas of the country. While it was not part of this trip, if I were to have seen the Temple of Monkeys in Jaipur on a side trip, for example, getting a rabies shot would have been recommended.

Since this was my first business trip overseas, I was paired with one of the managers who was a more seasoned traveller. Being accompanied by someone who frequents India for work also meant lounge access in Dubai for a more comfortable layover. I probably could have navigated around just fine if I was travelling on my own (though, I wouldn't have had the perk of the lounge), but it's far less nerve-wracking to travel that distance with someone else. Since I hadn't yet earned regular visits to fly business class as per company policy, I had to book economy seating, so having a luxurious rest to look forward to in Dubai seemed worth the long flight in coach to get there.

Seattle to Dubai

The Emirates flight to Dubai was pleasant despite it being my first 14-hour flight. The longest flight I had been on prior to this was maybe four hours. During the flight, I found the choices of food to be tasteful and the portions plentiful, so I never found myself hungry. Alcoholic beverages were free, so I would occasionally have a small bottle of wine to help me relax, even if I couldn't sleep. Though Emirates is a fine airline, coach was rather uncomfortable. The roaring noise of the airplane, closeness to strangers, and small seats hampered any possibility of sleeping. To prevent muscle cramps, I had to occasionally take a stroll up and down the aisle to stretch while I did a little people-watching along the way.

Most of the other passengers were Indian or Middle Eastern. One passenger in the aisle to my right was a Muslim man dressed in traditional Muslim wear who quietly read the Qur'an during much of the flight but whispered prayers from it during the morning hours. Some of the Indian women were dressed in beautiful saris in rich colours and had ornate braids going down their backs. The overall aroma of a full flight with ranging standards of hygiene did present a less-than-desirable smell, but it was only noticeable for the first couple hours of the flight before becoming less potent (or maybe because I just got used to it).

As a knitter and crocheter, I was disappointed to learn that I couldn't bring either knitting needles or crochet hooks on board. Prior to leaving, I was envisioning all the knitting and crochet work I could get done on the flight, so I had to settle with listening to music, watching movies between meals and occasionally checking the in-flight map on the screen in front of me to see where our current location was in the world. It was fascinating to see that our flight took us north over British Columbia and the Northwest Territories of Canada, around the North Pole, down through Russia, Kazakhstan, Turkmenistan, and Iran until we reached Dubai in the United Arab Emirates before our connecting flight to Delhi.

After landing in Dubai, we sat in the airport's cocktail lounge for a few hours where I had drinks and food from the buffet and listened to what sounded like Hindi and Arabic in the background mixed with the melodic chants of Muslim men echoing from the prayer lounge. To hear this for the first time was strange, beautiful, and haunting all at the same time. This was my first realisation that I was truly out of my element, far away from the familiar, and about to embark on unfamiliar experiences.

The Imperial

After our evening layover in Dubai, we arrived in Delhi in the middle of the night after a three-hour flight. Once I picked up my luggage and stepped outside, the first thing I noticed was the air. It was so thick I could see it, even in the night. It also smelled distinctly sulfuric, something like matchstick smoke. Stray dogs wandered outside the airport terminal and seemed both skittish and hopeful that someone might pay them even a quick moment of attention. As we waited at the kerb for the taxi to the hotel, one dog in particular—so skinny its ribs protruded from its sides—looked back at me and stared for a moment as if to say, "Welcome to my world; though, you may not like it," before trotting off. At that moment, I knew there was no turning back and that I needed to prepare myself for the possibility of seeing things I may find disturbing and could easily become imprinted on my memory for the rest of my life.

The taxi ride to the hotel was my first encounter with the wildlife in Delhi. I remember nodding off slightly before I heard my colleague say, "Oh, look at the monkeys!" I immediately perked up to see a whole group of them (maybe a dozen or so), sitting together in the middle of the road ahead of us. I can only assume the driver was used to seeing them out in the road because he maintained his speed as he approached them, at which point they all scattered to the side and up into the trees. I felt a bit angry at the driver for not slowing down but had to trust that he knew they would move. I only caught a few short glimpses of the monkeys, but long enough to be able to determine they were rhesus macaques.

Once we arrived at the hotel, it was roughly 3:00 a.m. I was in a strange headspace that I can only describe as annihilating exhaustion mixed with the exhilarating anticipation one might experience before going on a rollercoaster ride. However, the few energy particles I had left to formulate logical thought made me realise I needed at least a nap after a desperate need for a shower and a change of clothes. After reaching the privacy of my room, I did an underarm sniff test and I realised that either some of the airline aroma seeped into my clothes or that I had cooked up an odour all my own that I never knew I could, so there was only a fleeting acknowledegment of the beautiful five-star room I had just checked into as I wearily shed my clothes and shuffled to the shower.

My nap didn't last long before my first Delhi sunrise broke through the linen shades of my room. Once I gave in to the daylight, I became quickly alert to the cacophony of sounds from outside that made me feel as though I awoke within an aviary. I got up to walk to the window to see an array of birds emerging and settling on trees and rooftops surrounding the cobblestone courtyard my room overlooked. It was a delightful feast of new sights that gave me the encouragement I needed to get ready for the day despite lingering fatigue.

On my way down for breakfast, I was more aware of all the beautiful details in the rich colonial-style hotel and artwork that I was too exhausted to notice upon my arrival only hours before. There were fancifully-framed paintings and lithographs filling each wall, pedestalled sculptures lining the hallways, intricately detailed textiles over glistening marble floors, soothing sounds of trickling water fountains at the downstairs hallway crossings, and ambient Hindi New Age music that tickled the senses just as much as the sweet smell of essential oils that filled the entire first floor of the hotel.

Breakfast at The Imperial is nothing short of exquisite. The display itself was something to behold, but the taste and freshness of all the food offered was something worth taking time to savour. Many of the food choices catered to Westerners with an omelette stand where a chef prepared them according to your preferences. There were also waffles, pancakes, eggs, hash browns, bacon, sausage, and fine, rich coffee. Each morning, I'd try something different, but I seemed to gravitate towards lighter choices of yogurt, fruit, and these delicious little granola bars that were prepared from scratch each day. They were so delicate; I think the only thing holding them together was honey. Of all the choices, I found myself looking for these morsels each morning and often reminisced on their flavour during other times of the day.

After breakfast the first two mornings, I'd usually stroll around the hotel grounds for exercise and to take in the sights, sounds, and smells. Upon first venturing out into the courtyards, I immediately noticed these large birds that would perch on the apexes of the building rooftops. I thought they were condors, but upon asking the hotel staff what they were, I was advised they were brown eagles. All the smaller birds would peck around on the lawns, then abruptly take off and settle in the trees surrounding the perimeter of the hotel grounds. The trees were whimsical and wrapped in vines, many with lazy branches that seemed to languor like ropes. I thought I might see monkeys in those trees, but the only commotion in them seemed to be coming from the birds.

The temperature before 8:00 a.m. was nearly 100 degrees with enough moisture in the air to make the outdoors feel like a giant steam room. I could only walk the entirety of the hotel grounds once before feeling weighed down by the humidity. I stepped back inside the air-conditioned hotel to the sounds of flute music and the relief of sweet scents emitting from oil infusers set at each hallway crossing. The difference between the smell of Delhi and the controlled scents of the indoors was striking. The constant honking of vehicles just outside the wall surrounding the lawns was also a stark contrast to the soft sound of music and voices of passing guests inside.

As I walked back to my room, every so often a hotel employee would greet me in passing with their hands together and say, "Namaste!" This is a sign of respect and is polite to return the gesture every time. I quickly became accustomed to doing this as I walked through the hotel, before leaving, and upon each return.

First Exploration

The day of my arrival, I spent much of the late morning and early afternoon exploring Delhi within walking distance from the hotel. To my surprise, I somehow generated an enormous amount of energy and wanted to see more while my colleague caught up on her sleep. When I'm in a new environment, my innate curiosity seems to supersede all other senses, compelling me to dive right in. Of course, it's important to be aware of one's surroundings, but in my opinion, life is too short to get too comfortable with the hotel and not comfortable enough with exploring the vast possibilities that await…*especially* when there's a new country to introduce yourself to.

Despite being a sun-deprived Caucasian, I still wanted to blend in as much as possible (though, in retrospect, I looked *completely* out-of-place and fresh-off-the-plane), so rather than use a hardcopy map to figure out where I was going, I decided to use my iPhone's 'Maps' application to track my whereabouts in relation to the hotel. When in new surroundings, I have a way of wandering aimlessly in wonderment, so this method of tracking prevented me from getting hopelessly lost.

I wanted to first visit a landmark close to the hotel, so I followed the concierge's recommendation and ventured over to Jantar Mantar (meaning roughly "instrument for calculation") which dates to 1724 A.D. To get in, I had to pay a nominal fee (as a foreign tourist, it was 200 rupees, which converted to roughly $2.00 at the time) then was assigned a tour guide who took me through and narrated the entire history. The grounds for Jantar Mantar looked a lot of an outdoor terracotta museum as all the structures appeared to be red-washed masonry and stone. Many were used for tracking the zodiac signs and others for solar and lunar positions throughout the year. To my surprise, a couple of these monuments resembled Rome's Colosseum. The tour took roughly an hour, at which time I began to really feel the heat beating down on me, but since I had plenty of bottled water on hand, I decided to trek on. I paid the tour guide a gratuity and went on my way.

Following the tour of Jantar Mantar, I felt (and probably looked) like a blushed and sweaty disaster on the brink of heatstroke. I could have easily headed back to the hotel, but I wasn't ready to throw in the towel yet. I was determined to find some craft markets first and see what kind of beautiful little things I could buy. I started walking back in the direction I came from, staying on the side of the street where trees shaded the sidewalk so I could have a momentary reprieve from the punishing heat. There were beggars occasionally holding their palms out as I passed, street food vendors, barber stalls, people selling odds and ends on meticulously-displayed spreads on the ground, and tuk-tuk drivers calling out to me to take a ride. One even followed me halfway down a block before parking and continuing on foot to try and get me to take a ride. The longer we walked, the lower the price got until it was only 20 rupees (about $0.25). Either I must have looked completely wilted to the point he took pity on me or he *really* needed the cash that day. After being hassled enough, I insisted I wanted to walk after sitting in airplanes for almost 24 hours. The man seemed angry at my insistence and waved his hands at me in an I-give-up kind of way before storming back to his vehicle.

As I continued walking along and returned to my own thoughts, my senses began to pick up details about the streets. The air was thick and carried smells ranging from incenses, curried foods, exhaust, sour milk, cigarette smoke, and occasionally the stench of defecation as I passed makeshift camps with one or a few inhabitants. Crossing streets was challenging and like being in a game of Leap Frog: you step off the kerb at your own risk.

Just as I began to wonder if I would successfully find the bustling craft markets I had been envisioning, a young Indian man (who seemed to have been walking in the same direction I was) approached me and started speaking to me. He must have seen my encounter with the tuk-tuk driver because the first thing he said was, "Sorry, not all of the taxi drivers are like that." I laughed and told him what I told the driver: that my ass was sitting in airplane seats for 24 hours and I just wanted to walk! I must have given off an air of suspicion then because the next thing he said was, "Don't worry, I'm not trying to sell you anything," to which I replied, "Oh good, I appreciate that."

This guy spoke excellent English, was tall, slender and well-put-together in skinny jeans, a button-down shirt, and sandals. We continued talking as we walked along. I told him I had just arrived in the country for work and was staying nearby and he told me he was a student at the University of Delhi, but was originally from Churu, Rajasthan, India. He introduced himself as Parveen and asked me where I was headed. I told him I was hoping to find some local craft markets and maybe some shrines. He gladly offered to take me, assuring me there were some of both just a few blocks away. By this time, I determined he wasn't trying to bait me for an organised kidnapping, so I followed along.

On the walk to the markets, I saw what I hoped I wouldn't see on this trip: a cat. I am a lover of all animals but since childhood, I have always had a special place in my heart for felines. I have two cats of my own and, between my house and my office, have enough cat paraphernalia to secure a place in the Hall of Crazy Cat Men if ever such a thing existed. Before I even left for India, I wasn't sure what to expect in terms of seeing any cat population, so I sort of half-joked with my co-workers that if I happened to see a poor, helpless kitten in the streets of Delhi, I would more than likely have no choice but to rescue it and fight customs tooth and nail to bring it back to The States with me.

Fortunately, the cat I saw was a full-grown adult (so, at least more self-sufficient than a kitten) walking along the top of a wall Parveen and I were passing and seemed to be carrying something large in its mouth. I thought, *Oh God, it's a mama cat carrying her kitten; must initiate rescue mission!* However, as I caught up with the cat on the sidewalk below, I noticed it wasn't carrying its baby, but a giant, dead pigeon. Immediately, all my distress faded when I realised that this cat was doing *just fine* before I saw it leap out of sight down the other side of the wall.

As Parveen and I got closer to the markets, I saw smaller shrines for Shiva and Ganesh lining the street. The markets themselves were unexpectedly nestled among temples where people gathered for daily prayer and meditation. As I passed underneath the lobed arches outside of what I was told was the Gurudwara Bangla Sahib, I could hear chanting over a loudspeaker that seemed to call everyone out from the heat of the day and the market bustle for a few moments of reflection. Parveen asked if I wanted to go in, but I wasn't too keen on leaving my shoes and satchel (which carried my passport, wallet, cell phone, and other valuables) at the door outside as was required by all who entered. I just looked on respectively and people-watched for a moment until we continued walking.

When we arrived at the craft markets, I stopped in at a textile shop where I hoped for a bit of inspiration by feasting my eyes on the ornate designs, range of textures, and luscious colours. I even caught sight of an old loom used to display one method for weaving. Materials used for many of the rugs and other woven ornamentals were cotton, fine wools, and silks. Parveen patiently waited as I shopped. At one point, I started feeling guilty and asked him if he had anywhere to be, but he insisted he could wait until I was done so he could show me the way back.

As an obvious tourist, one challenge I faced while browsing the markets was that I was pressured to buy something from *everyone*. After purchasing a small trinket from one vendor, the same vendor tried escorting me to the neighbouring vendor and so on. There was no such thing as unattended perusing. It was difficult, but sometimes I had to firmly say, "No, thank you" and walk away, even as the vendor may have continued rambling on with their sales pitch (or worse, trailed along after me) after I already turned to leave.

After two hours in the heat and humidity, I was beginning to crave a cold shower and a chilled India pale ale back at the hotel. Parveen took me as far as a block away from the hotel where we would go in our separate directions. I thanked him for his kindness and told him how fascinated I was at the randomness of our meeting. We exchanged *Facebook* friend invites and agreed to meet again one day. We are, in fact, still connected on *Facebook* to this day.

When I got back to the hotel, I took a long, cold shower before taking a nap that lasted a few hours. After I had a good rest, my colleague texted me after waking up herself and agreed to join me in the bar downstairs where we enjoyed some tapas-style food and drinks before calling it a night.

Delhi Traffic

As a backseat driver, I have to say that I truly admire the driving abilities of the shuttle car drivers that took my colleagues and I to the office where we worked for the week. The only way I could remain calm as a passenger in Indian traffic without leaving scratch marks on the seat was to focus on all the new sights and to take photos of anything I considered new and unusual (which was a lot).

On the roads here, you will find a mixture of cars, trucks, lorries, tuk-tuks (three-wheeled vehicles, also known as auto rickshaws), cyclists, motorbikes, merchant-drawn carts, horse-drawn carts, and even cows sauntering alongside it all, seemingly oblivious to the chaos around them. If there are traffic laws here, no one follows them; yet, it all seems to flow at a continual pace. Compared to the U.S. where our traffic is more confined to the lanes, yet excruciatingly slow, Delhi traffic is wildly disorganised but constantly moves.

At first, I underestimated how this could all work. You'd think with all the honking that there would be more anger and road rage, but horns seem to be used more as a way of saying, "On your left!" or "On your right!" like an audible alternative for the rubber barrier on bumper cars in a driving range. I also couldn't help but imagine the cars intermingling like the crabs in *Finding Nemo* that would say, "Hey hey hey hey!" with their pincers raised as a warning as they crossed one another's path. It's chaos, but it's an understood normal in India. It took me a couple days, but

I eventually had to trust that our shuttle drivers knew what they were doing, learn to relax, and tell myself that this was not how I was going to die.

Shopping

On most days after work, we would take to the streets to go shopping. This is where immersion in the real world takes place. You'll see extreme poverty, meticulous extravagance, smell sweet things and awful things, and have your social experience pushed to the limit...all at the same time. However, I could not fathom so much detail and colour in such concentrated spaces until now. It was like a supernova to the brain. My hyper obsessive compulsive disorder compelled me to process it all and I was frustrated that I just couldn't. I had to quickly learn to focus on one thing at a time so I didn't have a meltdown over missing something.

A sad truth is that children are trained to be little salespeople from a young age to help earn money for their family (or nefarious employer). The strategy is that their small, often cretin-like appearance will elicit sympathy from tourists, therefore maximising their income. Regardless of how ordinary the items they are selling (e.g. ballpoint pens), these kids know how to pull on your heartstrings until what starts as a granular feeling of guilt becomes this upwelling of emotions that will soon become a nuclear implosion rendering you this gooey pile of worthlessness for not buying their goods. However, if your guilt gets the better of you and you *do* open your wallet, expect to be selling to ALL the children within a two-mile radius because they network with their friends faster than high-speed internet.

Visiting India was my second experience (after Mexico) where I stuck out in a crowd like the tall, Caucasian sasquatch that I am.

I might as well have had a blinking neon money sign hanging over my head because the shop owners and market vendors probably saw me as a walking ATM, calling out, "Please, you buy!"; "Only 100, no only 50 rupees for you today!"; "American, come SEE!" as I walked by, trying to make as minimal eye contact as possible. Sometimes they just grabbed a handful of their merchandise and followed me for what seemed like an eternity through traffic, crossing streets, and even all the way back to the hotel gate.

One of the more unforgettable sights I saw while out shopping was a certain beggar. Beggars are everywhere you go but seeing this one man stuck in my memory more so than a little girl who was trying to sell me blue ballpoint pens. Seeing her was heart-wrenching, but this man (who was clothed in little more than tattered rags) lay in the gutter of a busy street. He was holding one of his legs up from underneath the thigh to show passersby where the leg was missing just past his knee. He held it with both hands to shake the few inches of what existed of his lower leg to demonstrate his disability, then would reach out with one hand. I saw him and immediately thought, *Was he born this way or did someone do this to him?* I hoped that whatever money or food he was given went to his benefit only and not that of someone governing his efforts. Knowing that there were plenty of other beggars watching, I refrained from stopping to give him anything but found myself feeling perfectly wretched for quite a while after that.

As we waded through the crowded sidewalks between shops and street vendors, I learned that shopkeepers tend to be less intimidating. Regardless of where or from whom you shop, developing a skill for haggling is a necessity. Though I initially despised all the effort required as it *really* took me out of my comfort zone, I was getting good at haggling rather than taking prices at face value. A few shops had 'FIXED PRICE' signs posted above their doorways, but I'd still challenge prices on items I was interested in and often came away with bargains. The key is to be persistent and to get a good sense of the conversion rate and what you feel would be fair market value for an item in the currency you're accustomed to.

Musings

I find it particularly amazing how women in their elaborate saris can ride side-saddle on the back of motorbikes without getting the fabric stuck in the gears. These beautifully-adorned women seem almost misplaced as their garments, to me, are extraordinary fashion in an unexpected setting. Helmets also seem to be optional while riding motorbikes, for both adults and children.

While there is a lot of poverty here, it's remarkable to see so many vibrant colours, even in ordinary circumstances of ordinary people. People may not have much, but they seem to have a heightened consciousness of the clothes they put on their backs, especially women. Not even clotheslines are dull. It's a visual richness that matches the same complexity of flavour in their food, even if in small pockets of space.

In India, cows are regarded as sacred. As symbols of wealth and sources of prosperity, these animals are left to roam as they please. Even in the bustle of urban life, you will see them *everywhere*. They walk along roads in heavy traffic, graze in agricultural fields, and herd through intersections without any care in the world. They seem to *know* they are held in holy regard just like cats have never forgotten they were once worshipped by Egyptians. It's one of the many culture shocks I've experienced to see an animal that is such a huge source of meat for us in The States to be so respected in a place where you'd think their supply of beef could vastly alter hunger in the abject poverty. Although I already eat very little beef, seeing the level of respect Indians have for cows makes me want to give up beef entirely.

Reflection

On our last weekday in Delhi, we finished our work and left the office a bit later than anticipated. I was chomping at the bit because my work was done and I was anxious to cram in as much last-minute shopping and sight-seeing as I could before heading back to the airport later that night. Our flight was due to leave at 2:00 a.m. which would put us back in Seattle around noon a day earlier since we were going back in time.

In pursuit of sari silk yarn for my knitting and crocheting, we had to take a tuk-tuk (which was a first for me and even my seasoned India-travelling colleagues) to a place that was said to have it. Turns out it didn't, so we shopped for other gorgeous things which was still worth the wild ride there and back (think Mr. Toad's Wild Ride). Back at the hotel, with all shopping bounty combined, I could barely fit it all in my luggage after a long game of Tetris. If I tried packing one more box of incense, my luggage may very well have burst at the zippers. I was still a little disappointed that none of it was the sari silk I wanted to find, but I hoped there would be a next time to bring back an abundance of sari silk yarn and perhaps other loose fibres to add to my stash.

I was truly grateful to have had the opportunity to see India as my first overseas experience, even if just a small part of it at first. As overwhelmed as I was touring the markets, India is a place you want to introduce yourself to slowly, respectfully, and with an open mind and heart. It can be as ugly as it is beautiful and depressing as its colours portray a happiness...something like how a wake celebrates a life while relieving sadness of death. A visit can be a meditation just as much as its controlled anarchy is intimidating. I let the art, music, flavours, and incenses consume my senses, but I could not ignore the heartbreaking truths. I saw images that I will not soon forget.

I have a renewed gratitude for the wealth of fortune we have in The States despite our own ugly truths. Only a retreat from our own norms will make us truly see the tiny worlds of comfortable routine we live in. Trust that there is enlightenment that comes from an unknown we may fear at first, but once we've overcome it, the new perspective of the world and sense of self we gain will be permanent.

Manifestation or Coincidence?

As I was working on this section of the book, I decided to pull my travel journal off the shelf to see what sort of room I had for transcribing the experience. At first, I just felt the outside of it and mused at the tactile aesthetic of it like I often do with my journals; the quality of the leather and the detail in the tooling of the image of a compass embedded on the front of it. It's almost as if a special energy emanates from journals filled with original thoughts and ideas, perhaps from emotions felt during the writing process.

After opening and reading the introduction I wrote on January 14, 2003, I noticed that at the end, I had made a list of all the countries I wanted to visit in my lifetime. Mind you, I hadn't opened this journal for years, so it was much to my surprise that India was first on my list. I enthusiastically checked off the box I had drawn next to it, then wondered if it was merely coincidence or if there was some magical manifestation at work here.

Ganesh atop a frieze of gods in the Hindu pantheon.

A cow insignia on a milk stand.

Middle men.

Tow tricycle.

Side-saddling.

There's always room.

Lines of colour.

Family fun.

Mobile ballpoint pen salesgirl.

Pedestrian diversity.

The kids will be fine.

Adventures in tuk-tukking.

A Return to India: Culture, Inclusion & the Trek to Agra

"There is more to life than increasing its speed."
-Mahatma Gandhi

Familiar Arrival

What seemed like a long wait for my luggage, I didn't check into my hotel room at Shangri-La Eros Hotel until 5:00 a.m. I felt much more alert upon arrival this time around and managed to unpack and lay out all my things and scout out all the working electrical outlets in my room (only some will actually receive plugs on Western appliances, and of those, only one or two will successfully operate your appliances; e.g. a cell phone charger, flat iron and blow dryer). After a shower that felt like pure ecstasy, I slept for what I knew would only be a short nap.

As soon as I stepped out of the terminal at Indira Gandhi International Airport in the early morning hours, the familiar smell of matchstick smoke hit my senses. The mixture of fog and carbon-thick air shone like yellow cones under the lamps around the airport. The temperature was a mild 62 degrees (*vastly* desirable compared to the heat and humidity of June) and the sounds of tuk-tuk and car horns rose throughout the streets. Once I left the airport, the night grew calm as my taxi car reached quieter roads on the way to the hotel.

After a long wait for my luggage, I didn't check-in to my hotel room at Shangri-La Eros Hotel until 5:00 a.m. I felt much more alert upon arrival this time around, managed to unpack and lay out all my things and scout out all the working electrical outlets in my room. Only some received plugs on Western appliances, and of those, only one or two successfully worked. After taking the shower that I had been longing for, I slept for what I knew would only be a short nap.

I woke up around 8:00 a.m. feeling some fatigue, but nothing greater than the numbness in my backside. I literally couldn't even feel it after sitting for so long, so, as I knew I would, I greeted the day enthusiastically, ready to walk about to explore and exercise some feeling back into my glutes. There's no better remedy for a numb butt than getting out for a stroll.

After getting ready for the day, I went down for a light breakfast of yogurt, fruit, vegetable quiche, and copious amounts of strong coffee. The dining area was familiar from when I had dinner there on my last visit but was now bustling with an array of foreigners—English, American, Australian, and Japanese. I'm sure there were many other nationalities, but those were the few that I could determine based on the languages and accents I was hearing. Americans are the easiest to pick out because we're so goddamn loud.

After breakfast, I went back to my hotel room to change before greeting the wilds of Delhi. I looked out from my hotel room window to see a whole day ahead of me. My room overlooked thick trees for miles with what I believe were office buildings within immediate proximity to the hotel and dome-topped gurudwaras nestled in the distance. I saw tourists walking the sidewalk below and was eager to join them but not necessarily to follow them. I wasn't sure where I would go, but I was anxious to find out.

Shangri-La

The Shangri-La – Eros Hotel stands as a giant beacon of a high-rise in the Connaught Place district in central New Delhi, not far from The Imperial. As you enter the lobby, you step across a floor made of shimmering marble that looks to be polished nightly. Above it are chandeliers made from what appear to be hand-blown glass in elongated, individually-affixed teardrop-shaped pieces that, with the help of embedded illumination, give the illusion that the glass is dripping from the ceiling. Encompassing the base and dotting the underside closest to the floor are coloured pieces of glass in pinks and reds that look like lily pads. A number of these chandeliers accent the ceiling throughout and give a sparkling allure of extravagance and a paradise after which the hotel is so named.

Despite missing the courtyards, gardens, and lawn expanses of The Imperial, bordered by whimsical jungle trees that always left me in anticipation of seeing rhesus macaques, Shangri-La had its own bustling ambiance. Its vibe was modern, more closely connected to the busy world outside its gates and had an energy apart from the quieter, zen-like sanctuary of The Imperial. While The Imperial has The Imperial Book Shop where I'd find myself at least once daily during my first stay, Shangri-La has the Shopping Arcade. Within it are two stores next door to one another, each very similar to the other in the merchandise they carried: rugs, Pashmina scarves and shawls, figurines and statues, jewellery, and other trinkets.

Salutation, Slums & Spice Markets

After gaining confidence to venture out on my own during my first trip, I had few reservations about doing the same on this trip. Once I finished breakfast and changed clothes, I headed for the streets. Passing through the hotel's security gate to the outside always gives me the feeling of leaving a comfort zone (like, *This is it; you've voluntarily released yourself into the unknown*), but it's important to challenge this and make it so that you feel that returning to the hotel is merely comforting from the perspective of personal care. As a co-worker friend put it, "Hotels are only for the four s's: sleep, shit, shave, and shower."

Knowing that Shangri-La wasn't far from where I stayed at The Imperial, I naturally headed in that direction to revisit some of the markets and perhaps the Gurudwara Bangla Sahib, the Sikh temple that I meant to return to for a proper visit. As with my previous trip, I had to decline offers for tuk-tuk rides because I wanted to start the day by walking (I thought, *Unless I'm specifically hailing you, can't a guy just go for a walk?!*). I headed down a path of residential complexes toward the markets and was again approached by a friendly, polite young man. "Don't worry, I'm not trying to sell you anything!" was the first thing he said. I thought, *Seriously?* This seems to be the stock phrase when approaching foreigners, so the *déjà vu* of it made me laugh. "Where are you headed today?" he added. "Oh, I'm just taking in the sights," I said and asked where he was headed to. Apparently, he was just getting off work from the National Museum and was on his way home. Getting off work from a museum in the morning seemed strange.

We had a brief conversation about where I was from, why I was in India, and what my plans were. We walked past dilapidated brick buildings with patches of copper-coloured stucco and bare brick showing in places. I saw a young man operating a levered water pump to wash his hands, so I stopped to take a picture, holding my phone up first and raising my chin to motion in a may-I-take-your-picture? kind of way. He and another man standing nearby said, "Very old! Very old buildings!"

The young man supposedly from the National Museum and I walked farther down until we reached an intersection where I could tell that he was preparing to leave me to head off in his own direction. At that point, the markets were just across the street, but he hailed a tuk-tuk for me and told the driver that, for 20 rupees, he was to take me to different markets. He agreed, I waved farewell to the young man and got in the back seat. I wasn't *entirely* set on seeing what I had before, so I took it as the Universe saying, *Remember, while you're here, you should experience what's new and different, not what's familiar. Go on; you won't regret it.* I guess I just need a little nudge now and then to shed that cocoon feeling I enjoy (perhaps owing to having been nearly 10 months *in utero*). I could have easily spent a far less colourful day had I followed my mindset of, *Well, I'll start with what I know already, stay there for a while, and slowly make my way to something I haven't seen.* If you ever have this feeling while travelling, ignore it. It's no different than wasting time by lazily snoozing past your alarm clock on an important day.

The general consensus among the young man, my driver (who later introduced himself as Parkash), and eventually myself was that if I was to spend a successful day out in the real Delhi without being incessantly hassled by beggars and merchants was to look less like an American tourist and more like an honourary citizen by changing my outfit from khaki pants, a blue button-down shirt, and a pair of Chucks. While we briefly discussed this prior to rumbling away in the tuk-tuk, there was a lot of staring and finger-pointing at my feet between the two of them, so I think the Chucks were probably the worst offenders.

The first stop was at a handicraft bazaar very much like the Nirula Handicraft Bazar I visited on my first trip. The shop had three levels: the first was reserved for garments like kurtas, saris, tunics, scarves, and shoes; the second: small objects like wooden and stone figurines, devotional statues (I saw Ganesh, Shiva, and Vishnu), wooden and stone boxes inlaid with precious stones (marble, lapis lazuli) and metals (copper, gold, silver), bells, and a room for jewellery; the third: a space reserved for a painter who specialised in an intricate method using single-strand brushes on paper or silk screen.

I spent much of my time on the first floor where I decided to invest in a couple of nice kurtas. My first choice was a light, airy cotton in a warm beige colour with intersecting red lines as the pattern. I ended up wearing this one out of the shop. The second was a slightly heavier cotton in a deep forest green with thick, black pinstripes running vertically with intricate, light green embroidery around the collar and the buttoned part going down the chest. This one appeared more formal and decidedly perfect for wearing either to the office one day during the week or to dinner. Both kurtas fit me perfectly, but on-the-spot tailoring was offered for any I liked that needed alterations.

I was invited to peruse the rest of the shop where I settled on buying some loose masala chai tea, smaller knick-knacks as gifts, and a couple of paintings. I was brought a fresh-brewed chai to sip while the painter showed me his work. The paintings were done over old manuscript sheets with various forms of what looked like Arabic and Sanskrit calligraphy, with large stamps above the painted figures. He kept laying piece after gorgeous piece on the table until one with a white tiger appeared. "That one!" I said. "I'm definitely taking that one." I went on to explain to the poor guy how much I like cats to the point where he probably thought, *Just pay me and get out.* I also bought a painting with an elephant. The artist's name, Sachin, agreed to frame these for me and deliver to my hotel so I wouldn't have to carry fragile items around the rest of the day. While viewing all these zoomorphic images, I learned about the six symbols of India: elephant for good luck, horse for power, cow for happiness, camel for love, tiger for energy, and peacock for peace.

After the bazaar, Parkash came back to pick me up and asked where I wanted to go next. Having nothing specific in mind, I simply said, "Anywhere the tourists don't go; I want to see the real India." We drove around Delhi for quite a while, never really getting anywhere fast in all the congestion. I would occasionally see areas that piqued my interest, so we'd stop to walk around so I could take pictures. Some of my favourite images were what the outside of people's homes looked like, regardless of how modest or ill-kept they were. I saw a little boy sitting in a building nook that looked like it could have been a garage for a small car, but he was working on a sewing apparatus unlike any sewing machine I've seen before. It was noisy like an engine and had belts going from wheels on the machine, down through a slot in the desk the machine sat on. Next to the machine sat a wooden box filled with spools of thread in a variety of colours. The boy looked to be only seven or eight years old and paid unbroken attention to his task when I stopped for a moment to marvel at the whole operation. I asked an adolescent peer of his standing outside what he was making. "Shirts," he said.

The next (and probably most significant) stop we made was at a makeshift camp. I didn't know exactly what it was at first, but I could tell it was some sort of encampment. Parkash parked the tuk-tuk outside and we walked in. I instantly drew heads, but people seemed only mildly curious and took a moment from whatever they were doing to glance inquisitively. There were oxen and goats blanketed in cloth with geometric designs, young men walking an ox and a horse on lead ropes, a pigeon coop, children playing, women in saris conversing together on cots, and pitched tents constructed from tarps and wooden posts surrounding the perimeter of the lot. Tire-fitted carts were parked in one area (presumably drawn by the oxen), and clotheslines were strung across in different directions holding an array of different clothing. Instantly, so much of what I have that I regard as necessary for comfort and contentment now seems like clutter—props for comfort that are often just an illusion. Before we turned to leave, we passed the women on the cots who were saying something in our direction in Hindi. I asked Parkash what they were saying, but he seemed to refrain from telling me exactly what.

Delhi has its unpleasant smells, but a truly rich olfactory experience can be had at spice markets. We stopped at one that I was told was a hidden gem away from all the usual tourist traps. We walked along a row of spice merchants who had their shops set up under tarp coverings like those I saw at the encampment. Underneath were tables filled with burlap, canvas, and plastic mesh bags full of loose spices such as caraway seed, clove, coriander, curry, ginger, mustard, pepper corns, star anise, and turmeric that were piled high above the brim. Before even approaching the displays, you can smell the mixture of all these spices from down the street and are greeted by mounds of yellows, oranges, reds, browns, and blacks once you get there. I never had a more extraordinary experience where I could nearly taste the flavour in the aromas and visual feast of colour.

After the spice market, it felt like a good time for refreshments, so Parkash took us to a small street restaurant that was just a knockabout place the size of what a small pizza joint would be in The States. I admitted that I was a little suspicious of street food despite it being hot and cooked. Instead, I decided that I would eat back at the hotel and settled on having a Thums Up. If you've ever seen *Eat Pray Love*, you might remember Liz having one, claiming it was, "…five times sweeter than Coke." When the waiter came back with a bottle of Thums Up and cracked it open, I remembered Richard from Texas saying in the movie, "No lips on the bottle. First rule in India: never touch anything but yourself." I asked for a straw, but they didn't have any, so I decided to just go for it and drink straight from the bottle. I took my daily stomach pills with breakfast, so I considered it a mild risk. For the record, Thums Up tastes no different than regular Coke (at least to me). While he ate and I drank my Thums Up, Parkash and I shared photos on our cell phones of our separate lives—family, friends, and our homes.

It was endearing to be able to connect on a personal level.

After lunch, I was ready to head back to the hotel for a tea and shower detox. Spending the late morning and good part of the afternoon out in the Delhi hustle and bustle means also being exposed to a tremendous amount of pollution and dust. I asked Parkash how he deals with all the pollution while driving a tuk-tuk as his full-time job. "I have trouble with my lungs certain times of the year," he said, "but I love it when the rain comes because it cleans the air." For an out-of-towner, the pollution is intense. The blessing, though, was that the temperature throughout the day was perfect—in the 70s and dry. The pollution is certainly something to contend with, but somehow the sights and sounds help you to forget it at times while your other senses are distracted.

Back at the hotel, Parkash and I exchanged numbers and *Facebook* invites. Having seen a fair portion of New Delhi, I expressed an interest in seeing Old Delhi. I've been told Old Delhi is more crowded, louder, and a far greater magnitude of sensory overload, but I was willing to accept the experience for whatever it might be and make it as extraordinary as I could. After Parkash agreed to take me to Old Delhi, the plan was made for this to be the Sunday morning adventure before later joining new fibre artist friends. It was only day one of my second visit to India, but I already felt like the second part of the adventure of experiencing this country would only continue to inspire, intrigue, and delight me.

Friendships

My first Valentine's Day in India was a day of new friendships. Some were made on my own while, interestingly, others were the manifestation of a connection made back in The States. I was pleasantly surprised to find out that many people in India celebrate Valentine's Day. I refer to it now as Single Awareness Day, but for me, the love between old friends and the kindness shared with new ones carries just as much weight and significance as romantic love.

The first of these friendships, is with the then-33-year-old tuk-tuk driver, Parkash. Over the course of the entire trip, I came to know more about Parkash aside from his current profession as a tuk-tuk driver. In fact, he has a degree in Tourism Studies which shows strongly in his ability to delight and entertain while imparting his vast knowledge of the many wonders of Delhi. When I asked him if he ever wants to use his degree toward a related job, he explained that it's often difficult to even land interviews without any direct experience. Meanwhile, he drives a tuk-tuk around town as a means for income. Many of his fares are locals, but he told me about some of the tidbits of other languages he's picked up just by driving around tourists from places like France and Japan. I taught him some phrases in Spanish like, *"¿Como estás?"* ("How are you?") and, *"Muy bien, y tú?"* ("I'm good, and you?"). He taught me, *"Aap kaise ho?"* ("How are you?") and, *"Shukriya"* ("Thank you"). (It should be noted that *shukriya* is taken from the Urdu language and is often used as an alternative to *dhanyavaad*, which is a Hindi word).

One of the unfortunate side effects of being a full-time tuk-tuk driver in Delhi is the constant exposure to the pollution. There's no escaping it. When I inevitably find myself in traffic in the relatively much-cleaner air of the Pacific Northwest, I have the benefit of keeping the recirculation turned on so that I'm only breathing the air that's in the car rather than sucking in the exhaust from the cars ahead of me. Even turning it off for a moment to defrost the windshield allows a sharp stench of fumes in. I take shortened breaths to avoid taking in too much while the intruding dirty air fills the car, but at some point, I have to breathe some of it in.

Then I think of Parkash having uninterrupted exposure to the polluted Delhi air, day in and day out. Sometimes between his responses during our conversations, he would let out laboured, dry coughs. *Poor guy is only a year older than me and coughs like a chain smoker*, I thought. Though Parkash is not a smoker, I'm not sure there's much difference between being a regular smoker and taking in all the dust and pollutants that pepper much of Delhi's air. However, despite the unavoidable job hazard, Parkash has probably one of the most positive and uplifting outlooks on life. Rather than bemoan his circumstances, he accepts life for what it is without any complaints. He is genuinely grateful for what he has. Many others (including myself) could take a page from his book.

Outside from being a tuk-tuk driver, Parkash is also a brother, father, husband, and an uncle. Originally from Kathmandu, Nepal, he lives in northern Delhi with his mother, his wife, his son, his brother, his brother's wife, and their two daughters and an aunt. When he was young, his father moved he and his family to Delhi for better work opportunities. Unfortunately, his father passed away from tuberculosis and asthma. After the loss of his father, Parkash and his brother became the sole breadwinners for the family.

One night after work, Parkash gave me the great honour of inviting me to meet his family at their roughly-500-square-foot apartment. When I returned to the hotel from Noida, Parkash was already waiting there with his tuk-tuk. I ran upstairs to change, knowing that this would be a perfect occasion to wear one of the kurtas I bought. I decided on the forest green one with the black pinstripes and embroidery. Once I was dressed and ready to go, I was a bit distressed that I didn't have something to bring as a gift for Parkash for the kind gesture of inviting me into his home after having known me for only a few days. I couldn't exactly run down to a corner store to pick up a bottle of wine (besides, Parkash told me that he didn't drink alcoholic beverages, so I had a feeling the rest of his family didn't either). Instead, I decided to stop in one of the shops in the Shopping Arcade to get him a grey Pashmina scarf that I thought would be very fitting for a young man like him. When I met him outside, we hugged and he seemed very grateful when I handed him the package with the scarf in it. When he opened it, he was moved, but for some reason he didn't want to accept it and said, "Hold on to it and give it to my mother. She'll like that." I wondered if I had violated social etiquette about giving another man a gift, but then I thought that that might have been too ridiculous and figured he just wanted me to be more appealing to the matriarch of the family as a gift-bearing guest.

The tuk-tuk ride to Parkash's home in north Delhi took roughly an hour. He said the rush hour traffic made the drive longer. I wondered what the roads would look like when it wasn't rush hour; they always seemed to be a steady stream of vehicles except during the early morning hours while driving to and from the airport. I didn't mind the traffic though. To me, it was all about the journey, not rushing to the destination.

As the sun set on Delhi, I enjoyed watching the city come alive at night as we passed through it. At one point, we were heading into a particularly thick cluster of vehicles when we came up alongside a bus on the right as it was pulling away from the kerb. As the bus sped up to our left, the space between us diminished and caught a motorcyclist and his passenger in the pinch, causing them to slide against our tuk-tuk with an abrupt *CRUNCH*. It merely startled me and fortunately no one was hurt. Parkash immediately turned in his seat to ask if I was okay and I think I said something like, "Oh yeah, I'm fine. With the way the traffic is here, I'm surprised I wasn't involved in an accident sooner" very matter-of-factly. Parkash seemed very collected about the situation as he pulled over to examine the damage and talk to the motorcyclists while I stayed in the tuk-tuk. The hit only grazed the tuk-tuk and there didn't seem to be much damage to the motorcycle. Parkash asked if they were okay, but the driver of the motorcycle seemed angry as they exchanged some heated dialogue I couldn't understand and some New York-style *Hey-I'm-drivin'-here!* gesticulations. It was obvious that the motorcyclist tried speeding between us and the bus but miscalculated his timing before there wasn't enough space left to squeeze through. The bus also stopped, but once the exchange between Parkash and the motorcyclist was over, everyone went back on their way. As we drove on, I asked Parkash if accidents like that happen very often. "Sometimes," he said, "but they are not usually bad because you never go very fast."

After the collision, we came to a stop light that seemed to take forever to change. The locals must have known this because there were throngs of people weaving between the rows of idling cars trying to sell armfuls of various goods at car windows. Some were selling single-stem roses wrapped in clear plastic, packaged snacks, and balloons while others were merely begging with palms out then pinching their fingers together and motioning back to their mouths. Some did cartwheels on the street while others danced in place with bells around their ankles.

Two young girls who must have been around eight or nine years old spotted me in the back of the tuk-tuk and immediately ran over with their balloons. They briefly poked their heads into the shell of the tuk-tuk to get a good look at me then tried offering me a balloon for 20 rupees, then 10 when I shook my head and smiled to politely decline. They started talking to Parkash in Hindi and would look at me between phrases with the biggest smiles on their faces. I asked Parkash what they were saying and he said, "They want to know where you are from." I told them directly while Parkash translated for me. When the light turned green and the vehicles ahead of us started to move, the girls tried again and even more insistently to sell me a balloon. I almost wanted to buy one so I could tease Parkash by tying it to his tuk-tuk, but I knew if I did, we'd be swarmed at the next light. I waved as we drove off and the girls waved back before they turned to wade through the moving cars toward the sidewalk.

As we neared Parkash's home, he had to stop at a little shop to pick up some bread, milk, and other items for the house. The side street we were on was dimly lit, but the shop we parked outside of was brightly lit with florescence. I stayed in the tuk-tuk while Parkash went in. As soon as I noticed the business next door to the shop was a dog clinic, I spotted a cat. It was a beautiful, slender black cat that scuttled out from behind a four-sided sign that had 'DOG CLINIC' printed on each side in giant red letters and the same picture of Golden Retriever puppies. The cat paused for a moment but then trotted off. I felt a pang of sadness for the cat and followed it with my line of sight for as long as I could before it disappeared into the night. This was the first and last time I saw a cat on this trip.

We rumbled along side streets and through dark alleyways before reaching the place where Parkash lived. Parkash parked the tuk-tuk at the bottom of a flight of stairs inside a courtyard of a plain cement apartment complex. The air was filled with the smell of campfire smoke as the flickering of little fires could be seen at the exposed facades of many of the units in the complex as people cooked their meals. Children were running around in the dusky courtyard where the collective smoke of the residents' fires made it look foggy under the meagre lamplight. The children's footsteps and voices could be heard echoing off the walls of the building as Parkash and I climbed the dark, damp stairwell to his apartment.

When we reached his floor three levels up, we went through a black security screen that protected the walkway to his front door. Lines of laundry were hung overhead, so I used my hands to part my way through some of the garments before I got to the front door. As Parkash invited me in, I walked into a large room with a twin bed against the wall to the left and a king-size platform bed straight ahead on a raised part of the floor. There was a child sleeping at the end of the king-size bed. I was told it was Parkash's niece, Shristi. She was fast asleep with a bright green and yellow blanket over her and didn't stir at all from our commotion.

Each bed had colourful and elaborately designed blankets and the walls were a dusty pink with abstract paint designs that looked like strategically-placed paint splatters in blues and purples. I could hear voices of children and women in another room. The twin bed was also being purposed as a sofa as Parkash welcomed me to have a seat while he went into the other room to announce our arrival. I sat on the bed, physically collected, and looked around the room for as many details as I could absorb. I felt a nervousness that a first-time guest would feel and wondered what the rest of Parkash's family would think of this kurta-clad American sitting in their living room. From what it sounded like, most of the time was spent in this other room I had not yet seen and determined the area in which I sat was reserved for sleeping. Across from me was a large armoire and to the right of that in a corner, a television set that had Hindi commercials on at a low volume. To the left of the doorway to the other room was a sink and to the left of that, a small, slender door to what I assumed might have been the loo.

Parkash soon came out from the other room and sat next to me and we began to chat until a young woman came out with tea and biscuits. Parkash introduced her to me as his wife. I smiled and said, *"Aap kaise ho?"* She smiled and giggled, which made me wonder if I said something other than what I had intended to say, then she went back into the other room. The interaction between them didn't seem as close as one might expect with a young husband and wife; I sensed a formal and mutual understanding of their roles in a platonic way rather than a joining of souls.

Parkash and I continued chatting. We were waiting for his brother to get home from work. Meanwhile, his mother came out to meet me. She wore a beautiful women's kurta (a kurti), glasses, and had a kind face. She hardly spoke any English, so Parkash translated while we had a brief exchange. She looked at me with curiosity and had a warm smile that made me feel welcome. I gave her the scarf Parkash asked me to give her. She held it and nodded with gratitude and took it into the other room to set it down. She came back out with a child in her arms, Parkash's newborn son, Yagya (they call him Yug for short). She bounced him in her arms a bit while we continued speaking through small talk before the conversation dissipated.

I was then invited into the other room to hold the baby. In this room was a carpeted den area to the right and a small kitchen to the left. There was a sofa against the wall to the right of the doorway, so I took a seat and reached up to cradle Yagya as he was passed to me. It had been a while since I held a baby. He was calm and observant, looking first at me inquisitively then all around the room. After about five minutes, fussiness kicked in, so I handed him back to Parkash.

Parkash's brother came home shortly thereafter. He looked very much like Parkash and was about the same height. He introduced himself as Bhoopraj. He and Parkash starting to speak to one another in Hindi as if to catch each other up on each other's day. They seemed like two jovial comrades. Bhoopraj was just as friendly and outgoing as his brother. When I asked him what he did for work, he said that he worked in an office. He then began to ask me about my trip, recounting some of the details Parkash shared with him prior to my coming over. I'm usually a little reserved around new people, but because the brothers showed so much interest and were so full of smiles and laughter, I was put at ease in record time. They also carried a distinct sense of pride. They told me about how they were born into the Brahmin caste. The Brahmin caste is believed to be comprised of priests, teachers, and protectors of sacred learnings. Even as a tuk-tuk driver, Parkash seemed knowledgeable about life in an almost otherworldly way and is wise beyond his years, so being of the Brahmin caste seemed very fitting.

After the three of us talked for a while, Bhoopraj went into the other room to see his wife, Srijana, and their eldest daughter, Vaishnawi. By now, Shristi began to wake up and started to climb all over the bed. She wore a beautiful sweater Parkash and Bhoopraj's mother knitted for her. It was full of vibrantly-coloured yarns and matched her dark skin, black hair, and long eyelashes in an adorably doll-like way.

By now, dinner was being prepared in the kitchen. Potent aromas of spices drifted from the open door to the other room. Parkash went in to check on Yagya as Bhoopraj came back out to talk with me some more. At one point, the air became so thick with the spices that my eyes began to burn, so I had to excuse myself out to the patio that overlooked the courtyard. I was embarrassed and apologised as I meant no offense, but Bhoopraj said even his eyes were beginning to sting a little. "It smells amazing," I said, "but

I'm not quite used to all the spices that go into a lot of the Indian cuisine." I'm always more than willing to eat spicy food, but this was my first time being present for the actual preparation of a spicy dish before the stronger ingredients had a chance to mellow in the actual cooking.

As we continued chatting about the work I was doing in India and what things I had seen and done so far, I looked out onto the courtyard where many of the children had now gone inside, presumably to eat dinner. The air seemed to have thickened considerably from the small cooking fires I could see in the exposed units all around the complex. The yellow light of the lamps had their own swarms of flying insects and illuminated the contents of the air with cone shapes like the ones I saw at the airport. The open fires burning on the concrete slabs in many of the shanty units, along with the haze and wandering of stray dogs made this place look unsettlingly dystopian. I'm sure it looked much different in the daylight, but the night gave it a primeval appearance.

As I stared ahead, I sensed movement out of the corner of my right eye, between the hanging laundry just past the security gate. A young boy was standing in the hall underneath a single cone of white light from the exposed bulb in the ceiling above. Bhoopraj and I went out through the gate to say hello. It was a neighbour boy who wanted a look at the American wearing the kurta (or so Bhoopraj told me). Bhoopraj seemed to know the boy as they spoke Hindi in a familiar way. A little girl (who must have been no older than five) appeared from the doorway behind the boy, taking a long, uncertain look at me. I smiled and waved before she shyly giggled and retreated through the door. Parkash stepped out to say dinner was ready, so we said goodnight to the boy and went back inside.

Parkash, Bhoopraj, and I ate dinner at the twin bed. They sat on each side of the bed while I was given a chair to sit in, facing them. The meal consisted of white basmati rice, dahl (a dish made from split pulses like lentils, peas, and beans, often prepared with a variety of spices and vegetables), a spicy chutney and a plate of warm roti bread for the dahl. Their mother sat with us as we ate while the wives and children stayed in the other room. Parkash and Bhoopraj ate with their hands while I was given a spoon. They must have known that I was accustomed to eating with utensils, but halfway through eating, I became aware that I was being watched as I ate. Parkash and Bhoopraj laughed and Bhoopraj said, "We know you are used to eating with forks and spoons, but in India, we eat with our hands." I laughed and attempted to eat the rest of my meal by scooping up my dahl and rice with pieces of roti. I could only have a small amount of the chutney as it was indeed spicy but flavourful. Its preparation must have been what made my eyes water. The dahl was also a treat for my taste buds and the roti not only served to collect the food to bring to my mouth, but also helped to clear my palate so every bite was just as delicious as the last. When I started to get full, they insisted I eat more—and I did—but after a few more bites, I had to refuse any more as I was now completely stuffed.

I think what humbled me the most was that Parkash's family had so very little in possessions, but the food was plentiful. Their mother took our dishes after we finished and disappeared into the kitchen. I felt a little self-conscious to be waited on, but the welcome, kindness and generosity their family showed was something I'll never forget; it left an indelible mark on me and a smile in my heart.

By the time we finished dinner, it was nearly 10:00 p.m. Parkash said we should leave so he could get me back to the hotel as there was still an hour's drive ahead of us. As best as I could, I expressed my sincerest gratitude to his mother for preparing such a fine meal and said goodbye to the rest of the family. I was very melancholy when I left because I wasn't sure if and when I might see them all again. To be invited to Parkash's home to meet his family and share dinner with them was an extraordinary honour. I am forever grateful for such kindness. It just proves that it's not always what you say to people that conveys kindness but the gestures that show it.

※ ※ ※

The second friendship (which subsequently led to others) is with my fibre artist friend, Neena, who knits and crochets. The delightful power of *Facebook* led our mutual friend, Stacy Mann, to connect us via *Facebook* when Stacy learned that I was headed back to India. When I landed in Dubai on the way over, I received a *Facebook* message and friend request from Neena. I accepted her request and we made a plan to meet while I was there.

In the afternoon on the day of my arrival, I received another message from Neena to tell me that her nephew, Karn, was visiting from Melbourne, Australia with his fiancé (now his wife), Jess, to celebrate his birthday with the family. I was delighted when she invited me to this event that was being held at her son, Sohrab's, home in a high-rise in Noida. I was to be picked up at the hotel by Neena's sister, Meera, and driven over.

The day of the birthday party, I decided to wear one of the blue kurtas I bought while out shopping on the first day. The weather was sunny and comfortably warm. I had been out with Parkash in Old Delhi in the morning hours and was racing back to the hotel to make sure I could freshen up and change before meeting Meera downstairs. We were a few minutes late to the hotel, but I ran upstairs to get ready before I dashed downstairs to meet Meera outside. When I passed through the hotel gate and started walking down the sidewalk, she flagged me down from her car parked in an area of the road where the tuk-tuks pull over to idle or pick up and drop off passengers. Unless Neena showed her a picture of me beforehand, I must have been easy to pick out of the crowd. She drove a little silver Tata with the driver's side on the right and a stick-shift on the left as most cars usually are there.

After I got in and we introduced ourselves, we started wading through the traffic that would make the trip to Noida about an hour long. As difficult as it was for me to learn the stick-shift, I marvelled at the setup of having to shift with the left hand while sitting on the right and accomplish smooth shifting with all the continual stopping and going in the congestion. I know shifting left-handed should be easy, but the combination of all this backwardness made it seem really confusing to me. I think I even remarked to Meera how she made it seem so easy. It was Sunday, but even on the weekend, mid-day traffic is just as bad as it is during the week.

When we arrived at the high-rise in Noida and took the elevator up to Sohrab's floor, Karn and Jess were arriving at the same time, so we made introductions in the hallway. I also met Sohrab, his wife, Saumya, and their then-two-year-old daughter, Dia. Neena and her husband, Virender, were there along with Neena and Meera's sister, Rita, so there were many people to get to know and speak with. Neena, Meera, and Rita have another sister named Prerna, but she was not in attendance. Everyone was incredibly warm and welcoming. As a visitor of a family event, the last thing I wanted was to divert attention away from the birthday boy, so I sat off to the side and spoke with Neena and Virender for a duration of the visit. Naturally, there was a great deal spoken about fibre crafts with Neena and discussion about the work that brought me to India and sightseeing plans I had in my off hours.

Great company often comes with delicious food—and there was plenty of it. Lunch consisted of goat meat pulao, fish curry, potato curry, and naan bread. I was warned not to have the fish curry because it contained a lot of bones. I heeded their warning, but it smelled enticingly delicious. Everything was home-cooked and, by evidence of the rich flavour, it seemed that a lot of time and care went into the preparation of each dish. Next to the meal that Parkash and Bhoopraj's mother cooked for my visit, this meal was another exquisite culinary treat. For dessert, chocolate cake was brought out as Karn's birthday cake. Water and tea were served as beverages. I felt a bit self-conscious when I was hesitant to accept water when it was offered to me, but they assured me that it was filtered. As a guest in someone else's home, I didn't want to seem picky, but they understood that my system wasn't accustomed to some of the stuff in the water. Fortunately, I had no issues with anything I consumed while in Delhi and Noida.

After everyone had full, happy bellies, Meera was next to leave the party (after Virender, who had disappeared earlier). Instead, her sister Rita would be taking me back to the hotel. After goodbyes, Rita, her granddaughter, Prakriti, and I made our way down to the street where Rita's car was parked. The day had warmed up considerably and felt a bit dustier. There were other cars and cyclists occasionally passing by on the road. The high-rise development was set back from the business sector of Noida, so it wasn't nearly as crowded. Once we drove back into the Noida bustle and onward to GT Road, across the Yamuna River, past Red Fort, and onto Netaji Subhash Marg towards Connaught Place, there was a lot of time spent sitting in traffic. It turned out to be a great opportunity to get to know Rita better. Prakriti would occasionally speak to Rita in Hindi from the backseat, but Rita insisted she use English, especially since there was a native English speaker in the car. I think Prakriti was curious to know more about me because Rita would often reply to say, "Ask him yourself. You need to practise your English." Prakriti seemed annoyed by this, so she remained silent for most of the drive. I imagined that it was awkward for Prakriti to speak to me directly, so I could see why she wanted to direct her questions to me through her grandmother.

I learned that Rita is a wonderful storyteller. She recited stories from Hindu mythology in remarkable detail. I learned about the two incarnations of Vishnu: Rama and Krishna. When I mentioned having seen rhesus macaques on both my first and present trip, she told me all about the monkey god, Hanuman. "We revere many animals here," she said, "so many of our gods are represented in the form of animals." I had previously known this of the Hindu pantheon but hearing more about the relationship of the Hindu religion and the natural world was very endearing. I've always thought of the sacred undercurrents of life very much connected with nature, so stories of the Hindu religion fascinated me.

Somewhere between Red Fort and Connaught Place, we were stopped at a light when beggars began to weave between the cars with their palms out, some pressing their hands up against car windows. I had gotten used to this, but it's never something you grow comfortable with. A woman with a sleeping child in her arms approached Rita's car and began doing the hand-to-mouth motion. I noticed that many of these female beggars were often carrying 'sleeping' children which prompted me to ask Rita about this pattern. With all the commotion of traffic—engines running, the hum of voices from the crowds, horns honking—I wondered how any child could sleep through all that. Rita explained to me that it's common that these children are not, in fact, the children of the women holding them; rather, 'borrowed' children that have been given opiates for them to slip into a comatose-like state to act as props in order for the beggars to elicit more sympathy from those they beg. "It is a problem," Rita said, "because many of these children grow up to be dependent on drugs and often become beggars themselves. It puts a further strain on the system. It is very sad." I was shocked by this and didn't know whether to feel sad, disgusted, or angry. Probably a mix of all those emotions. It made me wonder what the government was doing to mitigate this issue, but Rita added that there is so much corruption within the government that people who need the most help never receive it, making problems like this a systemic norm. I pondered this and noticed the faces of people I saw on the streets of Delhi seemed to sum this up with just a blank, passing stare.

I was particularly curious about the treatment of women in India, so I took this opportunity to ask Rita—a woman of an older generation—what her perspective was on this point. I was a little hesitant to ask because I wasn't sure if this was a sensitive topic to broach, especially because I'm a male foreigner, but I felt that it was relevant to ask because I wanted to hear it from a woman living in India. Rita considered the question for a moment, then began to tell her story in that regard. I understood (and wasn't surprised to hear) that it's still very much a patriarchal society where men tend to have more freedoms than women. Women must often marry young and learn to live with their in-laws as living separately with their husbands is not traditional. Men are the workers while women often remain home to tend to domestic responsibilities like cooking and raising children. Getting an education is difficult since domestic life takes precedence over anything else. I then asked how social customs have changed since Rita was a young woman. She went on to explain that change has been slow since she was younger, but things *are* changing. Arranged marriage is still very much a custom, but there is also a shift happening in the younger generation where more women are seeking their education to have a greater potential for employment and possibility for independent lives, or at least a greater say in how they want to lead their lives.

Once we arrived back at Shangri-La, I said my goodbyes to Rita and Prakriti and wished them a safe drive back through the Delhi traffic. By this time, it was nearly sunset and the cars, motorcycles and tuk-tuks were driving up and down Ashoka Road with their headlights on. Meeting Neena, Rita, Meera, and family was one of the most memorable days of my trip.

Arranged Marriage

During my visit, I was asked (mainly by folks in older generations) when I was going to get married in the way a parent might ask their live-in, unemployed 18-year-old when they plan on getting a job. After being asked this the first two times, I had to develop a canned response something along the lines of, "Well, I'm very independent and enjoy the peace and quiet of solitude." I'm not sure how well-received that response was, but that's the best I could come up with considering the time and place. It's not something I'm customarily asked in The States but understanding that marriage is a big part of Indian culture, I could see how it would arise in conversation.

Just about anyone who knows me knows that I'm gay (and now, so do you). To me, it's just a natural, inherent part of me, but isn't necessarily *who* I am. It's no different than being born with a birthmark; it's there with me from the beginning, but I don't feel the need to make a point of talking about it unless asked and it doesn't dictate the kind of person I am now, will become, or what the rest of my life will be like. I wasn't comfortable enough yet with my new-found friends to explain exactly why I wasn't espoused to a woman and didn't think I was in any suitable place to do so.

Arranged marriages are still very common, so to be a single then-32-year-old without any ring on his finger was probably cause enough for the enquiries. There was talk of marriage (well, even somewhat of a pseudo proposal one night with a blurted out,

"Marry me!") with an ex of mine, but I knew in my gut that it just wouldn't have been right. There was love there for a time (and even a fleeting thought that getting married *might* be something that we did one day), but even a discussion of marriage after only six months of dating felt too hasty. I think my long-held and sacred independence made the idea of marriage more daunting than it should have been. I may be destined to be the fabled Crazy Cat Man instead (which I have no problem with), but perhaps the right person might make me feel differently about that someday.

Despite the heartbreak of the breakup (both for him and me), there were choices made. In India, choices regarding relationships (and marriage) are often superseded by custom, both for men and women. Being introduced to the concept of having your life partner chosen for you makes one's own choices seem very much like a luxury. In Western culture, it's almost unheard of to *end up* in a situation where your life has been forged with a complete stranger where you not only have to learn who they are, but also figure out their entire family that you're now living with (certainly many can relate to how in-laws can sometimes be a royal pain-in-the-ass) and, on top of all that, you're expected to have little humans with this husband or wife person that you're bound to for the rest of your life. It all seems so transactional.

After asking Parkash about arranged marriages, he presented me with a very different take on the arranged-versus-chosen argument that I had never considered before. From his perspective, people in America are always getting divorced (which I think is a fair statement considering the divorce rate sits around 40 to 50% for first-time marriages with an even higher percentage for subsequent marriages); they get to know each other a little bit first, then they get married for love, but they often don't learn to become friends first. In the case of arranged marriages, union occurs between two people who barely know one another, if at all. With the pressure of domestic life and future children, learning to become friends over time is necessary and often grows into a longer-lasting love than the first-comes-love-then-comes-marriage approach.

This new perspective changed my attitude on the topic of arranged marriages. While social norms seem to be changing in India with the newer generations, arranged marriages will likely still be a part of Indian culture, but perhaps not as ubiquitous a custom as it has been in generations past.

Humayun's Tomb

One afternoon after work, I texted Parkash on the way back to the hotel to say that I felt like going out. By the time our shuttle brought us back from the business district in Noida to the hotel, Parkash was waiting outside in his tuk-tuk. I ran upstairs to shed my work clothes and jump into one of my kurtas. It was warmer that evening, so I chose linen.

I started developing almost dual, self-assigned identities while in India where I'd dress in my normal American clothing and put my poker face on for the office. However, once each day was over and I was free to explore the city wilds of Delhi, I'd always change my clothing and mentally check-in to this frame of thought like, *How many new experiences and places can I fit into the hours I have left before it's bedtime?* Frankly, there were few limits and the distance I could go only depended on how far the tuk-tuk would take us.

I didn't have any idea where I wanted to go when I went down to meet Parkash. It had been a particularly stressful day at the office and I just wanted an adventure. Parkash, in his all-knowing, Brahmin wisdom, must have sensed that I needed to see something extraordinary and something to marvel at that night. I didn't bother asking where he was taking me because I had a feeling that it was to be somewhere profound. We went south from Connaught Place, past India Gate and soon reached our destination: Humayun's Tomb. We left the tuk-tuk in a small parking lot, paid nominal entrance fees and began walking the long garden path to the monument.

Completed in 1572 for the Mughal Emperor Humayun, this was the oldest structure I ever visited, after one of the smaller monuments leading up to it, a tomb complex of Isa Khan Niyazi, an Afghan noble in Sher Shah Suri's court of the Suri dynasty, who fought against the Mughals, constructed in 1547. The centuries-old vibe of this place was immense against the mere then-32 years of my natural life. The beginning of the pathway leading up to Humayun's Tomb was flanked by expanses of lawn, Amaltas trees, and flowering bushes. Once we passed through the main gateway and reached the Char Bagh Garden, the cement pathway became red earth. Through it ran a central water channel toward the tomb itself. This was just one of the bisecting central water channels in the quadrilateral layout of this Persian-style garden. Manicured bushes marked each quadrant of the garden that were each their own expanses of lawn dotted with trees.

As it was nearing closing time, there were few others walking the paths. It was dusk and most were heading back toward the entrance, snapping what last-minute photos they could. It was quiet except for faint city noises from the distance and the raucous birds in the garden as they flew from the tall palms around the walls bordering the garden to the Amaltas trees. On a number of occasions, I would stop to look back so I could glimpse views of the setting sun in the west with different angles of the garden and architecture. The evening sky was hazy, with some wisps of clouds high above in the darkening blue sky.

There was a slight sense of urgency as Parkash and I were the only ones walking towards the tomb. Not knowing if I would be coming back to Humayun's Tomb on this trip, there was no way that I was going to miss walking up the steps to the platform of the tomb upon which the entire structure was built. There seemed to be just enough time left to do a quick walkabout. Once we took the several steps up, we noticed there were still some visitors looking around and a few uniformed guards pacing around restlessly. There was a group of young Indian men and a foreign couple who sounded English.

I walked the perimeter of the western half of the platform, marvelling at the incredible size of this man-made structure and profoundly intricate details in the facades. I walked to the west-facing edge to look back out on the garden. It felt like I was much higher up than I was. Birds circled overhead, shrilling and squawking as they had been doing in the garden. The chamber dome was closed for viewing, so I took in as much of the exterior as I could before it was time to go. The guards began to blow their whistles as the exit signal to all of us left meandering on the platform. I was standing still at the northwestern apex of the platform, looking up at the dome when Parkash walked back over to me to ask if I was ready to go. I became very conscious of my ephemeral presence and savoured the last few moments I stood on that platform to this 16th century wonder before we were ushered toward the stairs.

We were the second-to-last to leave as the group of young Indian men followed us back through the garden toward the entrance. It had become twilight and the birds had become quiet as the red earth turned to paved pathway again on the last stretch through the lawns with the Amaltas trees and flowering bushes. We again passed the older tomb complex of Isa Khan Niyazi where I stopped to turn around and have one more distant view of Humayun's Tomb through the arches of the successive gates that led to the Char Bagh Garden. The platform where I stood only moments ago seemed so far away and already a distant memory.

Before heading back to the hotel, Parkash and I decided a chai would be a nice treat before calling it a night. We stopped at a little nook along a street within view of Shangri-La. Its ceilings hung low and had seating for perhaps a couple dozen people. It was almost filled to capacity with a congregation of men who were watching a cricket game on telly. I got a variety of looks from everyone, but generally accepting and benevolent ones. Parkash ordered a potato samosa with his chai while I opted for just a chai as I was to meet my co-workers for dinner in one of the hotel restaurants. We got our chai and Parkash his samosa and settled into two of the few remaining open seats to watch cricket.

I had never watched cricket before, so I sipped my chai and tried to figure out what this game was all about. At one point, I noticed that everyone else with chai had theirs in much larger glasses opposed to the little paper cups ours was served in. At first, I was a little annoyed by this, but when I asked Parkash about it, he said that we were served chai in paper cups because the proprietor recognised that I was a foreigner and didn't want to risk me getting sick by drinking from a glass washed with their water. "The chai is fine," he said, "because it is very hot, but the glasses are not always clean to drink from." It was a simple gesture, but I was very touched by this.

When Parkash dropped me off at the hotel, I met my colleagues at Grappa's for finger food. They were already halfway through their meals when I arrived, but they were kind enough to order me some choices to go with the wine they knew I would undoubtedly want. I seemed to be the only one consistently wearing traditional Indian clothing, so they started acknowledging me as a good candidate for an ambassador to India. I'm not sure how serious they were, but I was quite proud of the idea.

Agra & Taj Mahal

Knowing that I was going to see the Taj Mahal on this trip first reminded me of an AP Art History course I took in high school. This was my favourite course of all time, taught by one of the most influential, passionate, and adorably quirky teachers I ever had, Mary Baldwin. I have no idea where she is today, but I learned that she retired not long after I graduated in 2002.

My textbook for this class, *Gardner's Art Through the Ages: Eleventh Edition*, is a beast of a book, measuring 11.5 inches tall, 9.5 inches wide, and 2.5 inches thick and weighing something like 20 pounds. This book covers history of the cave paintings all the way up to modern art. After consuming the better part of this book during a semester in this class, I hoped that one day I would be able to feast my naked eyes on some of the man-made marvels I studied in this book. This course was by no means easy; I sacrificed many, many hours of sleep and became a regular fixture in local coffee shops where I drank gallons of coffee to be able to earn my 'A'. If there was ever an INSANITY® workout in the form of a class, this would have been it.

I don't recall spending a lot of time on Islamic art in my AP Art History course, but I do remember that it intrigued me. I think a lot of my interest had to do with the details in the calligraphy, pointed arches, and domes in the architecture. There is, of course, the romance behind the creation of the Taj Mahal, but there was also a remarkable amount of thought and calculation put into the design of the structure. *Gardner's Art Through the Ages: Eleventh*

Edition sums it up perfectly:

> The most famous of all Islamic buildings in India is the fabled Taj Mahal at Agra. This immense mausoleum was erected by Shah Jahan (r. 1628-1658) as a memorial to his favorite wife, Mumtaz Mahal, but the ruler himself eventually was buried there as well. The central block's dome-on-cube shape is descended from that of the Samanid mausoleum at Bukhara and also reflects the basic form of the mausoleum of Sultan Hasan in Cairo. But modifications and refinements have converted the earlier massive structures into an almost weightless vision of cream-colored marble. The Agra mausoleum seems to float magically above the tree-lined reflecting pools that punctuate the garden leading to it. The illusion that the marble tomb is suspended above the water is reinforced by the absence of any visible means of ascent to the upper platform. A stairway, in fact, exists, but the architect intentionally hid it from view of anyone who approaches Mumtaz Mahal's memorial.
>
> The Taj Mahal follows the plan of Iranian garden pavilions, except the building is placed at one end rather than in the center of the formal garden. The tomb is octagonal in plan with arcuated muqarnas niches on each side. The interplay of shadowy voids with gleaming marble walls that seem paper thin creates an impression of translucency. The pointed arches lead the eye in a sweeping upward movement toward the climactic balloon-shaped dome. Carefully related minarets and corner pavilions enhance, and stabilize, this soaring central theme. The architect achieved this delicate balance between verticality and horizontality by strictly applying an all-encompassing system of proportions. The Taj Mahal (without the minarets) is exactly as wide as it is tall, and the height of its dome is equal to the height of the facade. The perfect harmony and

balance of dimensions were carried over into the complex as a whole. For example, the bright white mausoleum is flanked by twin red sandstone buildings. One (at the left) is a mosque, but the other is an empty replica, constructed solely to provide compositional symmetry. Rarely has so grand a building been erected just to achieve an aesthetic effect.

❉ ❉ ❉

The van ride down to Agra started on Friday afternoon from Noida. It had been a long week at the office, so everyone seemed anxious to get out and enjoy themselves. The trip would have normally taken about two-and-a-half hours, but a stop for beer (there are no open container laws for passengers), frequent stops for roadside pees for the men and a gas station stop for the women made it roughly three-and-a-half hours.

As the city turned into vast countryside, the air began to smell a lot cleaner. To the west, the sun was getting lower in the sky and was becoming obscured by low-lying moisture in the air. The farther south we drove, the more humid it felt. The long stretch on the Taj Highway/Yamuna Expressway that heads south-southeast past Hathras through the state of Uttar Pradesh was an uninterrupted straightaway. Aside from our stops to take care of nature's calling and roadside photo-taking shenanigans, we'd have to stop occasionally to pay tolls. The stretch reminded me a lot of the I-5 through Bakersfield, California: the air smelled like agriculture and there was farmland as far as the eye could see on each side of the highway.

Of the two vans carrying our group to Agra, I was selected to be part of the 'party van' (no, nothing to do with drugs). This surprised me because I've always felt like that kid who was picked last for dodgeball when it comes to party-anything, probably because my reserved nature throws people off. During one of our first stops, they switched out one of our more conservative attorneys for me because the consensus was that I could handle the crude jokes they were holding back on with said-attorney riding along. Truth is, I'm quiet, but I love crude humour. Give me a few drinks and there's little holding back on the crudeness that often comes with being an Ochs.

The best part of the drive was that we also became the karaoke van. One of the guys, Avikash, pulled out his phone with an inexplicable amount of music on it given how quick he could pull up tunes based on whatever anyone was requesting. Most of what we collectively sang to was American songs like George Michael's "Freedom" and Santana (featuring Rob Thomas)'s "Smooth." I thought we needed some Michael Jackson, so there was "Thriller" and "Billy Jean." We also had some Bee Gees' "Stayin' Alive" and Donna Summer's "Hot Stuff" thrown in. While I love good American classics, I hoped for some "Aaj Ki Raat" from *Slumdog Millionaire* or "Jimmi Jimmi Jimmi Aaja" from *Disco Dancer*, had I only been able to remember the names of the songs at the time. I wanted to enjoy Indian culture as an American while in India, including the music. However, a bunch of Indian guys singing "Freedom" lyrics at the top of their lungs was genuine, unforgettable hilarity.

When we arrived in Agra, we drove through dense, narrow streets filled with roadside vendors, a hoard of people walking the streets and the familiar sight of cows and tuk-tuks. It was around

9:00 at night and the city was bustling and well-lit with streams of headlights and fluorescence from the multitude of storefronts. Our vans came to a slow crawl as we waded through the crowds. We continued to listen and sing to a variety of American hits until we pulled up to the hotel where we would be staying for the night.

The ITC Mughal in Agra was just as opulent as Shangri-La and The Imperial hotels. The pathway to the entrance had beautiful reflecting pools on either side of it and an abundance of lily pads and reeds growing in them. Flowering plants also grew in spaces between the white marble flanks and the pools. Orange strips of neon light ran along the ground on either side of the pathway making it look like a botanical catwalk. The lobby was even more exquisite with glistening white marble throughout, and plush, velvet seating areas in front of the concierge desks and under a magnificent chandelier made of individual glass globes that formed a large conical shape protruding from an internally-lit circle in the ceiling. The concierge desks were also extraordinary in that they were a series of rectangular, dark-wood fixtures with unique, ornate carvings in each. In the middle of the lobby stood a large, round pedestal table with tall bouquets of flowers reaching nearly as high as the lowest-hanging point of the chandelier. Like the other hotels in Delhi, the ITC was a perfumery of exotic scents that ambiently floated throughout the common areas.

I had a bit of a panic attack when I went to check-in because, for whatever reason, we were required to show our passports. I had left mine back at Shangri-La where we would be staying when we got back to Delhi until we flew out the next night. The only passport I had on me was my passport card which is only valid for international land and sea travel between the United States, Canada, Mexico, the Caribbean, and Bermuda. As suspected, they didn't accept it. After some back-and-forth and waiting for hotel staff to make phone calls to management, they allowed me to check-in, but needed me to send them my passport information electronically once I was back in possession of my passport booklet. For a moment, I thought I would have to sleep out in one of the vans but was fortunately granted a room.

Once we were all checked-in, the plan was to drop our things in each of our own rooms and head down to the buffet for a late dinner. My room was down a long corridor from the lounge on the first floor. Like my rooms at The Imperial and Shangri-La, my room at this hotel was overwhelmingly luxurious. I almost didn't want to touch anything because it all looked so perfect. I felt like a pollutant that had drifted into a pristine biosphere. I set my things down anyway and had a quick look around before I dashed out to meet everyone for dinner.

The extravagant array of food was also a bit overwhelming. There were curries, dahls, soups, salads, sautées, meats, and vegetarian options. There was also a separate area for desserts like yogurts, fruits, cakes, pies, fudge, and little cup desserts with tiramisu and cheesecake. I started with small portions, but this only led to three servings before I even ventured into desserts. Wine and other alcoholic beverages were copious; happy people and laughter were abundant. I don't think a finer hotel dining experience was had on this trip. It had already been a long day of work and travel time to Agra, so we were all in need of delicious food and beverages.

After dinner when we were all thoroughly full (and a little inebriated), we went to the hotel rooftop to try and get a glimpse of the Taj Mahal. We were told that on some nights, it could be seen lit up if the moon was big enough. It turned out to be hazy that night with clouds hiding the moon, but some of us were able to discern the dome and the four minarets. I was able to see a vague silhouette. I knew I would be seeing the Taj in its full glory the next day, so I was more interested in seeing what lay just beyond the grounds of the hotel. I could hear some ethnic music playing in the distance and a collection of elated voices from what seemed to be coming from a party. Agra seemed to be much darker than Delhi, save for a smattering of dim lights from modest residential areas.

The next morning, I awoke with discomfort in my gut—the colloquial 'rumble in the jungle.' I had an instant flashback to when I had visited Tecate, Mexico with my grandparents as a teenager when I made the unfortunate mistake of drinking a soda with ice made from their water and eating tacos with lettuce washed with the same water. I don't know if it was one or both that did it, but I had the worst case of Montezuma's Revenge the night we returned home to San Diego. It was not only a horrible experience in unmentionable ways, but the pain in my gut was like digesting barbed wire. What I remember the most was trying to live through the pain while writhing in bed (when I wasn't spending long spells in the bathroom) like some poor, possessed soul. Sleep was impossible, and the only mildly comfortable position was staying bent over on my knees with my face planted in the pillow. For whatever reason, I didn't go to the hospital and all my parents could do was give me household pain medications.

I remember this lasting for at least a couple nights, all the while not eating a thing. I felt like that injured animal you find that is so far beyond saving that the only humane thing to do is to euthanise it.

What I had, however, didn't give me the same sharp pain (thank all that is holy) but, let's just say, had me confined to the bathroom for the better part of the morning. Fortunately, I brought along an emergency prescription in the event of this magnitude of sickness, so I quickly took one of the pills and prayed for mercy. At first, I was almost in tears because I was afraid that I'd have to stay behind at the hotel while everyone else got to go see the Taj—there they'd be, marvelling at 17th century marble while I was becoming one with porcelain. I was upset at first, but after a few trips to the loo, it just became laughably ridiculous. The worst part was dealing with the embarrassment of texting my manager to let her know what was happening and to find out when we were leaving. Thankfully, I had about an hour before everyone would meet in the lobby to check-out.

For that hour, I literally had to coach myself through the rest of the ordeal, all the while trying to figure out what the hell I ate that did me in. I did have a great deal of different foods the night before, but I eventually concluded that perhaps it was due to having never been in Agra before, so something that came from the city that went into the making of one of the foods was probably what got to me. I also realised that I hadn't taken my pills the day before. Eventually, within 10 minutes to spare, the medication kicked in and calmed the beast. When I was able to go through the motions of dressing myself without feeling the onset of another aftershock, I deemed myself well enough to leave the room. When I met my manager and boss in the lobby, I would have preferred they didn't mention it at all but having people I work with acknowledge it out in the open was insult to injury despite their good intentions. I skipped breakfast, taking only water with me, and thought it ironic how I managed to avoid Delhi Belly all this time but fall victim to what I decided to call Agra Aggravation.

Driving to the point where we would park the vans to get to the Taj Mahal took only a matter of minutes. I was excited to see the streets of Agra in the daytime. They were still bustling with people as if the city had never slept. Some of the roads were a little bumpy, so I had to brace myself with breathing exercises and drink water, hoping that the medication would hold out for the rest of the day. The jungle thunder had subsided, but my insides still felt ravaged. At this point, diverting my attention to all the sights around me was helping.

We parked on a side street and walked a few yards to where camel-drawn carts were waiting for us. Rather than walk the long distance to the ticket boxes, we decided to take this mode of transportation. Sadly, these camels were not in the best condition, yet they stood before their carts with stoic obligation. They had rope nets for muzzles that connected to rope harnesses with reins that stretched back over their humps to the handlers. They wore shoddy A-shaped wooden frames over their humps with horizontal planks of wood running the length of these frames as footing for whomever would want to ride atop the camels. My manager, being an animal-lover, ventured onto the camel drawing our cart, despite the smell. I thought it would have been neat to say that I rode a camel while in India, but I was too afraid of upsetting the belly again, let alone contracting some sort of crotch-rot if I straddled one of these poor creatures.

The smell of these unfortunate beasts was almost unbearable as plastic burlap poo sacks were strapped under their tails to collect their excrement. If the sickness I had that morning came with nausea, I surely would have been vomiting on the side of the road. The distance to the ticket boxes spanned the length of an American football field, so I was willing to walk there in my sympathy and guilty disgust for these animals, but because we were now entering a tourism area, the beggars were out in force and especially persistent. I decided to swallow my pride and ride with everyone else.

Once we exited the camel carts, the crowd of beggars seemed to double in size. Other tourists had also crowded together. The day was overcast, the muggiest of days on the entire trip and with the humidity came a hoard of midges that descended upon everyone like a biblical plague. Before we left the vans, we applied an oily insect repellent which, mixed with sweat, only turned me into walking fly tape. Before long, I was freckled with these little black bugs. I didn't have sunglasses that day, but wished I did because I was worried about these things flying into my eyes. The only alternative was to walk with my head tilted down and one hand shielding my eyes. I'm sure I inadvertently ate some of these; it was inevitable. In all honesty, I wasn't really enjoying myself at that point, but hoped the sights I was about to see would be redeeming.

Once we were herded through the packed line that meandered through a maze of barricades, we emerged like cattle to pasture with our tickets. The packed entryway at admissions turned into broad cement pathways that cut through expanses of lawn and shrubbery. Once we were all accounted for, our tour guide led us to the front of the towering main gate that we would pass through to reach the formal garden of the Taj Mahal. For a moment, we stood there while the guide recited some history about the four gates and the Taj itself before we merged with the throngs through the gate to finally see the entirety of the Taj in the distance.

There is no preparing you for the sight of the Taj Mahal in person, especially if it's your first time seeing it. I would have preferred to walk slowly through the gate to make the approach as appreciable as the sight of the Taj itself, but I was forced to go with the pace of everyone around me. Once I passed through the archway of the gate and out of the main foot traffic, I stopped and just stood there. There, in the distance, was the ultimate architectural display of love and devotion. All that ran through my mind was, *My god, I made it. I can't believe I'm actually here.* It's in moments like this that you become instantly aware of your short existence on earth. I then thought, *Humans—people—made all this, and in such extraordinary perfection centuries ago.* Once you come to terms with the sheer magnificence of it, then you start to contemplate the logistics of its construction and wonder how this was all accomplished with such mathematical precision and symmetry.

Before we descended into the garden from the gate platform, the tour guide's photographer wanted to get photos of us in a group, individually, and in smaller groups for the separate company employees. I wasn't feeling particularly photogenic after being sick that morning, but when it came time for me to do silly tourist poses in front of the Taj Mahal, I was less than enthusiastic, but did so solely out of being a good sport. After photos, we listened to another recitation from the tour guide before our walk through the garden to approach the Taj. I was glad to have seen Humayun's Tomb first because I was able to draw many comparisons between the two. It was also very fulfilling to apply what I learned from *Gardner's Art Through the Ages* to real life. I wished that I was in touch with Mrs. Baldwin because I wanted to share the experience with child-like enthusiasm. I very clearly remember sitting in her class all those years ago, thinking, *I wonder if I will I ever see any of these places we're studying?*

Having no idea what the agenda was for the tour, I didn't expect that we would go *in* the Taj Mahal. I was enamoured just to be able to ascend the platform and see the mausoleum from the outside. When we reached the base of the platform, we were asked to remove our shoes and drop them off at a station like those in a bowling alley, or place shoe covers over our feet that were given to us for an extra fee when we got our tickets. There are two reasons for either removing your shoes or wearing covers over them: 1) The sandstone building to the left of the Taj is a mosque and the Taj is a tomb, so it is a sign of respect and 2) It's practical given all the millions of feet that walk the platform and interior of the Taj every year, so preservation of the site is of utmost importance so it continues to be a place worth visiting for its symbolic, historic, and architectural value. I was suspicious about parting with my shoes entirely, so I used the shoe covers that are the same as those doctors and nurses use.

Being awe-struck at first sight of the Taj Mahal from the gate was nothing compared to being atop the platform upon which it stood. The vastness of the Taj is immense and, together with the intricate details within plain view, it leaves you reflective and speechless; it's a struggle to find the words to memorialise the experience while there. Despite the collective voices of the crowd, I felt withdrawn into my own moment, taking in every possible detail while feeling so completely shrunk in the presence of the thoughtful grandeur that went into the making of this place.

As we entered the south, garden-facing side of the Taj, we stopped to marvel at the lapidary along the walls. Precious and semi-precious stones were cut to create the floral motifs that adorned the panels designed at human height. I used the tip of my index finger to trace the lines, imaging the hands that made them. We walked into the Taj to darkness except for the light coming through the marble jali screens at all sides of the mausoleum. We followed the crowd around the octagonal chamber that housed the marble caskets for Mumtaz Mahal and Shah Jahan. The chamber itself was paneled with marble jali screens having lapidary borders with similar floral motifs as the panels outside. The only way I was able to see some of these details was because of some of the natural light and the firework show of camera flashes. Photography was not permitted, but people took photos anyway. The roaring cacophony of echoing voices was a little aggravating and made me wonder how this could be a suitable resting place with the constant visitation of noisy tourists. Fortunately, however, the bodies of Mumtaz Mahal and Shah Jahan are interred in a crypt beneath the inner chamber, so I had hoped that the regular traipsing of tourists didn't disturb their eternal slumber. *I'd be one angry ghost if I had to listen to this every day*, I thought.

It was an extraordinary experience to be in the Taj Mahal, but the cattle crowding of people around the chamber in darkness was a little unnerving after a few minutes. On the way out at the north side, I quickly stopped in a narrow alcove with a marble jali screen at the end of it. I walked toward it to peek outside through the piecework voids and wondered how many people have done the same at this exact spot over the years. It was one of the few areas near the exit where there was no one else, so I wanted to seize the opportunity to claim a solitary moment of my own. I wanted at least a few minutes alone to quietly acknowledge the significance of being at one of the Seven Wonders of the Modern World.

I hadn't realised that the Taj Mahal sat along the bank of the Yamuna River. I exited the north side and walked the length of the platform between the two minarets standing the northwestern and northeastern corners. The 180-degree view of the river gave added scale to how large the Taj really is. This position also gave me a greater view of the sandstone mosque to the west and its replica to the east, both stoic structures and remarkable in their own rights.

Our group convened at that point and we made our way to the steps down the platform where we made our way through the eastern edge of the garden. Running hoses were laid out to water the lawns and white cranes meandered along the streams flowing from them. I was already getting sad to leave and, like I had done at Humayun's Tomb, began to relish every moment on our way out. It's an exasperatingly rushed feeling because you know that at some point you must leave, but there is tremendous concern because you don't know when you might again be in such a magnificent place. You try to make every footstep count.

After we left the Taj Mahal, we stopped somewhere in Agra for lunch before we embarked on the long drive back to Delhi. The restaurant was an Indian buffet with a setup like that of the ITC with just about the same foods. Considering I was going to be boarding a plane in about 12 hours, I didn't get too adventurous with what I ate, still a little weary in the gut from earlier that morning. Though I wanted to eat everything in sight because it all smelled so good, I was conservative and stuck with rice, a mild chicken curry and heaps of naan bread. I was a little envious of everyone else as I watched them enthusiastically eat all those foods I wanted to eat.

Somewhere along the drive on the stretch of the Taj Highway/ Yamuna Expressway, we stopped at a gas station for restroom breaks and to organise the vans so that those of us heading back to the Shangri-La had our own van while the others heading to Noida had theirs. It was nighttime by then and fatigue had already begun to set in. I wondered how I was going to stay awake until it was time to leave for the airport around 2:00 that morning.

Since we left the restaurant, I had been texting with Parkash via *WhatsApp* to give him updates on when I might get back to the hotel. We wanted to see one another one last time before I headed back to The States for however long before my next trip back to India. It was nearing 9:00 then and I was growing impatient with the drive. As expected, we hit traffic coming back into Delhi which created an even longer delay. Once we reached the Delhi limits, I was antsy, but I felt my brain wanting to doze off like a computer goes into sleep mode. I think I might have slipped into a light sleep with my head against the window before we arrived at the hotel.

As we pulled up to the gate of the Shangri-La, I saw Parkash waiting at his tuk-tuk in the same place where he always picked me up. He must have known that it was us as we stopped to let the guard inspect our van as they do with all the entering vehicles. Knowing how late it was and how far he still had to drive to get home, I felt so incredibly touched by his friendship and realised that such kind souls are rare to meet in one's life. When we parked, I went back outside the gate to greet him. We hugged and I briefly described my experience seeing the Taj. He came bearing a gift which was a large bag of masala chai tea that he knew I loved. It instantly reminded me of the chai we shared while watching the cricket game just a couple days earlier and then back to when we were sitting down for drinks and sharing photos of our separate lives. I was tired, grateful, and sad all at the same time.

Ashoka Road was alive with headlights and horns, but it became melancholy then, losing that vibrant appeal I had associated with it before, knowing that I would have to say goodbye and let Parkash go on his way; his lonely drive back to northern Delhi and I to my mechanical, obligatory packing and preparation for the drive to the airport in a matter of hours. Farewells were made and waves exchanged after we went in our own directions. It was a very definitive mark of the end of the trip, but I had to remind myself that the trip wouldn't have been nearly as remarkable had our unique lives not come together that day I was musing around town. It's the people you meet in life that make the time spent in fascinating places extraordinary experiences.

The Quest for Silk & New Creative Pursuits

My search for sari silk did not pan out as expected. I had hoped to find loads of pre-spun sari silk yarn that I could use to crochet, knit, and weave into garments, but I couldn't find any of this—not in the bazaars, markets, or any of the shops. Because I am also a hand-spinner, as in spinning yarn from wool and other natural fibres, I sought loose sari silk for spinning by itself or blending it with other fibres in my ever-growing stash. I learned that I would have to go to Kashmir—a disputed territory north of India—to find such fibres. However, due to ongoing conflicts between Kashmiri insurgents and the Indian government in this region, the probability of going to Kashmir for textile materials is minimal. The distance from Delhi is also well over 500 miles, so that in and of itself was off-putting. I may have to temporarily set aside the search for sari silk, but I intend to maintain a keen eye for the vibrant potpourri of colour that is trademark of this beautiful fibre.

Since returning from India, I have experienced a revival in my interest for manual typewriters. It all began in March after I took my only typewriter out of a cabinet in my roll top desk where it had been sitting for at least two years without much use. It's a 1945 Smith-Corona Clipper that I bought in mint condition in 2012 and is one of my most prized possessions. I took it out to get some air and decided to write a letter on it after I hadn't done so during those two years. Because I had this typewriter put away for so long, I think its charms were simply out of sight, out of mind. When I opened its case, it was as if pent-up inspiration had been released from it, immediately becoming my muse to write.

After I had written the letter, I began to wonder what other makes and models of typewriters would feel like. The next day, I went on Craigslist and found what would become my second typewriter. Since then, I've been amassing a collection of these mechanical marvels. As of this writing, I have 70 typewriters— an Adler, Brothers, a Cole Steel, Coronas, Hermes, an IBM Selectric II, Olivers, Olivettis, Olympias, Remingtons, Royals, a Sears, Smith-Coronas, and Underwoods. They all have their own look, feel, smell, and even vibe. They also have their own unique histories—some known, some a complete mystery.

When I learned that Godrej & Boyce, an India-based company, was one of the world's last manufacturer of typewriters, I became interested in seeking out shops in Delhi that might still carry secondhand typewriters from the glory days of typewriter production in India. When I did a quick search online, I was pleased to find business names in Delhi such as: Chawla Typewriters, Universal Typewriter Company, Delhi Typewriters, Kharbanda Typewriter Company, and Crown Typewriter Company, to name a few. Most didn't seem to have a website, and those that did hadn't maintained or updated theirs for a long time. I wasn't too disappointed by this because it just meant that I have another exploratory adventure to look forward to on my next trip.

The goal is to find a portable manual typewriter that I can bring back with me to The States as a carry-on item. If possible, I would also love to find typewriter operators on the street who still provide document services for those who do not have a typewriter themselves or the means to own a computer. Conversing with these skilled service providers would be extraordinary for not only myself, but for many of the other typewriter enthusiasts I know here in The States. The Antique Typewriter Collectors page on *Facebook* is a favourite virtual hangout where fellow enthusiasts share information, photos, knowledge, and camaraderie on the topic of our favourite machines.

While sari silk continues to be an elusive find, the search for just the right typewriter to bring home can certainly serve as an exciting alternative. In my collection and use of typewriters, I have also found that acquiring typewriters also begets the desire and need for stationary. While plain white paper will always suffice, the art of composing such things as letters on these machines should not stop at the typing of them alone. I have learned that the material upon which you impart your sincerest thoughts is every bit an expression as the words themselves. For that reason, my search would extend to any fine papers that might be available. Nepal, a neighbouring country to the east, is known for producing unique, handmade paper, so I hoped to find some of this in the shops and markets of Delhi. Typewritten messages on artisan paper is sure to brighten up anyone's day when found in their mailbox.

A Hint of Dubai

On the journey home, Emirates would take me back into Dubai for a layover before departing on the 14-hour stretch home to Seattle. By the time the plane landed, the sun had risen to illuminate the desert sky. From what I could see through the windows across from me, it was hazy with desert dust, like the many sunrises I've seen after overnight drives from San Diego, California to Tucson, Arizona where I would stay to visit friends and chase thunderstorms during the monsoon season. As I waited for the first half of the plane to exit, my mind wandered for a moment and wondered what it would be like to ride a camel out across the rippled desert dunes (and not one burdened by cart-pulling or a poo sack tied to its butt).

Rather than de-plane through a sky bridge, we instead took ramp stairs from the plane to the ground below where buses waited to take us to the terminal. I had never exited a plane this way. My understanding from the announcements was that the airport as particularly busy with incoming flights that morning, so many had to park just off the tarmac and bus their passengers to the terminal they were originally intended to arrive at. When I stepped out of the plane onto the platform, I had to wait in a line that had accumulated to the stop of the stairs while passengers were boarding the buses down below. I had a spectacular 180-degree view of Dubai at that point and could smell the dry, morning air of the desert not far away.

Once I was on a bus, it drove on for what seemed like half-an-hour as it meandered between different terminals, employee parking lots, and airport administration buildings. Toward the end of the ride, we drove along a chain-link fence that separated the airport from the city bustle of Dubai. There was an array of office buildings, retail shops, and an abundance of expensive cars on the roads. At one point, between a clearing of buildings, I caught a glimpse of the Burj Khalifa—the mighty skyscraper of Dubai—glistening silver in the morning sunlight. I kept my eye on it until the bus turned, photographing the image into my mind, not knowing when I might again see it again with such clarity.

The bus eventually reached the terminal where I followed the crowd inside to find out which terminal I would need to be at for my long flight back to Seattle. Meanwhile, I indulged in a bit of last-minute shopping at the cornucopia of shops that line the interior of the Dubai airport. My favourite shops are the perfumeries where I find new and exotic colognes to bring back with me—"stink-pretties" as I call them thanks to a friend's humourous influence.

Connection

Sitting down to write this portion of this book proved that I have grown a strange bond with India, one that I never expected to happen. The first trip seemed to be the challenge of whether I would be receptive to everything it had to offer (and didn't): wealth and poverty; extravagance and modesty; perseverance and despair; colour and drab; beauty and ugliness. All of this is so unapologetically intermingled—shamelessly dependent opposites. You can either take it for what it is—all the synchronicities and contradictions—or fight it and risk being completely overwhelmed.

Despite the oppressing weather on my first trip which made the bad seem even worse, I chose to embrace it all. Similar to meeting someone for the first time, why start off on a note of pessimism? Coming back to India for the second time was like seeing a familiar friend. I feel as though I passed the test on the first trip and now I felt less reserved about venturing about to fill every spare moment. India has a way of rushing in on you if you're not prepared or willing to embrace it, but when you do greet it with open arms, you feel that you're no longer going against the grain.

However many times I return to India, I hope that it will always have something new to show me. Some things may remain the same and familiar as does home whenever one returns to it after time away—the smells, the sights, the way people welcome you back—but frame of mind and order of the arrangement of moments-lived will undoubtedly be different. I can only hope so as returning refreshed—along with an open mind—is the spirit of presentation one must bring with them when travelling to and within India. Being in the present with an open heart and mind is what attracts the moments and experiences worth remembering. Just as it's nearly impossible to overlook happiness that emanates from truly content, balanced people, the Universe has a knack for knowing who is open to adventure. It will therefore show those who seek it fulfilling wonders and sublime connections that will leave them forever changed and perhaps enlightened in ways they never imagined. This is true for me and the anticipation of enriching my life by imagining the vast 'what else', is exciting and immeasurable.

Street-side shave.

Fetching water.

Sachin and his many manuscript paintings.

M&Ms: check.

Young labour.

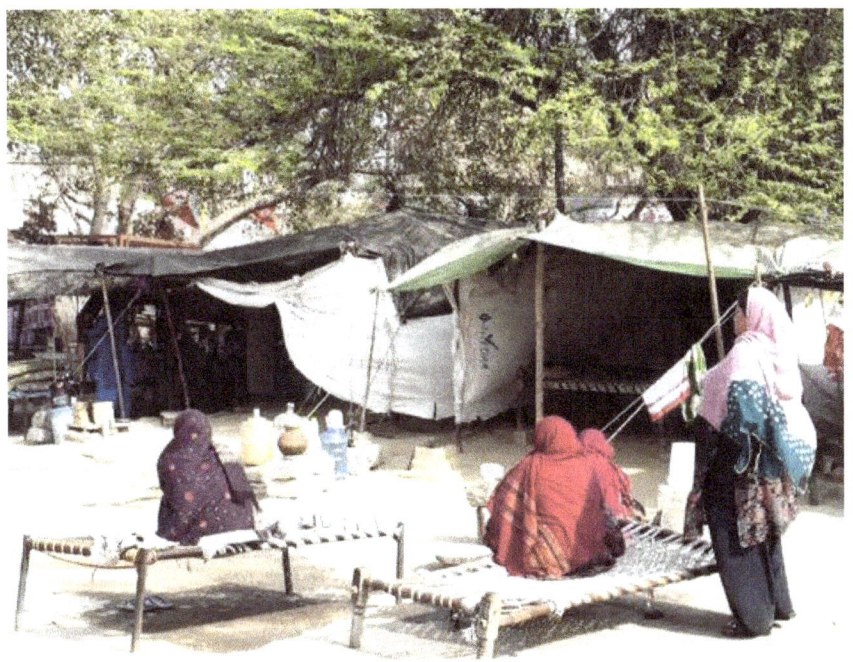
Women in repose.

Clothed cow.

Garmented goat.

Going somewhere.

Stand of spice dunes.

Ready for a close-up.

Dog days.

Piled pomegranates.

Family monkey business.

Humayun's Tomb.

Yagya ("Yug") and the Yankee.

Inquisitive.

Feeding time.

What to make of these Westerners.

Ladies in red.

Wrong end of the camel.

Magnificence.

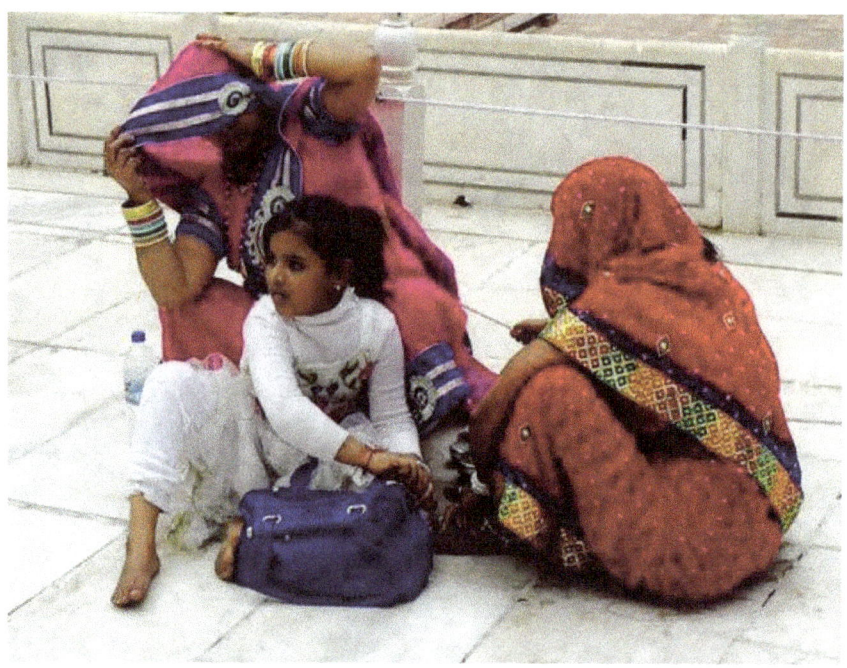
Visitors of the Taj.

Visitors of the Taj.

Scary Sikhs.

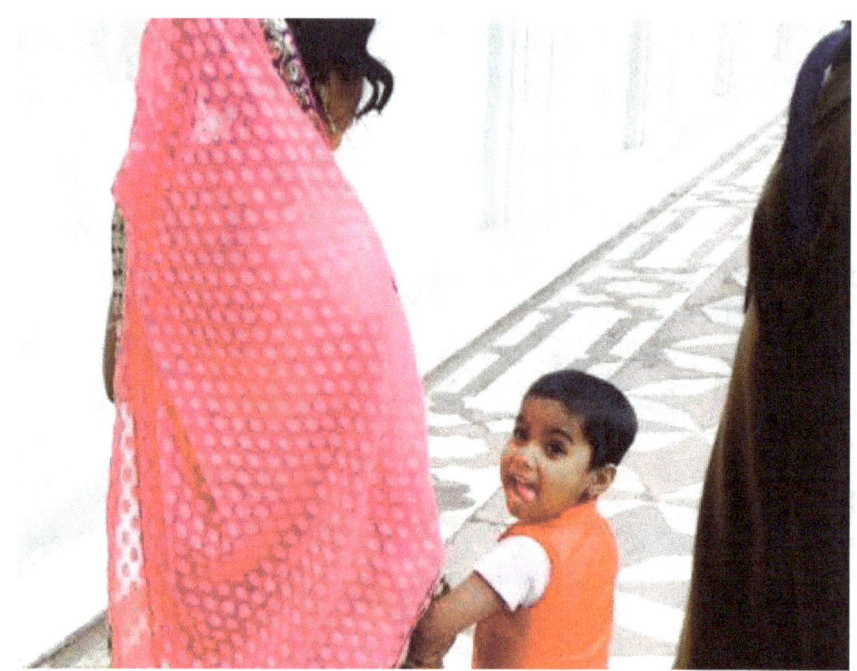
Cheeky.

Juxtapose.

Sweet indulgence.

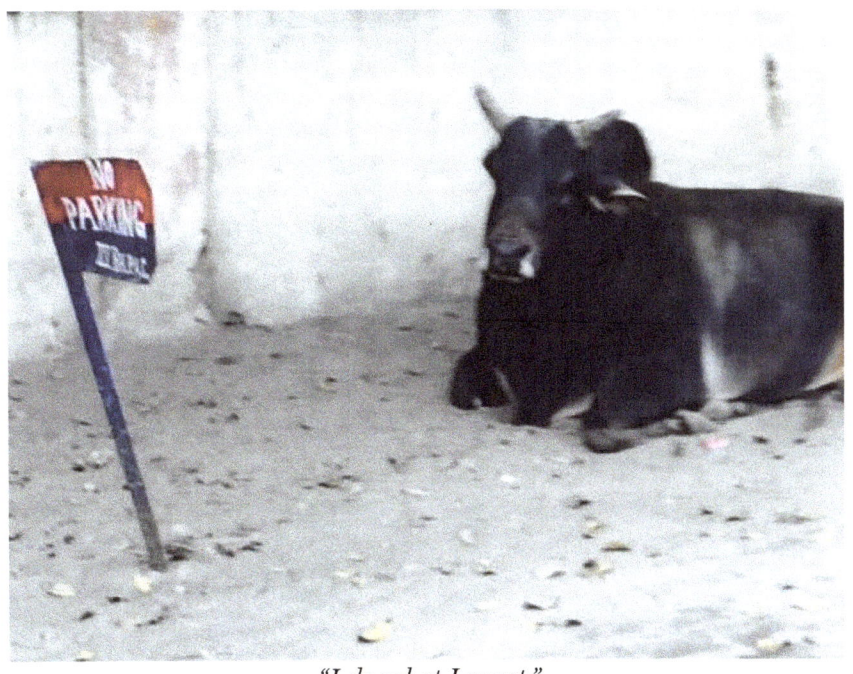

"I do what I want."

Gem-laying craftsmen.

There Is No Time Like the Present

*"A nation's culture resides in the hearts
and in the soul of its people."*
-Mahatma Gandhi

"It is better to travel well than to arrive."
-Gautama Buddha

When I landed at Indira Gandhi International Airport for the third time, the mid-October sun shone down brightly through the haze. I had just come from autumn in the Pacific Northwest, so even the mid-morning temperatures in Delhi felt like the heat at high noon in summer. It was dry though, so it felt more like the desert heat of Arizona than the suffocating monsoonal moisture that sat upon this land just a matter of weeks ago.

Parkash was to pick me up from the airport in his tuk-tuk but was not within immediate sight after I walked out of the terminal, so I waited outside with my luggage. This was my first time arriving during daylight hours, so it gave me an opportunity to people-watch and examine the airport surroundings. Everything was the same as I remembered it from my last trip—the smell of the air, the sounds of different pitches of horns, and English was replaced almost entirely by the chatter of Hindi and other Indian languages.

I stood under the overhang of the terminal to keep cool while throngs of people passed by me with their rolling luggage to either wait at the kerb for their transport, or flag one of the many waiting taxis across the cement island that separated the thruway for pick-ups from the area for idling vehicles. I occasionally looked down into the oncoming traffic to see if I could spot Parkash's green-and-yellow tuk-tuk rumbling down with the rest of the autos.

I stood there for a great deal of time before I started to sweat, and I wished I could change out of my closed-toed shoes but was not of the mind to open my suitcase in the middle of the crowd to excavate my flip-flops from the tightly-packed contents. After some time, I received a *WhatsApp* message from Parkash to say that tuk-tuks were not allowed down the thruway for arrivals. Instead, he had to park in a separate lot and take the shuttle to the area where I waited between columns 14 and 15.

Before long, a familiar voice called for me from over my right shoulder and there was Parkash, as jovial as ever, and looking very dapper in a bright white kurta and pajama pants. We hugged, and he helped me with my luggage on the walk back to the shuttle that would take us to the lot where his tuk-tuk was parked. The shuttle itself was nearly packed as Parkash had me take a seat while he held on to one of the loop handles that hung from the top. The shuttle and all its passengers swayed from side to side as we drove along to the drop-off station. Some passengers were chatty, while others remained in an exhausted, post-journey stupor which could have easily been me, but I had a surprising amount of energy to spare and caught up with Parkash about the flights there, family, and all goings-on since we last saw one another.

The parking lot where Parkash's tuk-tuk was parked was a large, dusty expanse of asphalt where only his auto and a rough-looking tour bus sat. I wasn't sure if my large suitcase, carry-on, and backpack carrying my photography equipment were going to fit in the back and still leave enough room for me, but it did, and we were quickly on our way. I was happy to be back in that tuk-tuk, quietly reminiscing about the many fascinating places it had taken me before and I wondered where it would take me this time.

The day seemed to warm up considerably as it approached noon, despite the breeze brushing against my face as we swiftly cut through the air down roads and circling the roundabouts. When we'd join thick clusters of vehicles in the busier parts of the city, the heavy fumes overwhelmed my senses, along with the perpetual dust that is just as prevalent as the pollution.

Because of my height, my head sits up high in the dark green canopy of the tuk-tuk, so my view of the world outside is always somewhat limited, but on the drive to my home for the next two weeks, I could see the street sweepers tidying the black-and-yellow striped edges of the kerbs with their primitive, long-tipped brooms like large Japanese paint brushes that they would use to move piles of garbage and dirt from one place to another with one hand, all the while sending clouds of dust into the air that no doubt settled upon the passengers of motorcycles and tuk-tuks that sped by. There were also the many storefronts with langouring shopkeepers idling outside either staring blankly at the flood of passersby or smoking; the labourers outside their workshops hammering away at beams on the ground, mechanics working under the hoods of vehicles, and masons moving clay bricks into organised piles.

Amid all this rugged industry, there was the familiar (yet no less surprising) sight of glittering sari-clad women walking through, past, and among it all like semi-precious stones in desert sand. The contrast itself always makes me look twice because it's almost a traditional resistance to the daily drab surroundings; it's an effort to look extraordinary against the ordinary, and they achieve this with the utmost grace regardless of how sweltering the heat or overpowering the exhaust of motors that pass them by.

The ride to my Airbnb rental seemed to take an exceptionally long time, but then I had never taken a tuk-tuk from the airport to the Anand Lok colony. We went through the familiar maze of roundabouts and down along stretches of dusty roads until we arrived in front of the address where I would be staying. The plaque outside the metal, cast-iron gate read, 'BHANDARI' and I knew I was in the right place. The plan was that I was to meet my host, Malti Bhandari, upon arrival, but my travel time there took longer than expected. Through *WhatsApp*, Malti advised me of an earlier appointment she could not break, and that I would instead be greeted by her sister, Monica, until she would arrive.

Parkash waited with me after I rang the bell. A few minutes later, a short, stout man arrived at the gate to let me in. He wore a polo shirt, shorts, and blue flip-flops. I introduced myself and shook his hand. He simply said, "Raju." I determined his English was limited and guessed that he might have been some sort of domestic help. He assisted by taking my luggage down the driveway as I remained at the gate to say goodbye to Parkash. We agreed that I needed time to get settled and rest before venturing out. Parkash would be back later to pick me up once I messaged him to say that I was ready to go out. I shut the gate and followed Raju down the driveway through a small, cement courtyard, then around a row of plants to the front of my detached rental unit that I immediately recognised from the Airbnb listing. I opened the white, sliding French doors to go in and brought in my luggage to get settled. Raju smiled, nodded, and waved before leaving me to get comfortable in my new surroundings.

The rental was modest—not much bigger than 400 square feet. The walls and ceiling were white-washed. There was a small surface area and cabinet above it which served as the kitchenette with a microwave, hot plate, basic cookware, and eating utensils.

To the right of this was a side table that held a basket of snacks, cloth napkins, and a tea set. There was a selection of tea bags along with sweeteners in a container on top of the microwave with an electric kettle next to it for boiling water.

In a corner next to the kitchenette was a coffee table, two wooden chairs with seat cushions, and a long, cushioned bench with navy blue throw pillows with intricate geometric designs. The glass-topped coffee table had a little wooden dish shaped like a canoe that held fresh apples and bananas. Above the bench hung two portraits of Frida Kahlo. One was her famous photo on the cover of *Vogue*, except this print captioned one of her famous quotes: *"Pies, para que los quiero si tengo alas para volar"* ("Feet, why would I want them if I have wings to fly"). I dared not sit on any of this furniture because it looked more delicate than it probably was. Instead, I often found myself sitting at a round, cobalt blue table with a matching chair that were positioned in front of the kitchenette. This round table would be where I wrote my daily notes.

There was another portrait of Frida in the bathroom, picturing her wrapped in a red shawl, leaning up against a wall with a slight, knowing smile. The bathroom was marbled, had a spacious stand-up shower, two-door cabinet for storage, and a wide sink in front of a large mirror. I found the twin bed to be smaller than expected, but as I usually sleep in the fetal position anyway, it didn't seem to matter; the bed was one of the most comfortable twins I've ever slept in; it was firm but had enough padding to contour the body in any position. There was also a ceiling fan which was a relief as there was no air conditioning and the weather, to me, was uncomfortably summer-like. The quaintness of this place was exactly what I hoped for and was preferable to the overabundant and overwhelming luxury of the five-star hotels I stayed in before. Just as I had imagined, I felt like an honourary citizen. The rental had the basics of what I needed—no more, no less.

A few minutes later, a tall, dark-haired woman appeared outside. She looked young, and wore a casual, teal kurti. I left my unpacking to greet her outside. She introduced herself as Monica, Malti's sister. Monica explained that she wasn't directly involved in the Airbnb management of the unit, but she was warm and friendly and made sure I was comfortable until Malti returned home. Monica lived in the first-floor unit of a small, multi-level apartment complex just across the courtyard from the back entrance to Malti's house.

I found that I embarrassed myself when I asked Monica about the two unsealed water bottles that I noticed next to the kettle when I was examining the unit. I asked if I needed to boil tap water in order to drink, but Monica, who seemed surprised at is, assured me that not even the locals drank tap water and said that these bottles were simply re-used and filled with fresh mineral water from the dispenser in the house. If I needed to refill them, I could just go into the kitchen in the house to get more water. Having gotten sick on my last trip and being hyper-aware of possible risks of getting sick again by living, eating, and drinking like a citizen, I subconsciously felt that my enquiry might have sounded ignorant, but I thought it better to risk being rude than to end up confined in my rental with stomach illness at the start of my trip. After that was explained, I think I was forgiven. Monica also better introduced Raju as the domestic help who lived on the property in a small, contained unit next to mine.

Soon after I unpacked, had a shower, and a brief rest, Malti came home and walked over, calling for me. Malti was shorter than her sister (I found that I towered over her) with long, black hair with thin, tasteful strips of copper highlights. She had a thicker Hindi accent than her sister. Malti, like her sister, had one of those warm, welcoming auras that made me feel comfortable and quickly eliminated any initial awkwardness that can often come when two strangers meet. I noticed that she was one of those kind-but-direct personalities in the way her expression would change from a radiant smile to a stern and serious face. Malti seemed pleased that I had already settled in after looking in and explaining details about the rental, basic provisions, and what services and businesses were nearby if I needed to get cash, shop for food, etc. After introductions, I was asked to join her and Monica in the house for lunch that Raju was preparing.

The inside of Malti's home, or at least what I saw of it, had a small fluorescent-lit kitchen with white-tiled walls, grey marbled countertops and floor that could be accessed after a few steps from the courtyard and through a screen door. Because there was no means for refrigeration in my unit, I was allowed to use the kitchen at any time to store food or chill my wine in their refrigerator. A swinging door from the kitchen led to a long dining room that looked straight ahead into the sitting room and beyond that, the enclosed garden bordering the street. The ground was the colour of terracotta and was surrounded by tropical plants and overhanging trees. There was also a swinging chair that I imagined would be comfortable on cool Delhi nights when the mosquitoes weren't at their worst. The dining room was painted a calming cream white with lamps set at two buffet pieces that gave off soft, ambient light. There were also thriving houseplants that grew in pots. After walking through the swinging door, I could see two framed portraits of Hindi deities, one hanging about a half-length lower than the other. The heart of many homes resides in the kitchen, but in Malti's home, it was the dining room.

Sitting at Malti's table for lunch was the first of her many gestures that made me feel more like family than just a guest. As the first of a number of invitations to join them for meals, I felt an immediate sense of gratitude and an extraordinary detail-oriented consciousness of being there, and how it vastly differed from the ordinary routine of my life at home many thousands of miles away.

Lunch was set out on the table in separate dishes: dahl, white rice, peeled long-sliced cucumbers, and red onions. Raju would bring fresh roti bread out on plates over a folded paper towel, and they would keep coming when requested. They anticipated a Westerner sitting at their table as I had a place setting of utensils to eat with while Malti ate mostly with her hands. I thought I would follow suit by placing dahl over a bed of rice and use torn pieces of roti to scoop up the mixture in bites. The more I've eaten with my hands on my previous trips to India, the more I've learned that there is a certain sacredness in feeding oneself without the use of a fork or spoon. It's custom in India, so overcoming the American non-custom of delivering fingerfuls of loose food to my mouth (at least as a grown-up) has been a challenge. Not only that, but considering I'm an obsessive hand-washer, using my fingers like an eating utensil does not come as second nature.

Over lunch, we spoke of my previous trips to India and specifically how this visit was a fresh experience since I was there entirely of my own volition and expense. I explained how it was almost transcendent from a novice foreign traveller's perspective because if I could travel somewhere as far away as India, I could go anywhere I wanted in the world and have the courage to face whatever adversity I encountered. The first two work-related trips were warm-ups but left me desiring more authenticity outside of five-star lodging.

I told Malti that a number of acquaintances back home didn't understand why I would use my vacation time to go to India, rather considering more idyllic settings like white-sand beaches in the tropics or metropolitans of Europe as making more sense but that after two work-intensive trips, "I knew I had to come back and see India on my own terms." With the suffocating pollution, poverty, and frustrating overpopulation, one could hardly consider it idyllic, but I came to learn things, both about my surroundings and myself. The greatest lessons one can learn are from removing oneself from the familiar and comfortable. I'd find myself utterly bored if there wasn't something in new and unusual places that would challenge me in some way. I came to look, to feel, and to dive whole-heartedly into it all with a journalist's eye rather than to waltz about, care-free, for vanity.

My earlier shower and bellyful of home-cooked food gave me the energy I needed to finish the day. After lunch, I went back out through the courtyard to my room where I decided to take some initial photos of my surroundings so as not to forget to do so later.

As I did so, Raju walked by as he bustled around doing chores and said, "Nice picture!" which I interpreted as meaning, "Nice camera!" As I walked around the property, I became more aware of the details around me than I had been when I first arrived. The plants around the courtyard and the thick canopy of tree branches that hung predominantly over the seating area outside my room made me feel like I had my own little piece of a tropical paradise. Way up in those trees were a few brown eagles and flocks of more chatty birds that would settle once the eagles left.

To the left and right of the courtyard, there were separate apartment complexes that snugly bordered the walls around Malti's property. In the window nooks and patios of the square units were common pigeons that flapped their wings while clutching in place as they seemed to fight for roosting space with other pigeons. When they were calm and settled, they gave off loud chortles of what might have been contentment. I went back inside to take notes of the journey thus far.

The intermittent wailing and short bursts of horns from the street rose up and echoed off the walls of the neighbouring apartment buildings. I could also hear Raju shuffling around the courtyard with his pointed broom, sweeping along the brick edges of the planters outside my doors. Somewhere over the wall between us and the complex to the left, I could hear a group of men chatting loudly in Hindi. The neighbours behind us had set up some sort of square blue tent with different colours of lights and were doing sound checks. I assumed this was in preparation for a Diwali pre-party. In additional to all this, there were occasional sharp, reverberating explosions of firecrackers like artillery shells that would send whatever birds were roosting in the tree branches to flutter away in a panic. I wasn't sure if I would be able to sleep this first night.

※ ※ ※

In the warm afternoon, I sat outside to read in one of my light kurtas that I brought from home. I faced the neighbours to the back and would occasionally see heads popping up over the fence as they continued preparations for the party. Quick sound checks also turned into brief singing through the microphone.

A few paragraphs into my reading, I heard meowing before a long, slender cat appeared from out of the low jungle plants to my right. It was orange and white with defined stripes running from head to tail with a wide, thick head—clearly a male. He seemed cautiously curious at first, but when I lowered my hand, he came up to be pet, rubbing his body along the legs of my chair and butting my hand with his forehead. His voice wasn't as low as I've known male cats to have but it was definitely that of a tomcat. He lingered for a while until Raju walked past and took off. I could tell that they were not fond of one another. This was the first time a cat approached me in India and I hoped to see more of him.

※ ※ ※

In the evening, Parkash came back to take Monica and I to Hauz Khas Market. The neighbour's party was just getting started and the sound of firecrackers had escalated throughout the day, so the atmosphere felt ideal for celebrating. I knew I'd want some wine and was told that there was a wine shop in the market. Monica came along because she needed more Djarum Black cigarettes that she got specifically at this market. I was pleased to introduce Parkash to Monica because he had become like a brother to me, while Monica—after intermittent chats throughout the day—was already starting to feel like a familiar friend.

Hauz Khas Market was not far from Anand Lok—maybe a little under two miles—so after merging into the thick of traffic on August Kranti Marg, Monica and I thought that walking might have been faster, but we rode and talked in the tuk-tuk the entire way. The exhaust was considerably thicker than on my drive in from the airport, chemically souring the air, mixed with dust kicked up by the motorbikes, and a vague stench of stagnant water. I joined Monica in having one of her clove cigarettes so the sweet, spicy fragrance would combat some of the smell.

Hauz Khas Market was a busy area with fluorescent storefronts, carts strung with packets of snacks and condoms, and covered spaces along the sidewalks where outdoor merchants sold products one might get at the gas station: cigarettes, cold soda, toiletries, and grease-fried foods. Some merchants sold fruits and vegetables in large, stacked mounds. There were also heaps and strings of marigolds being sold ahead of Diwali; I could only smell them if I walked real close. It was a loud, bustling shopping centre where a thick vein of cars, motorbikes, and other autos passed slowly through the street in both directions while pedestrians cut through at a quicker pace whenever they could.

The dim yellow and bright white headlights illuminated the particles in the air to show the murky mayhem of Delhi streets at night. Parkash stopped the tuk-tuk on a side street and waited as

Monica and I wove our way through the street on foot, cautiously avoiding being caught in a pinch between bumpers or hit by motorbikes buzzing through from the sides. Your safety as a pedestrian is entirely your responsibility. Unless there are traffic lights (which should still never be taken for granted), the concept of a pedestrian's right-of-way is non-existent.

What would become my frequent go-to for wine, the aptly-named Wine & Beer Shop was familiar as a liquor store only in that it was fluorescent-lit, long, and narrow. You had to walk up to a counter to ask for what you wanted, and you had better know exactly what you wanted with your money ready, otherwise you'd be loitering behind the crowd in stupid awkwardness. Fortunately, my height worked to my advantage, so, while fairly minding my order of arrival, I used my towering mass to make my way through. When I got to the counter, I could barely see what was on the shelves, so I asked to duck under the counter to take stock of their inventory. I specifically wanted an Indian white wine, so after a few minutes of looking and getting bumped by the back-and-forth of shopkeepers, I chose a 2015 SULA Vineyards Chenin Blanc. I'm traditionally a reds drinker, but considering the weather was making me constantly blushed, chilled whites were a fine exception. I handed one of the shopkeepers two bottles and scuttled back out from under the counter to pay—750 rupees each which is approximately $11 per bottle.

I saw Monica waiting for me behind the crowd and we hurried our way back to the tuk-tuk for the ride back. In the crowded mess, I could see the faces of men, women, and children, and how they would see me—an obvious foreigner well outside any area where foreigners usually gather to stay (I had seen none since the airport)—and held expressions in their lingering stares of blank indifference but seemed curious all the same. I'd smile whenever possible and sometimes got slight, cracked smiles or nods in return but quickly understood that I was merely another addition to the masses despite being in that fresh, euphoric state a new arrival in a foreign country sometimes feels. I can sum up the message as: *You're nobody special, foreigner, but you're still odd-looking enough to stare at.*

Back at the house, we said farewell to Parkash for the night and sat at the round table in the courtyard for a drink before Monica and Malti would be leaving for a party. As we drank and chatted, the tomcat showed up to join us. Monica called him a "she" and believed him to be a she for as long as he had been coming around. Pointing at his behind, I said to Monica, "Look, you can tell it's a he because he's got furry nuggets." I learned that he was a regular visitor to their courtyard and made it his territory, often fighting off other cats that would encroach upon it. The tomcat took to Monica most of all and was somewhat of a wild pet in the way he came and went. He was intent on affection whenever he was around, nudging legs with the side of his meaty head, then his whole body before inviting himself onto the lap of whomever was available and accepting.

I could also tell that the tom was semi-feral in the way my hands and arms often became prey to random and unexpected love nips that sometimes felt more like a small-scale version of a lion's takedown of a wildebeest; I'd sustain some light damage but learned not to tolerate it or to leave any limbs dangling as I idled. It wasn't until later during my visit that I began calling him Scrappy Tom.

After Monica and Malti left for their party and the night wore on, the party just behind the house grew louder with bass, fast-paced Hindi music, and muffled singing through the microphone. I was in bed before midnight because I knew I needed the sleep, but I fought the temptation to get dressed and invite myself over to meet these people. Ultimately, it was the concern of not speaking Hindi to be able to adequately explain that I was a visitor next door and thought I'd join and hope that it was okay to do so that prevented me from going. Before long, I was comfortably in bed with earplugs in and drifting off to sleep with the vibrations of bass against the walls, and the occasional blast of an explosive.

※ ※ ※

The next morning, I woke early to the sound of men clamouring about to clean up after the party, and metal clanking as they dismantled the tent frame. Car horns were almost nonexistent this time of day. The only other sounds at 5:00 a.m. were the occasional passing vehicle along August Kranti Marg, the whirring of the ceiling fan, and the hissing of the kettle after I got up to boil water for tea. A packet of Typhoo black tea seemed like it would have the most caffeine.

I sat at the blue table next to the kitchenette to drink my tea and read. I had the double doors swung open with the sliding screen doors shut and began hearing a variety of birds filling the voids of silence. There was also some sort of Hindi techno that began resounding throughout the courtyard from a small digital source repeating a tune as if coming from someone's cell phone as their morning alarm. Residential New Delhi was waking up.

My first breakfast consisted of tea, a granola bar, dried apricots, blueberries and cranberries, roasted almonds, and banana chips I brought from home. During my e-mail exchanges with Malti prior to the trip, she told me that there were grocery markets nearby where I could buy enough food during my stay. Because I wasn't sure when I would be getting to these markets after arrival, I wanted to bring enough food to sustain me until I could get to one. I brought enough dried produce and other non-perishable foods to last me about a week if I ate three times a day and not to get full. The selection was nutritious and wholesome, but I knew it would become bland repetition. What I really wanted, though, was some coffee. I had only ever seen chai stands and shops which stand equivalent to how The States has a proliferation of cafés, but I hadn't yet discovered a place where I could get my daily cuppa.

After breakfast, I took a long walk down August Kranti Marg and side streets. The morning air had just a trace of moisture but was warm. As the many autos and motorbikes drove by, each would kick dust into the air that dispersed in their wake. I wore light khaki trousers, an undershirt, a salmon-coloured kurta that extended just past my knees, and tan leather sandals that I bought on my last trip. I could feel a layer of dust start to coat my feet and was glad that at least it wasn't monsoon season.

I must have either been perceived as a resident or because I was outside of any tourist area that I wasn't being incessantly flagged down by tuk-tuk drivers. I simply walked at my leisure as if I had been there all along. There were many schools, upscale residences, some street vendors, and barber stands. Along one quiet street, there was a sad-looking grey horse tied to the front of a cart parked on the side of the road. He looked worn out, tired of his dutiful existence, and flinched his withers as if trying to shake a perpetual itch. I stopped at the corner across the street from him, wishing to cross to see if I could console him—even if a little—from his depressed state, but I noticed that I was being watched by someone from the wall behind him who could have been his owner. I kept walking, occasionally looking back, hoping that this poor animal had seen at least a little happiness in his life.

I continued my walk along August Kranti Marg, occasionally taking a random side street to escape the noise of the growing traffic. I had it in mind to scope out closer markets so I knew where to buy necessities within walking distance, but mostly, I wanted to start building a mental map of my new surroundings. This led me all over, soon disregarding where I had just come from so that I could back-track my way to Malti's. I was comfortable enough knowing that I could always get a tuk-tuk back, so I wasn't nearly as cautious as I was on my previous trips.

By mid-morning, the heat had risen to the point where I began to feel sweat dripping down my back from the continuous walking. I could feel myself getting red in the cheeks to the point it was probably noticeable, so I decided to head back. I was on a side street somewhere off August Kranti Marg—my known go-to for directing myself back to my point of origin—but it had all become quickly unfamiliar. I wasn't terribly concerned; I just wanted out of the heat. I walked my way back to what I did recognise, waited carefully to cross August Kranti Marg, then went down the sidewalk to where I thought I had come from. Eventually, I found the street signs that led me back to the Anand Lok colony, but I had taken the long way to get there. I was pleased to see the 'BHANDARI' plaque outside Malti's when I found my way back, but I was even more confident that I had sketched out some of the area on my aimless excursion on foot. Sometimes I don't mind getting lost because it's a good introduction to new ground and takes out some of the scriptedness in plan-making by adding a flair of spontaneity.

Typewriters of Delhi

Later that morning, Parkash picked me up to go visit some of the typewriter shops I wanted to see. We first headed in the direction of Connaught Place where I knew Adarsh Typewriters was from my research. As I sat there in the back of his tuk-tuk, I was bubbling with anticipation over the novelty of looking for typewriters in a foreign country. It's a favourite activity of mine at home, so the possibility of what I might find in Delhi made 'the hunt' that much more exciting. I considered bringing one of my portable typewriters so I could start writing this part of the book, but with the potential for bringing one home, I travelled without.

Unexpectedly, before we arrived at Adarsh Typewriters, Parkash took me on a side trip to a nearby road that had two different typing schools, each the size of small shops. The first was open but empty of any students. Only a small, elderly woman occupied the school at her desk to the left of the entrance. Parkash and I greeted her before Parkash began to speak to her in Hindi, requesting that we have a look. He also mentioned that I was a typewriter collector and user—pointing to me—to which the lady smiled and seemed to react with approval. Parkash also asked if I could look at the typewriters that were sitting out.

Within immediate view from the entrance of the school was a long wooden table with a low partition running down the middle of it and semicircular endcaps. At both the front end and on each side of the partition sat 11 typewriters that were the dirtiest, most worn-yet-working typewriters I had ever seen. Each were spaced about a foot apart and sat above square stools where students would sit. These rough-looking, standard-size models did not have covers over their spool housings and looked as though they had either taken a tumble down a chimney or survived a house fire. While they lacked any aesthetic beauty, they retained their utility like stoic, battered relics. Many of these were old Godrej & Boyce machines, an Indian company that once manufactured them. I also spotted an Olivetti Linea 88 and a jowly Remington. I felt for these machines the same way one might feel for orphans in rags. These typewriters had a place to reside and a purpose until they would no longer be mechanically useful. The woman at her desk seemed to preside over them in their idling quietness like a Mother Goose, and I imagined the clamour and echoing clacking of activity when class was in session.

To the right of the typewriter station were a few computers with giant monitors set up along a bench against the wall. They also idled—turned off—and were dirtied from regular use. I wondered if students began their typing lessons on the rigid action of the typewriters before they graduated to using the computers once they reached a certain proficiency on the mechanical machines. The typewriters certainly outnumbered the computers, so it must have been a school for beginners. Considering my constant exposure to computers, I was delighted to see a larger ratio of analogue to digital.

Parkash continued to talk to the lady while I looked around, examining each individual typewriter—the keys of the English alphabet, wondering how many people must have typed on them during the lifetime of each typewriter; the ribbon, and the typebars, imagining the cacophony of thwacks each would make on each typewriter during the orchestration of class in session. I had a thorough look at the entire arrangement of typewriters before meeting Parkash back at the front. The lady, who seemed pleased with our company in the lull between classes, smiled as we turned to leave. I put my hands together, nodded with a smile, and said, "*Shukriya*" before walking out.

Across the street was another, smaller school. This one, however, was alive with activity that I could hear pouring out onto the sidewalk when I was within audible distance from all the typing. Again, Parkash stepped in as interpreter to speak with a large, stern-looking man sitting at a desk just inside the entrance to what was barely a small room with similar bench surfaces upon which similar typewriters sat, this time with students sitting before them. The man was agreeable to letting me step in to have a look at the students at work. Both young men and women clacked away at their typewriters with their backs to me as they faced the wall, following lesson prompts to their left. One young woman in a green kurti with a long, black braid running down her back, was using a Godrej & Boyce while a thin, young man to her left in a tight, white, collared shirt and blue jeans was typing on a hefty Remington. On the left and right of these two were another man and woman working on their prompts. The men occasionally spoke to one another as the snap of the typeslugs against the platens continued, all while the whirring of autos driving past and the occasional sounds of honking from the road drifted into the school.

I lingered only long enough to record a video of the students on my phone, but to avoid interrupting them, Parkash and I left after only a few minutes from our drop-in. The man at the front desk seemed like some sort of administrator for the school, so I thanked him for permitting me to briefly step in during the typing session so I could feed my curiosity. Not only was it interesting to see typewriters set up for use in the school environment, but they were used as a foundation for acquiring typing skills when, in places like the United States, learning to type by using typewriters is specific to older generations. While the U.S. seems to have cast typewriters aside in both school and office settings, they're very much alive and relevant in places like Delhi, India.

Back in the tuk-tuk, we drove through the dusty streets and roundabouts to reach Adarsh Typewriters in Connaught Place. I began to see more tourists and the day was growing warmer. The sun hid behind the same hazy sky that I saw the day of my arrival. Connaught Place was, as I remembered it from previous trips, bustling with autos and crowds of pedestrians. Shops were open and other green-and-yellow tuk-tuks, like bees, buzzed up and down the roads looking for fares, or carried seated passengers to their destinations. The air smelled of sulfur and foods like samosas (a triangular-shaped fried or baked pastry with a savory filling often consisting of spiced potatoes, onions, and pulses) and kachori (another deep fried breaded treat often served with *moong dal* or mung lentils). The sound of horns grew louder and the whole of traffic was a thunderous drone that reverberated throughout the Imperial-style buildings.

We parked just outside Adarsh Typewriters in a taxi zone and walked up to its orange sign that hung over a dark stairwell between two white pillars and a tall, narrow, wooden door that was shut. The sign read, 'ADARSH TYPEWRITERS, SALE & PURCHASE REPAIRS & HIRERS OF ALL KINDS OF TYPEWRITERS' with the subscript, '(APPROVED GOVT. CONTRACTORS IN MINISTRY OF DEFENSE, GOVT. OF INDIA).' There was also an image of a Godrej & Boyce standard typewriter pictured in a circle on the sign. Outside of the door stood a tall and skinny guard in a blue collared shirt, tie, and black trousers. Next to him on a stool sat another man that looked like another security guard. It appeared that we were in the right place as evidenced by the sign, but I wasn't sure if the closed door was the entrance or if we were meant to ascend the stairs. After Parkash spoke to the guards, we were told that the shopkeeper would be back but were given little other information except that he was, in fact, working today. It was getting on to lunchtime, so we assumed that he had gone off to lunch; we decided to do the same.

Even in the shade, I was starting to wilt in the heat, so ducking in somewhere for lunch and a drink sounded like a great idea. Near where we stood, I spotted an A-frame chalkboard sign that listed alcoholic beverages like beer and—wouldn't you know it—margaritas. I knew that Parkash didn't drink, so rather than go seek out this advertised place that sounded more like a bar, I started to consider where to go so we could both enjoy ourselves over some food (and I could get my drink). I began to sweat more than was comfortable, so I started asking Parkash about air-conditioned restaurants where I could at least cool my skin down from what was undoubtedly an angry pink.

As we were about to leave, we were summoned by the guards just as another man showed up and was unlocking the door under the sign. The shopkeeper had come back and started to bring out all his repair equipment from inside the narrow nook that the door had concealed. I was surprised by how he fit everything in there and wondered if this tiny space was the whole of Adarsh Typewriters. Along with his equipment, he brought out a few different typewriters and placed them in small cubbies in a display in the wall to the right of the door. Considering his shop's minimal space, I wasn't expecting many to come out, but there were three portables that he carried out for viewing. Primarily, it seemed to be a repair shop rather than a merchandise shop with a robust inventory.

The typewriter that caught my eye was a glossy red Brother portable. When the shopkeeper noticed me paying special attention to this one, he set it on his work table and motioned for me to have a seat on the stool to sit down and type on it. I had already dismissed the other machines as they seemed to be in only satisfactory condition, but this red Brother was the most intriguing. Though it had more plastic components than I usually prefer on a typewriter, something about it reminded me of a sleek, red, 1980s Corvette. The body of this Brother was also a bold, fire engine red, and the black keys like the black trim of the Corvettes. Aesthetically, it surpassed the other typewriters but still had minor signs of wear on the paint in inconspicuous places. I was considering buying it until I noticed the carriage return lever was broken off, but there was enough of it left to perform its intended function. Parkash and the shopkeeper watched as I continued to tinker with this Brother, trying to determine if it was worth taking.

It did come with a case while the others did not—most important, especially when travelling.

I typed on it some more and was enjoying the key action, imagining myself clacking away back at Malti's, but then I enquired about the price. *"Kitane ka hai?"* I asked. It was 28,000 rupees or approximately $418.25. I was gobsmacked. Given I had never spent over $300 for a *mint-condition* typewriter in The States, I couldn't believe the audacity to charge so much for a typewriter that had obvious flaws. I would not personally rank Brother as one of the highest-calibre makes of typewriters either, so it was like asking a new BMW's purchase price for a used Chevy. Disappointed, I got up to leave. Parkash asked if there was room to come down on the price, but the price was firm. I left empty-handed, but there were still other typewriter shops to see.

As we left, I wondered if the exorbitant price of the Brother had more to do with the fact that Connaught Place was a tourist area. During my second trip to Delhi, I began to notice this after shopping at various places there and buying goods in other parts of the city where the locals would shop and tourists rarely ventured. During both my first and second trips, Connaught Place became a comfortable and familiar destination, but on this third journey travelling alone to India and staying well outside and away from any of the tourist traps, I began to live each day like the locals, seeing less of what I already had before in favour of different surroundings. This was both challenging at times but mostly it was a relief. I was developing disinterest in Connaught Place.

Our next destination was Chawla Typewriters in Old Delhi. Before heading in that direction, Parkash and I first stopped to eat. I wanted a nice sit-down restaurant, so our choice was Berco's for Chinese food. I was relieved to find that it was comfortably air-conditioned, calmly lit, and had all the delightful culinary aromas of Eastern cuisine. While a chilled beer and a curried rice dish hit the spot, it was good to sit down for a meal with my friend again. Just as we had done after first meeting on my second trip, we caught up on more of what we missed discussing after I first arrived. Just three months apart in age, our camaraderie didn't seem changed in the least; he was still like my Nepali brother. It was clear that he is the wiser of us both which I attribute to his worldliness that far exceeds mine. Our cultural backgrounds are vastly different, but Parkash is one of those people that you don't need to spend an extended amount of time with before realising that you are in the company of a remarkable old soul.

After lunch, we rumbled along to the crowded wilds of Old Delhi. This part of Delhi always fascinates me because it's a giant step up from New Delhi in terms of an assault on your senses, but it has an endless supply of curiosities to the Westerner. The intermingling hoards of people on both sidewalks and streets mix with horse-drawn carts, bicycles hauling produce and other stacks of goods, motorcyclists, tuk-tuks, cars, trucks, lorries, and cows roaming and relaxing freely because, as sacred beings, they practically own the place.

There is an undeniable escalation of noise and pollution, and you better haul ass like the Devil's chasing you when you decide to cross the street through all this mess. There is a steady rush of workers, shoppers, and idlers that wait in clusters for the Tata metro buses to arrive. The chaos is never any less alarming, but

I've learned to channel the locals by taking the it-is-what-it-is approach to just get through it.

Chawla Typewriters was not immediately easy to find. I had the address, but the shop wasn't one that you could spot quickly while driving along Asaf Ali Road. There was a tall, cement, dirt-filled barrier running down the middle of the road, so after doing a number of U-turns and asking the locals where the shop was, we found the part of the road where we were supposed to be to find the shop. We parked on the opposite side of the road in front of a small dirt lot with bricks laid askew where a man sat and watched two black horses that stood and ambled over the bricks. One nearest the road was tied to a cylindrical metal rail with a lead rope and wore a bell on a string with large beads. The other stood in the shade next to a rustic-looking building with a terracotta roof and patches of cream-coloured stucco on its walls. This other horse had a white star on its forehead and seemed a little more agitated than the other.

Parkash and I quickly crossed the street, climbed the barrier along which other people stood while waiting for the bus. The speed at which motorists were coming down the road from the left side made it no easy task to cross, so one either has to wait a long time until there's a brief clearing in the traffic or dart across with your left hand up with the hope that the autos would slow down enough so you can cross without being hit. We reached the other side and merged with the rest of the pedestrians who were walking along the raised sidewalk or along the kerb.

Walking down the narrow sidewalk, intermittently tiled and set with brick, I saw the sign for Chawla Typewriters over two parked motorcycles, a stack of white-wrapped packages, and wooden crates that rested against a closed storefront. The sign read, 'CHAWLA TYPEWRITER' beneath which was listed, 'GODREJ-REMINGTON-FACIT.' Chawla was not an easily-recognisable storefront, but rather, was situated on the third level of the building complex it shared with other businesses. We took a few steps off the sidewalk that led to a long, dark, narrow corridor with other shipment packages like those that sat out on the sidewalk. Another sign over the doorway to the corridor read, 'CHAWLA TYPEWRITER' in bold, red lettering. Down the corridor were stairs that led to the other floors; we took two switchbacks before reaching the level where Chawla Typewriters was.

Before reaching Chawla Typewriters, I had the idea that it might have been arranged with a variety of typewriters on display for prospective buyers to look at and test. When we reached the top level of the building where Chawla Typewriters was, we walked out into a narrow outdoor area with the sun beating down. The first thing I saw was what I dubbed 'The Heap of Sadness' which was a large pile of old, scrapped typewriters of varying size and shape that were mixed in with broken wooden crates, tarps, cardboard boxes, random pieces of metal, and pipes. The heap was collected into a corner and nearly reached the entire height of the wall—roughly eight or nine feet. I wondered if they had just been cleaning shop or if this was a usual sight.

A tall, broad man came out from an office to greet us and introduced himself as Sunil Chawla, the owner. In Hindi, Parkash introduced us and told Sunil why we had come. Sunil switched to English and began to ask me what I was looking for specifically, so

I mentioned that I was a typewriter user and enthusiast looking for a working manual, portable typewriter to use while I was there in Delhi and bring back to The States with me. There were a couple other men working there, so Sunil summoned one of them to bring out some of their typewriters for me to look at.

Chawla Typewriters certainly wasn't what I was expecting, but it was a fascinating place nonetheless. It was almost like a multi-room warehouse from another era with manual typewriters, mostly boxed and stacked high against walls. While I waited for some of the typewriters to emerge from their storage for me to play with, I examined the surroundings intensely as I wasn't sure when and if I might visit again. The day had reached its hottest and I could feel myself dripping sweat under my kurta, and my face turning pink in the direct sunlight. It wasn't the most comfortable way to shop for a typewriter. Buying these machines should be an experience in which you take your time, test them out, and see which 'speaks' to you the most. In essence, it's a personal experience like shopping for a car: you want to test-drive, check out all the available features, and see if it feels right for you.

From the looks of this common area where there seemed to be the most activity, Chawla Typewriters must have been a supplier for businesses more so than for the individual enthusiast who was looking for aesthetic, functionality, and novelty. A third man carrying packages was quickly coming and going from space to space and up and down the stairs we had just come from, so the packaged inventory downstairs was likely theirs. Ahead of me at the other end of the outdoor space where we stood, the general office was on the left and a larger storage room through the adjacent wall next to it. In the centre, there were tables on the left and right with older, standard models sitting on them. I inspected the table on the left and noticed that, despite having been well-used and cosmetically worn over the years, these few were in the Hindi language. Up until then, I had only ever seen typewriters in English and Cyrillic (alphabet used by many Slavic peoples), so seeing Hindi characters on the keytops and on the typeslugs was fascinating.

The typewriters that were brought out were an Olympia Traveller De Luxe and another Brother, but a larger portable model. The man who brought them out set them up on the table to the right and began to type on each with remarkable speed, occasionally looking at me, then back at the typewriters to demonstrate their operability. Aesthetically, the Olympia was another house fire reject but seemed to work and was the smallest of the two. The Brother seemed to be in better shape but was missing a paper feed release lever and was composed of more plastic than the Brother at Adarsh Typewriters—one I called The Tonka Typer. The Olympia was priced at 3,000 rupees and the Brother at 3,500 rupees—approximately $45 and $52, respectively. These prices shocked me just as much as the 28,000-rupee Brother at Adarsh Typewriters because these two were in essentially the same condition but being sold for pocket change in comparison. I was more convinced that the price hike for the other Brother had a lot, if not all, to do with Connaught Place being the tourist trap I learned it to be.

The Tonka Typer was definitely staying, but I pondered heavily on the Olympia after realising the price was right. I played on it some more, hoping that with each touch of the keys, I might be further convinced to take it with me. It was also getting unbearably hot for me and I could feel the sweat beading up on my forehead and running down my back. I was both physically uncomfortable and faced with making the decision of whether or not I would be taking a typewriter with me. It was still the beginning of my trip, so I thought, *Well, it's not perfect, but use it while you're here to start producing some written work, then you can either sell it before you go, or take it home with you and see if having a typewriter from India might make it more of a novelty keepsake.*

I was not entirely convinced and found it difficult to believe there were only the two English typewriters to choose from. I asked for any earlier vintage typewriters. Initially, Sunil didn't understand what I meant by "vintage" but I gave him the date range of 1920s to 1950s. "Well, we have one," he said, "but it does not work." A little excited, then more discouraged, I waited for this one to come out of the dark storage room. This, too, was brought out into the light moments later, but the doorstopper set on the table in front of me was an absolute no-go. It resembled what might have once been an Underwood 4-Bank, Champion, or Universal from the 1930s but was sadly rusted and dirtied beyond recognition. This one might have been both a swan-dive casualty down a chimney before being salvaged from the same house that burned to the ground. I pitied it for what it must have once been, but it was now just a spoiled ornament.

I felt guilty for taking all the time I did to look, but I didn't take any typewriters with me that day. The rusted, nameless one left me a little broken-hearted, and passing The Heap of Sadness as we left didn't help either. I felt like I had just left a high-kill shelter, then guilty for not taking one of the two typewriters presented to me, then imagining the Olympia and Brother feeling dejected after seeing a typospherian turn to leave them to an unknown fate. I told Sunil that I wouldn't buy anything that day but that I was in town for two weeks and would think it over. I descended the stairs back down to the street a little heavy-footed, but I had to rationalise the fact that, as a collector, I set my hopes too high and that I had many more typewriters—beautiful, functional typewriters—back home in The States.

On my typewriter excursion through Old Delhi, there was also a man working on the street in front of a small typewriter station with a large Godrej & Boyce standard. His desk was just large enough to hold the typewriter and, next to it on the left, a stack of papers about three inches high in various colours, and with tabs sticking out on some. He sat in a dusty office chair on wheels, professionally dressed in a collared shirt with a sterile design like graph paper, and brown trousers and shoes. I walked up to him just as he pulled a completed document from the typewriter and handed it to a man standing on the sidewalk to his right. His next customer was what looked like a Muslim man dressed in a white kurta, white trousers, and flip-flops. He also wore a *kufi* (a brimless, short, rounded cap) atop his head and had a long, black beard. The Muslim man stood in front of the typewriter with his hands behind his back to wait while the typist filled out spaces on a form for him. The Godrej & Boyce was another dirty, decrepit-looking machine, but it seemed to keep up with the quick typing action of its operator.

The typewriters in the schools, shops, and on the street were not much to look at, but their use was still very much alive in Delhi. Their sole purpose was not to be mechanical eye candy, but to perform a job.

A Mehendi Party

More than anything, I went back to India for a wedding. When you receive an invitation to an Indian wedding—especially if you're a Westerner—it's an extreme honour, and all efforts must be made to attend. Now that I have been to one, I can tell you that they are not to be missed.

The wedding was being held for my friend Neena's niece, Shruti, and Ashish, the groom. While the wedding would take place on Sunday, October 23rd into Monday the 24th, 2016, the night before was reserved for *mehendi*. *Mehendi* is one of the pre-wedding customs where the bride is decorated with intricate henna designs on her arms and legs. The *mehendi* tradition is reserved for the bride's side of the family and friends only.

Both the *mehendi* party and the wedding were to be held in the Dwarka colony of Delhi, not far from Indira Gandhi International Airport. This was also not far from where Parkash now lived, so he agreed to take me there on his way home that night. While exchanging details of the *mehendi* party and wedding in online messages with Neena prior to my flight to Delhi, I Googled Dwarka which gave me the result of Dwarka in Gujarat on the northwestern coast of India. Previously, Neena told me, "The wedding is in Dwarka so you can just take the metro to come there." I looked at these results, which showed Dwarka to be about 830 miles and 20 hours away by car. I nearly had a heart attack. I wasn't anticipating having to arrange for such a long side journey to another region of India. Then I thought, *Wait a minute. What metro goes that distance?* I messaged Neena back to confirm and she clarified, "No no it's a colony in New Delhi only…that's also called Dwarka." Then she told me that the Dwarka in Gujarat is the birthplace of Lord Krishna, so I at least learned an interesting factoid out of that.

I was told that the *mehendi* party would be informal, so I wore jeans, a black collared shirt, and black dress shoes. "The 22nd is the informal night," Neena said. "Only the girl's side will be there, celebrating the last day of being unmarried. There will be a lot of singing and dancing and non-vegetarian food. Shruti is my husband's younger brother's daughter—the first wedding in their family. My husband and his family are from a region called Garhwal in the state called Uttarakhand now."

It had been a warm day. The evening was predictably to be the same, so I didn't bring a coat. I felt silly for having brought a few coats when I was told that Delhi would be cool in October, but when summers can reach upwards of 110 degrees Fahrenheit, the 70s and 80s would seem cool to those who lived there. Having just left from afternoon highs in the 60s and lows in the 40s in the Pacific Northwest, to my body, it was like revisiting summertime.

The party wasn't until later in the evening, so the sun had already set when Parkash arrived around 7:00 to pick me up from Malti's. The traffic was heavy along August Kranti Marg and I imagined it would be the same all the way to the party located at Jaggi Farms, Sector 24 in the Dwarka colony. Except for the early morning hours, I couldn't think of a time during waking hours when there wouldn't be a sea of traffic on every road. "Sea of traffic" because it hardly moves at its thickest but has at least some current to it as all the autos inch along at a glacial pace.

The drive over in the tuk-tuk was indeed long and tedious. Being in the thick of smog in the often stand-still traffic, I felt like I was being force-fed pollution. This was the farthest I had gone in Parkash's tuk-tuk in one sitting following the ride from the airport to Malti's. It was nighttime, but I still got to see a lot more of Delhi than I had before. I couldn't tell the exact route we took, but I recall the sights, sounds, and smells as if I were still on that rumbling fast-and-slow, stop-and-go ride. Despite the incessant exposure to all the emissions, dust, and occasional approaching beggars, tuk-tuks are a lot of fun to ride in because you feel like you're cruising along in a covered go-kart that someone else is operating. Whenever I ride in one, I always think of the segment from an Eddie Izzard skit where he talks about Italians riding around in their scooters: "…but most Italian people are always on scooters going *'Ciaooo'*." Why not do the same while riding around in a tuk-tuk: with a flick of a hand wave and wink at the cute desi guys going, "*Namasteee.*"

Much of the ride ran along busy streets with fluorescent-lit shops, some classy upscale retailers, while others were dark and uninviting that sold basic provisions and odds and ends. Because Diwali was only a week away, buildings were lit with vertical strings of lights that hung down from the roofs—some were multi-coloured, some only one colour; some were blinking in all manner of sequences, some were steady. In some of the finer shopping districts, strings of lights were hung over the streets in zigzags, illuminating the windows of cars driving under them and the crowds walking the sidewalks where trees were also warmly decorated with lights wound around their trunks and throughout their branches. To a Westerner, it was like Christmas in October.

There was also the familiar blur of the yellow, lamp-lit roundabouts and long stretches of the *margs*—dusty and murky with exhaust as they always seem to be—leading out of the more congested parts of the city. Soon the little food carts started popping up on the side of the roads, huddled groups of the poor appeared under the dim light, and the ever-present, lanky, mix-breed dogs trotted along the gutters or across the street when they could with their whip-like tails curled up over them. Mostly, though, the drive to the party was thick with traffic, and all there was to do was sit there and just hope that this wouldn't be one of those rides where we got sideswiped by another vehicle or motorbike.

Looking at the faces in the cars on either side, there's always a pensive look of determination on the driver and passengers to get through. Sometimes, others would catch my gaze and stare back for a long time until it was decidedly best to keep looking ahead. Other times, those riding the motorbikes would pull up right alongside us and look in, exchange some words with Parkash, then speed off when the masses of vehicles would jolt ahead again. Having barely any wiggle room between all the bodies of metal, I always found myself impressed with and at ease by Parkash's remarkable alertness and fluid reflexes when navigating this madness to get ahead with efficiency when I thought there was no such possibility. There are very few people in this world that I would feel completely relaxed with as a passenger under such circumstances, and Parkash is one of them.

I had the address for the location of the party in the Dwarka colony but being that it was nighttime and the surroundings were becoming quickly rural, it wasn't the easiest destination to find, even with a seasoned tuk-tuk driver and long-time Delhi resident in the driver's seat. Parkash had to stop a number of times, asking cart vendors, pedestrians, and other drivers *en route* for tips on reaching the specific destination. Parkash had a cell phone with GPS to get us most of the way but oddly, it became more deceptive and precarious the closer we got. Parkash's resourcefulness outside of the use of technology is also one for the books.

When we finally arrived at the destination, I could immediately tell that I was in the right place. The venue was surrounded by a wall but just beyond it, I could hear music playing and many voices. There were also lights strung everywhere, especially at the entrance where they were brilliantly blue-white and marked the way into where dozens of people were congregating. Parkash dropped me off at the entrance which was along a narrow residential street with cars and trucks parked on each side of it below what looked like either large homes or small, multi-unit complexes. There was enough noise coming from the party that I found myself wondering if the people who lived there were given notice of the party. Except for a few yellow street lamps, the curved stretch of asphalt was dark and without any commotion except for the collective sound of music, laughing, and talking coming from the party.

Because my arrival time was somewhere between 9:00 and 10:00, the plan was that I would just request an *Uber* to get back to Malti's that night. This was to be my first time using *Uber* in a foreign country, so I just hoped that my cell service remained strong enough to use the app and that I could convey well enough in English where I was going on top of whatever directions the driver's GPS gave. Parkash saw me in before leaving for home, then waved and left. I decided I'd just enjoy myself and worry about getting back later; I was sure I could figure it out but being on the complete opposite end of town late at night, and left to my own devices, was a little unnerving.

I walked in along a carpeted path that first led me to a few well-dressed strangers who were either standing in place and chatting or walking outside the venue for whatever reason. To my left, under a long overhang were cloth-covered tables set up with metal catering dishes holding all sorts of non-vegetarian foods. I decided not to eat yet and instead went to meet everyone first. I noticed that you could serve yourself, but there were also waiters walking around with trays of samples of the same food.

Inside the walls of the venue was a grassy expanse with covered chairs and sofa-like seating scattered throughout the lawn. The walls had an array of plants growing up them at their base but most striking was all the lights that were set up to illuminate the surroundings. Many ran vertically in long strings between strands of fragrant marigolds that seemed to compete with the savory aromas of the food. The closer I was to the decorative marigolds, the more intoxicating the air became. Just ahead of me from the food tables was a small stage set up for dancing in front of a music station between large speakers where a deejay was playing what I can best describe as entrancing Indian dance music—some recognisably Bollywood-esque. A few women in shimmering saris decorated the dance floor as the fabric of their saris moved in rhythm with their bodies and their bodies to the music. Children were also dancing with them.

Another thing I noticed quickly was that midges were swarming everywhere. In addition to the decorative lights, there were bright, industrial-grade spotlights that lit the entire area from the rooftops of the recreation centre buildings. The midges spun around each of these lights like blazing torrents of a hurricane. It seemed that the lit vortices of these midges kept them drawn to the spotlights, but they seemed to linger everywhere that night. Because all the covered seating was white, I could see the midges upon every surface and I would have to brush them off like excess sand whenever I was about to take a seat. It was a bit uncomfortable having to bat them away from my face all night, but it *was* an outdoor venue. Fortunately, it was cooler the later it got, so they weren't decoupaging themselves to me like they had that humid day at the Taj Mahal.

I soon found Neena sitting with family in the centre of the lawn, just a short distance away from the dancefloor. It was Neena, her son Sohrab, his wife Saumya, and their daughter Dia. Neena's husband, Virender, was also there, and his mother. Everyone greeted me warmly and I was introduced to Neena's mother-in-law, Tara, whom I hadn't met yet. I took a seat while Neena went on to explain to Tara that I was visiting from The States on holiday after my prior visits for work. Everyone had small disposable plates in their hands from which they ate an assortment of all the foods that were being served: sweet potato fries, fried cheese cubes, and fried green beans.

After introductions and a brief chat, I was encouraged to get a plate of food. I found that I didn't need to serve myself because anyone walking in the general direction of the tables with the hot catering dishes was approached by one of the waiters carrying trays with one of the food selections. I'd add some of one kind of food to my plate before another waiter came up with another food. I could have filled an entire plate with those fried cheese cubes, but I opted for variety. I ate more fried green beans because I knew I'd be stuffing my face without discretion all other days of the trip, especially at the wedding.

After I finished eating, Neena took me over to meet her niece, Shruti, who was having her henna done in front of a beautiful display of vertical strings of lights and hanging garlands of marigolds. Shruti was dressed in a sari and sitting very proud and still while intricate henna designs were being applied to her hands and arms. Neena introduced me to Shruti as her American friend here on holiday. I was met with a beaming, red-lipstick smile as Shruti looked up to greet and welcome me. Shruti looked young—probably in her early to mid-20s—and graceful as she sat there being decorated. There were a few other women sitting near her having their henna done as well. I had a close-up look and could see the henna artists—all young men—applying the shiny, dark paste of the henna mixture to the ladies' skin from carrot-shaped tubes of plastic, like bakers use to dress a cake with frosting. It was a detailed process, but the artists were quick about it as there were other women and children wanting to have their henna done.

Neena and Shruti must have noticed my fascination with all the detail before they both suggested that I get a henna design done as well. I was initially reserved about the idea because I knew that it was something only women did, but they insisted so that I could have the opportunity to enjoy the full experience. I agreed and before long I was sitting down to get my own henna done on my left hand. The artist chose an unusual botanical design with three swirls of what must have been flowers, surrounded by teardrop-shaped leaves like some sort of tropical plant, finished off with smaller swirls outside the leaves as vines with inward-curving, fern-like fronds running along my pinkie and index fingers, and a thicker, serpentine line running down along my wrist with four sharp protrusions before ending with a teardrop-shaped bud. The design was ornate but took all of 10 minutes to complete. It looked strangely like a scorpion that had burst into an array of plants. When it was done, I had to be extra mindful of my hand until the henna paste dried into a crust, at which point I could wash it off, leaving only the stained design on my skin.

I wandered around afterwards while I waited for my henna to dry. Music was still playing as people came and went from the dancefloor. It seemed to grow louder at times, then softer, then faster, then slower as different music was played for different kinds of dancing. The adults enjoyed dancing, but the children seemed to be the ones making the most of it in their own unique, interpretive ways.

After a while, I was invited to join Virender and a couple of other gentlemen in one of the recreational lounges for drinks. The room had a large, rectangular table in the centre with sofas, and it was brightly lit with fluorescent lights from the ceiling: not my idea of lounge lighting, but it was a break from the swarms of midges that proliferated outside. There were bottles of top-shelf whiskey and soda water on the table, so we all enjoyed whiskey sodas on the rocks. The servers were also ordered in on occasion to bring plates of the same food being served outside.

Since the U.S. election was just a little over two weeks away, the topic of conversation was both U.S. politics and the occasional comparison to politics in India. Politics has never been my favourite topic to discuss over drinks but given the nature of the contentious campaign over that last several months, I was curious to hear opinions from those abroad who were watching and listening to the campaign. Virender was the most vocal, eventually narrowing the conversation down to discussion between he and I. One of the gentlemen stayed for only a short time while the other sat across from me on the other sofa, mostly silent and occasionally sipping his drink.

There was fair mention of adoration for America from Virender, but I could sense some disdain as well. Virender loved America, but he thought the country was not doing itself any favours with all its wars, "leaving a mess" wherever it fought them, then continue to fight more wars. It's a tricky subject I hadn't come to my own conclusions on with absolute certainty, but I found myself chiding that some wars are necessary, and rhetorically questioning if there is such a thing as a 'perfect war'. I added that I didn't support all our war efforts—many, I thought, having disqualified the country from any deserved adoration—but that some invasions and raids were unquestionably warranted, namely that of Operation Neptune Spear to kill Osama bin Laden.

I might have been on my third whiskey soda when Virender suggested the notion that the U.S. caused the creation of the Islamic State. This wasn't an idea I had ever mulled over at length but one I had no definitive facts on. Still, he loved America and believed that India continues to look to America as an example.

Despite homosexuality being a taboo subject in India, he also believed that LGBTQ rights were improving because of the leadership America has shown in that regard. I remember finding this thought comforting for the LGBTQ community in India but considered it with reservation given how much progress there was still to be made in both of our countries. I was, however, proud that—despite our flaws—America provides a beacon of hope for other countries, in the opinion of some, especially one as large and diverse as India.

Having made another whiskey soda, I hardly noticed the servers coming and going as they brought in additional plates of food, taking empty ones out, and supplying more ice for the drinks. At that point, I wasn't in any state to properly articulate a political argument, so I mostly listened as Virender seemed to become more impassioned in what he was saying about the candidates, the campaign, and the upcoming election, despite our maintaining the same pace in drinking. He would say "you" a lot and point directly at me when referencing Americans in general, but I didn't take it personally and felt a bit removed anyway. I was probably too tipsy to take offense to anything I didn't agree with. Frankly, he gave Americans the benefit of the doubt. At one point, I noticed my henna had dried, so I excused myself to the bathroom to wash off the crusted paste to reveal the design underneath. It certainly did what it was supposed to do and left me with a beautiful tattoo that I still felt silly about but was glad to have the experience.

The music seemed to have gotten louder and more fast-paced as the night wore on. I looked at my phone and noticed that it was inching closer to midnight, so I decided to book myself an *Uber* back to Malti's knowing that the car ride would be at least an hour. My signal wasn't the greatest which left me a little panicked, so I walked out to the street where I got just enough signal to book the ride through the *Uber* app. Once booked, I waited for several minutes to see if the little car icon was heading in my direction on the map. After about 10 minutes, it wasn't moving, so I called the driver to see if he was on his way. I got no answer. Frustrated and a bit worried, I cancelled the ride and re-booked it, hoping my booking would be assigned to another driver that *was* responsive. To my surprise, it booked the same guy named Manoj driving a Tata Indica. I called him again and this time got an answer. "Elo?" he said, before mumbling something in Hindi. I wasn't really expecting an English speaker—nor did I have any right to—but I said, "Hi. I just wanted to make sure you're on your way. *Shukriya*" before hanging up. I felt stupid on top of being inebriated and was ready to go back inside to have Neena make the call for me until I noticed the car icon on the *Uber* app started to head in my direction. I heaved a sigh of relief and headed back to say goodbye to everyone before Manoj arrived, if he were to arrive at all.

Everyone still seemed to be in full-swing of festivities, but the dancefloor had cleared out a bit. I went back into the lounge to say goodbye to Virender and to thank him for the drinks; then Shruti, congratulating her and letting her know that I would see her at the wedding tomorrow night; then Neena and her immediate family, mentioning that I ought to get back so I could get enough rest before the festivities would begin again at the wedding. I walked back out under the canopy of lights at the entrance and waited under a yellow cone of light along the street. The night had grown quiet, the streets more still, and even the swarms of midges seemed to have dissipated as the air grew cooler.

Around 15 minutes later, a Tata Indica pulled up. I stepped up to the passenger-side window to look in, then opened the rear passenger door. "Manoj?" I asked. He nodded, so I got in for the ride back. He had a cell phone clipped to his dash with a GPS map running. "Sorry, but I don't speak much Hindi," I said, with a slight laugh, understanding the futility of speaking before I even spoke. I suppose I just wanted to express that I meant well. He looked up into his rear-view mirror with a vacant stare and did one of those bobblehead nods Indians do as an acknowledgement gesture that Westerners can't decipher between 'yes' or 'no'.

It felt like a long, awkward ride back to Anand Lok where there was absolutely no conversation and only shared exhales of frustration as we hit inexplicable traffic along the way. I felt more awkward for Manoj because it's me who should know at least some of his language, not the other way around. Westerners who are met with English-speaking Indian nationals while in India—despite English being a widely-spoken language—should treat it as a luxury and a courtesy, not a right.

Chanting, Faith & Gratitude

The next morning, I decided to take a walk throughout the colony to get an idea of the layout of the neighbourhood. It was warm and sunny with just a bit of haze in the air. I wore another one of my kurtas over light khakis to stay cool. August Kranti Marg was already bustling with traffic and the birds were flying between the trees, making all pitches of noises.

As I walked through the courtyard to leave through the gate, Malti saw me and came out to chat about the *mehendi* party. Malti noticed the henna design on my left hand and seemed disapproving of it. I noticed this and told her that I already knew it was a custom usually reserved for women but that it was suggested that I have it done for fun and the experience of it. "Usually women only have it done, but you're visiting," she said, "so it's okay," letting me off the hook. "You usually want to get it done on the inside of your hand though. Otherwise, when it fades, it starts to look like a skin disease." *Great*, I thought, *I'll be going home looking like I contracted some sort of skin rot.*

Before I left, Malti invited me to go with her and a friend to a Buddhist chanting group in the area. She said she thought it would be a good experience for me and something I'd enjoy. I immediately jumped at the opportunity because how often does one get to go to a Buddhist chanting group in India? It was about 9:00 a.m. then and we would leave in a couple of hours, so I said I would be back in time after I took a walk through the colony and to find some breakfast.

On August Kranti Marg, I could feel the warm, dusty air sweep against my sandalled feet as I walked along the sidewalk against the rush of the autos. Colony guards in blue button-down shirts and brown trousers sat listlessly in plastic chairs in front of their respective addresses. Some read newspapers; some napped; some just stared blankly with their legs crossed in front of them. I zigzagged along the sidewalk to avoid stepping in the exposed squares of dirt around the trees. These dirt patches, confined by surrounding bricks, smelled foul and often contained pieces of plastic garbage. I appreciated the sight of trees planted down the sidewalks—perhaps to provide shade for pedestrians in the hotter months—but it made walking over the uneven bricks and concave areas of dirt a little precarious.

After walking past several homes and a bank, one of the entrances to the colony streets appeared to my right. It had a manual boom gate that was operated by another colony guard similarly dressed as the others and sat in a plastic chair with another guard sitting next to him. They saw me turn to enter and said, "Good morning!" with beaming smiles before raising the barrier pole to let me through. I would see these gentlemen just about every morning on my walkabouts; they were always very friendly to me.

Anand Lok is an upscale colony organised very much like a gated community. The streets are all paved and lined with luxury cars like Audis, BMWs, Jaguars, and Mercedes-Benz as the domestic help washes them. Most of the homes are set behind gates or walls of their own and are of modern, multi-level designs. Many of the stately residences seemed to have guards of their own like the homes I passed along August Kranti Marg. At the centre of the colony was a gated park with green lawn and shrubs and trees surrounding it. There was some exercise equipment in one corner. If it didn't get too warm, I thought that it would be the perfect place to bring a book to read.

I walked down the middle of the streets so I could take in all the sights. There were lush, tropical plants growing everywhere along the sidewalks and over the walls and gates from the residents' yards. Occasionally, there would be someone walking down the street alone, in pairs, or with children; many of them were women, so I imagined the husbands must have been off at work for the day while the wives went about their errands and enjoyed the surroundings. I'd smile in passing, but the women typically didn't acknowledge me. The domestic help would often stop and stare at me with expressionless faces while the guards were typically the ones who would wave and say "Hello!" or "Good morning!"

After I went right-left-right-left between the rows of homes, I could see one of the other entrances/exits of the colony. I could smell food, so I knew there must have been a market or restaurant coming up. Before I went farther to the boom gate, I saw a large plumeria tree to my right just outside someone's home. On one of the leaves was a beautiful black butterfly with spotted white accents running across the base of its black, lobed wings. I stopped briefly to marvel, then moved along, knowing with absolute certainly that I had chosen the most perfect place to stay.

As soon as I approached the boom gate, to my right was the source of all the aromas of food. There was a small market and a restaurant called Diggin along Siri Fort Road before it joined with August Kranti Marg. I knew immediately that this was where I would be having breakfast. Diggin seemed to cater to Westerners in both its appearance and menu. It reminded me a lot of a café one might find in New Orleans with its French-style patio and hanging potted plants. The interior had a beautiful wood floor and brick walls. Upon entering, the most prominent wall was painted a creamy white and had a large, whimsical tree painted over it that covered almost the entire space. Lights hung from the ceiling that rose high above and seating was organised evenly and comfortably apart from other tables. The overhead music was new American pop and rock hits.

I took a seat at a table near the large windows that overlooked the patio. A small Asian woman waited on me. I ordered a coffee before even looking at the menu. When the coffee came, it was smooth, rich, and invigorating to drink just after a few sips. I placed an order for blueberry yogurt since I already ate one of my granola bars and some dried fruit back in my room. When the yogurt came, it was pearly white, the consistently of smooth ice cream, and had blueberries at the bottom with almond slices sprinkled on top. The coffee gave me the energy I needed to start the day while the yogurt cooled me down afterward for the warm walk back to Malti's. I ate my yogurt slowly, savouring each spoonful like one should do with any kind of food while on holiday. The streets were bustling outside, the day was warming steadily, and I was getting excited for the wedding that night.

When I got back to Malti's, it had already warmed up enough to the point I needed to change again before we left for the chanting group. Because I would be doing an awful lot of walking in what was essentially summer temperatures to *my* body, I would be going through at least a few outfits a day. With an invitation to a Buddhist chanting group, of course I wanted to be fresh and presentable, especially while participating in a new spiritual practice.

We would be taking Malti's silver Scorpio SUV which is a tall, squarish, and spacious vehicle that I've seen frequently in India. Malti's young, freelance, physiotherapist friend had arrived to go with us. I was invited to sit in the front while Malti took the wheel and her friend climbed in the back seat. Raju came out to open the gate and close it behind us once we left. Once out on the busy August Kranti Marg, wading through the traffic in the Scorpio felt like riding an elephant through a sea of people. Naturally, because we were riding in a Scorpio, I mentioned being a Scorpio, so that kick-started an astrological conversation: what our signs meant and how much we identified with the stereotypical aspects of them.

Our destination was not far away. We parked in a residential area past a boom gate in what was probably another colony right by an entrance to a park area. We took a short set of stairs that led to a meandering pathway through lawns with massive trees that provided shade to the area. It looked like a prime location for transient monkeys—and I looked for them high in the tree canopy as we walked—but saw only brown eagles and other birds. There were benches along the path and I thought this would make for another ideal place for quiet reflection or reading.

The Buddhist chanting group was held at a residential complex. We entered through a gate and walked up to an open front door where pairs of shoes were left on the floor and on shelves at a landing. We took our shoes off and left them in open spaces before we descended a dark and narrow staircase that led to a large, plain room that was white-washed, lit with long, fluorescent lights, and had tall ceilings with spinning fans hanging down. There were single-file chairs set up against the walls to the left, right, and back of the room. Almost all the seats were already taken, including much of the floor space where others sat, amounting to almost 30 people. In the front of the room sat a woman in a chair with her back to the other attendees. In front of her was some sort of shrine assemblage and lit votive candles. This woman was leading the men and women of this group in a unison chant through a microphone.

Once I took a seat in the back of the room on the left, Malti came over with a copy of a newsletter of Buddhist teachings where she wrote *"NAM MYOHO RENGE KYO"* on the back of it, pointed at the words, then went to take her own seat. I read these words and they immediately resembled what everyone was chanting in an echoing, persistent resilience before I joined the almost hypnotic rhythm that sent enlightening chills down my spine. Our chanting of *nam myoho renge kyo* was swift and deliberate and, with eyes shut, began to feel more like a temple then a plain white room. I hadn't chanted with this much dedication in a long time, so to join a group of strangers and instantly begin doing so felt awkward and perhaps a bit silly at first, but I soon relaxed, surrendered discomfort, and let the vibrations of everyone's collective voices envelope me.

After about 15 minutes of chanting these words, it felt as though I had been subdued into a delicate but conscious trance. The woman leading the group drew the chanting to a silent close before striking a small bell that resounded like a gong throughout the room. Everyone, including me, seemed to draw into themselves and sat reverently in their places until the woman at the front of the room turned to face us and began to speak.

The woman introduced herself and thanked everyone for their attendance. She also welcomed any newcomers and asked that they stand and introduce themselves to the group. There were a few of us, myself included. I suspected that I might have to introduce myself, so—despite being a bit nervous—I made sure I had something to say. When it came to be my turn, I told everyone my name, mentioned that I had come with Malti whom many seemed familiar with, and meekly stated that I was visiting on holiday from the U.S. and was grateful to be there. I felt awkwardly tall in that room among everyone else and obviously stood out and could feel that everyone might have already had time to acknowledge my presence after I walked in earlier, but the welcome I felt was tremendous. The energy I perceived from everyone there let me know that I was among friends—very balanced and enlightened friends.

What seemed like mostly a benefit for the newcomers, there was some brief instruction on some of the basic teachings of Buddhism and how it shapes our daily lives for those who wish to make it part of daily practice. There was also an explanation of *nam myoho renge kyo*: it is essentially a vow to oneself to summon strength and determination to cultivate our Buddha-like nature that will guide us through challenges. Chanting *nam myoho renge kyo* with others is done because this mantra is also an expression to help others adopt this law for their own lives so they too can overcome obstacles and find happiness.

On the Soka Gakkai International (SGI) website, "a community-based Buddhist organisation that promotes peace, culture and education centred on respect for the dignity of life", it further explains:

> Nam-myoho-renge-kyo *is a practical way for all people to focus their hearts and minds upon this law and manifest its transformative power in reality.* Nam *comes from the Sanskrit* namas, *meaning to devote or dedicate oneself.* Nam-myoho-renge-kyo *is thus a vow, an expression of determination, to embrace and manifest our Buddha nature. It is a pledge to oneself to never yield to difficulties and to win over one's suffering. At the same time, it is a vow to help others reveal this law in their own lives and achieve happiness…*Myo *can be translated as mystic or wonderful, and* ho *means law…*Renge, *meaning lotus blossom, is a metaphor that offers further insight into the qualities of this Mystic Law. The lotus flower is pure and fragrant, unsullied by the muddy water in which it grows. Similarly, the beauty and dignity of our humanity is brought forth amidst the sufferings of daily reality…*Kyo *literally means sutra and here indicates the Mystic Law likened to a lotus flower, the fundamental law that permeates life and the universe, the eternal truth. The Chinese character* kyo *also implies the idea of a 'thread.'*

After introductions and a discussion of Buddhist practices, a few of the attendees read aloud their own personal stories of gratitude, accomplishment, and happiness, and how the law of *nam myoho renge kyo* has helped shape their lives. Even though it was a very supportive spiritual group full of enlightened and enlightening people, I listened to the narratives that were read and thought that those who were reading them were incredibly brave. Some of these stories were very personal while all were genuine and heartfelt. I thought that I ought to practise *nam myoho renge kyo* in my own life to see what changes come about. In whatever form, chanting, faith, and gratitude can only help manifest more beautiful things, especially if more people incorporated these practices into their lives.

After the last story was recited, the gathering was concluded with another chanting session before everyone rose from the floor or their seats to leave or mingle and speak with others. I met a few of the attendees: a middle-aged gentleman who works in textiles; a young woman who lives in San Francisco and works in education, having just earned her Masters degree; and the woman who led the group after Malti initiated the introduction before we left. I also left with two small yellow-and-pink lotus-shaped candles and a scroll of paper with a yellow ribbon tied around it. It wasn't until I returned home to The States before I untied the ribbon to open this scroll. It was a list: "Ten Key Points to Apply to Your Buddhist Practice," by Jeanny Chen (from the November 2000 issue of *Living Buddhism*):

1) FAITH

There are several things we can do to strengthen our faith. First, we can practice vigorously to get results or benefits. Second, we can attend SGI discussion meetings and listen to others' experiences. Third, we can study SGI publications to deepen our understanding of Buddhism. Fourth, we can connect with seniors in faith to receive encouragement and advice.

The benefits of the Gohonzon are expansive, infinite and know no bounds.

2) MISSION

What's our mission in Nichiren Daishonin's Buddhism? The first mission is to become happy ourselves. The second mission is to help others become happy, which is what we call Kosen-ruru or world peace. It's very important to support our mentor SGI President Ikeda and the SGI's mission of peace, culture and education and also to help develop capable and positive successors for the 21st century.

3) GOALS

The third point is having a Goal. We often hear that goals should be specific and detailed. We can set bold, ambitious goals. The more impossible they are, the more rewarding they become when we reach them. We can also set goals that we feel comfortable with. Basically, we set goals to overcome hardship and create value.

4) DETERMINATION

Now that we've converted our dreams and desires into very concrete goals next is my fourth key point: Determination. We have to be determined to change, determined to never give up and determined to take the correct action now. Let's talk about determining to change. It means to do Human Revolution. It's important to shift our fundamental life tendency in order to change our destiny and our karma. If we don't, we'll just repeat the same life pattern.

5) DAIMOKU

So far, we have faith, we understand our mission, our goal is set and we're determined not to give up until we reach our goal. Now on we need lots and lots and lots of Daimoku. Key number five is Daimoku, chanting Nam-Myoho-Renge-Kyo. Besides morning and evening prayers, we have to chant as much as possible. Abundant prayer is the key.

6) TAKE ACTION

Next, we have key number six: Take Action. Everything is empty without action. In Buddhism, we have to take action, to say: "I'm the one who has to do it. It's my karma, my destiny. When my goals are fulfilled, it's my joy and my fortune."

7) STUDY

The seventh key point is Study. This Buddhism is meant to be studied. Each day we should study even one sentence or paragraph as if every single word is directly intended for us, for our lives. When things don't seem to be going our way, or we find ourselves in a crisis, it is an understanding of the Buddhist life-philosophy that keeps us going till we win. I believe everyone knows the importance of study.

8) SHARE BUDDHISM WITH OTHERS

The eighth key point is to share Buddhism with others. The will of Nichiren Daishonin is the peace and happiness of all people on earth, through the propagation of his Buddhism. Nothing is a greater cause than chanting Daimoku and sharing this Buddhism and the SGI peace movement with other people. We have to make such a great cause in order to transform our own karma.

9) SHARE MY EXPERIENCE WITH OTHERS

Now, we come to the ninth key point: Share our experiences. We should share the essence of our experiences, not just the results. I would like to encourage you to chant for the wisdom to share your struggle, your determination and the efforts you made so people will have the concrete information they can walk away with—knowing how they also can do it. In this way, we create the most value out of our precious experiences.

10) CONTINUE MY PRACTICE OF FAITH THROUGHOUT LIFE

It's 'Continuing in our Practice' of faith. The goal of this Buddhism is to bring happiness to oneself and to others. When we have achieved our personal goals, we have more capacity to help others. In a deeper sense, it's the real beginning of our practice, not the end. The lamp we light for someone else illuminates our own way. When we make efforts for the happiness of others, we are helping ourselves simultaneously. Once we achieve our dreams and goals, we should not slacken in faith. There is continual struggle in life between the negative and positive, between good and evil. This is where a benefit can turn into an obstacle if we stop polishing our lives. It's also very important to support our organization in every way we can.

❈ ❈ ❈

After the chanting group, we dropped off Malti's friend. Both Malti and I needed some provisions from the market, so we went to Hauz Khas Marketplace. It was busy but during broad daylight, it wasn't the zoo it was when Monica and I went. I found a little shop where I bought things I needed for my room, as well as wine from the same, plainly-named Wine & Beer Shop. On the way out, Malti pulled up to a fruit stand to the left of the exit and spoke across from me to the vendor to ask about a certain fruit and the price. After a quick exchange, Malti handed me some cash to give to the vendor before the vendor handed me a bag of mangoes.

While leaving Hauz Khas, Malti turned to me and said something that I will never forget. Matter-of-factly, she said, "You know, I only just met you and I feel like I've known you before." I had only been a guest of Malti's for a couple of days. It was probably one of the most complimentary things I've ever heard from a new acquaintance.

The afternoon was wearing on when we got back to Malti's. I decided to lay out my outfit for the wedding before taking a nap after I was told that the festivities could last well into the night. I brought a teal kurta with embroidery around the neck that I thought would make a fine choice for the wedding. I had also bought some white-and-gold khussa shoes with gold trim and a cream-white scarf to drape around my shoulders as an accent. Under the kurta I would wear white pajama trousers that hugged and collected around the lower legs as traditionally worn. It would be the first time that I would wear the full kurta outfit without some Western element.

I napped the rest of the afternoon so that I would be energetic for a long night ahead. I also made sure my camera's battery was fully charged as I would not only be attending as a guest but also as a photographer as I agreed to do.

An Indian Wedding

The sun began to dip low in the sky when I woke to my alarm set to allow enough time to get ready. Arrival time was loosely scheduled for 9:00, so to make the trek across Delhi to get to the Dwarka colony in time, Parkash said he would arrive to pick me up around 7:30. I was excited about wearing my outfit for the wedding, so I got dressed and fixed myself up with the same enthusiasm I do for holiday festivities.

Earlier in the day, I had prepared a gift for Shruti and Ashish. I had asked Neena what was appropriate as a wedding gift from a guest visiting from abroad. She told me that guests and friends can give money but only in specific denominations, and always ending with a '1'. One meaning for this is that to end an amount in '0' would be inauspicious as '0' symbolises an end. To add an additional rupee to a gift of 100, 500, 1,000, or greater is auspicious for a new venture and denotes prosperity. It also symbolises 'additional value added' and wishes of growth and abundance to the bride and groom.

As Neena's invited guest, I was told that 1,001 rupees (approximately $15) would be appropriate. I wondered how best to present this gift so I wasn't just tactlessly handing cash to them at their wedding. An ordinary envelope certainly wouldn't do. This is where Malti's advice came in handy. She told me that presenting the cash gift in a decorative, ornate envelope was ideal and provided me with some options that she happened to have. On the flap of each was an embedded, silver one-rupee coin to conveniently turn the enclosed cash into the desired odd number. Being that I'm naturally drawn to reds, I chose a scarlet-coloured one with intricate gold designs.

I got myself ready quicker than expected, so after I was comfortable in my outfit—hair combed, and one final spritz of cologne, I walked out into the courtyard where Malti saw me and came out to have a look. I was pleased to find that I looked nearly authentic and was given an enthusiastic seal of approval. Monica also came out of her apartment to have a look and gave me her sign-off as well.

Scrappy Tom must have also been nearby to hear our echoing chatter and soon showed up, caterwauling to announce his arrival as he usually did and contribute his company before I left for the night. It was about 7:15, so I had some time to spare. I went back to my room to pour some SULA wine (remembering the wedding itself would be a dry event) and sat with Monica at the table in the courtyard for a moment to chat and give Scrappy Tom some attention. Given he had a habit of randomly attacking fingers, I kept my arms above the table so I wouldn't arrive at the wedding with fresh wounds.

Parkash soon messaged me to let me know he had arrived. I said goodnight to Monica as she went back to her apartment and I headed down the driveway and through the gate to the congested and headlight-lit August Kranti Marg. I toted my camera's backpack along with me and set it in the compartment of the tuk-tuk behind me. Before we rumbled off, Parkash turned around in his seat to get a good look at my outfit. He had a big smile and was very delighted, saying, "You look like you belong here!"

The tuk-tuk ride to the wedding seemed longer and more intense than the previous night's ride to the *mehendi* party. The convergence of autos on the road throughout the city seemed thicker, pumping all their pollutants into the air. The worst was stopping at an intersection and having a motorbike or car's tailpipe pointed in the direction of the back of the tuk-tuk. I thought again how poor Parkash has to deal with this every day, so I have no right to complain. Of all things, I started to worry if my cologne would wear off and how much I might sweat by the time I got to the wedding; I still wanted to be fresh by the time I arrived as I anticipated meeting a lot of new people.

We took the same general route to the Dwarka colony as we did when going to the *mehendi* party; the wedding was not far from where the *mehendi* party was held. Once out of the main congestion, the roads were again long and dark. Some straightaways were clouded with dust as I'd see headlights from another vehicle coming up from the opposite direction like torch beams in a dusty attic.

Parkash and I would occasionally chat but because of both the tuk-tuk motor and other road noise, I felt like I had to yell when we were in the thick of traffic. I could barely hear what he was saying from the front anyway. I'd usually just sit sideways, cross-legged, and watch the other motorists passing, staring—some with their car windows rolled down blaring Indian music—; others with windows closed against the dust and exhaust, their drivers and passengers sitting and staring blankly ahead.

As we got close to the wedding venue, we could see where it was because of the beaming halo of light that stretched into the dark sky. Shortly after 9:00, we turned onto the road where the entrance was. It was undeniably the place where I was supposed to be. There were a few well-dressed people walking in the direction of the venue but not the volume of attendance I was expecting to see flocking in at that time of the night.

I grabbed my backpack from the back of the tuk-tuk, hugged Parkash, and thanked him for another long ride across the city. "Have a good time and I will talk to you tomorrow," he said, waiting for me to walk in before he left. Before walking through the white-and-gold lobed archway that led to a cement path leading down to the main entrance, I looked around and, despite it being dark all around, I could see a big expanse of open space around me. I could hear it too and felt it in the way the air moved. The air had a slight dampness to it and smelled like agriculture.

The cement drive that led to the entrance of Jaggi Green Gardens was bordered on each side by black-and-white striped kerbs. To my left was a stretch of dirt behind the kerb where shrubs and thin-trunked trees grew, reaching high and canopying over the drive. To the right was a long wall of thick hedges about my height that ran the length of the drive from the start all the way down past where a car was dropping off guests at the entrance. Strung in front of this hedge wall was a grid of yellow faery lights that stretched from larger trees that were planted about 50 feet apart. Around each of their trunks was wrapped a coil of rope lighting: some in yellow; some in a brilliant neon blue.

Through the spaces between the trees, I could see the green turf expanse of the wedding venue. It was predominantly lit by towering square columns that held square rod frames above them with brilliant white spotlights projecting from each side. Hanging down from those frames were strings of more yellow faery lights. Midges swarmed the white lights above in a frenzy. I hoped they would stay aloft and keep from disrupting everyone below.

Tables and chairs were set throughout with white, purple, gold, and fuchsia iridescent cloth covers. Through the sparse crowd that had assembled thus far, I could see a pavilion-style building painted white with golden accents. Its roof was flat and had bulbs all along the top like those of vanity mirrors. Bay trees and palms were scattered throughout in their own designated places; each had their own spiral of rope lighting around their trunks in a balance of the same yellow and blue that I saw along the walk to the entrance.

Before I reached the front gate building, I stopped to kneel down to get my camera out so I could start snapping photos before entering. More people began to arrive and walked down the drive behind me. I started to feel a little self-conscious then, thinking to myself, *they must be wondering what this white guy in ethnic wear is doing here, fiddling with a camera on the outside*. I smiled and nodded as they passed. They seemed friendly and welcoming just by their expressions, even though we didn't exchange any words. Everyone was dressed beautifully in traditional clothing.

The entrance matched the intricacy of the pavilion I saw adjacent across the turf; it was painted white and had flowing, organic engravings on the gold cornice. It had lobed arches on the outside and inside with a dark-wood pergola between them. The front arch was decorated with thick garlands of white and red flowers that swooped down from the centre and parted like curtains. Hanging on each side of them were vertical strands of cream-coloured flowers with brass bells on the ends. Manicured palm fronds were placed in curved formations above all this like a complementary window dressing. As I walked in through this brick-laden space, golden, sparking fountains—one against each wall—trickled softly and had petals and votive lights floating inside them. Sweet fragrances hung in the air, emanating from the abundance of flowers.

Once I was in the venue and began to walk around to survey the space, separate details, and the guests, the number of people seemed largely disproportionate to the amount of space. I thought, *This has got to be just a small portion of the attendees*, because everything was set up to look like an Academy Awards after-party. It felt special to be there, like a secret feeling of being part of the in-crowd, even though no one yet knew that I was part of this crowd and only acknowledged for my effort to at least try and look dressed like everyone else.

I hadn't walked far yet but with just a few glances around, I could tell I was the only American there. I found this a little unnerving at first because I do not like drawing unnecessary attention to myself in a crowd of strangers, but I reminded myself that to be out of my element—comfortably, if possible—was part of the experience. I had a backpack with a camera, so I imagined that I might have been presumed to be one of the hired photographers.

None of the people I saw yet were familiar as I scanned the faces to see if I could find Neena, Virender, their son Sohrab and his wife Saumya, or Meera. After putting my camera away for a moment, I realised I probably also looked suspicious meandering aimlessly while carrying a black backpack. I even started *feeling* that I looked suspicious, so I stopped at a table to message Neena that I had arrived. She messaged back, "Right. We are coming soon."

Meanwhile, I retracted into myself and felt the sense of obligation that occasionally came over me during the ride over: I volunteered to photograph the event, but I also wanted to absorb every detail I could through photos and observing with my own eyes because, I thought, *How often am I at an Indian wedding*...in *India*? I was carrying that backpack for a reason, so I pulled out the camera again and started taking photos of as much as I could. I was glad to have arrived early because it allowed me the opportunity to capture much of the exquisite arrangements before more people arrived. To be there to see everyone arrive in small and large numbers was also a visual feast.

After walking the perimeter of the venue to take some initial photos, I took a seat at another empty table to wait for Neena's family to arrive and to sit back and marvel at the outfits of the new arrivals. Women wore elaborate saris in every possible colour and stitching and woven intricacy that defies imagination; men looked classically dapper in sharp-cut, fitted suits and silk kurtas. It was like being at a Bollywood red carpet show. The click-flash-flash of the other photographers' cameras made it seem like it truly was.

Soon Neena's family arrived and we all convened at the table that I had picked out. Sohrab and Saumya also brought their daughter, Dia, who was dressed adorably in a sparkling red-and-gold, long-sleeved dress with gold khussa shoes. Neena wore a dark cyan sari, as did her sister, Meera, but in a lighter version. Saumya's sari was a peacock blue with gold. Sohrab wore a handsome purple-

and-black brocade jacquard kurta with matching pajamas and khussa shoes. Virender wore a sophisticated black suit—a very proud uncle of the bride. When they were all standing together, the many colours of the fabrics of their attire were a brilliant, glittering spectacle.

While Neena and her family visited at the table and spoke with others, I continued walking around with my camera to capture more of what everyone was wearing—especially the saris—separate gatherings of friends and families, and the collective excitement of everyone assembling for the wedding. It was difficult to look anywhere and not find something worth photographing. The care and attention to detail put into everything—the colours, the lights, the arrangement of seating, table dressings, fresh floral garlands, and an exquisite selection of foods.

Across the green lawn in the lit pavilion was where the food was. I had never seen such an array of Indian foods in all my life; the quantities were clearly prepared for hundreds of people in mind. Rows of catering dishes were set out over cloth-covered tables with all sorts of rice, curries, dahls, samosas, and other foods in the Indian cuisine that I had yet to taste. There was also an entire row dedicated to desserts, including my favourite gulab jamun, which are milk solids covered in dough that is deep-fried, then soaked in a sugary syrup that's prepared with green cardamom, rose water, and saffron.

Outside the pavilion was a separate station where naan and roti bread were made fresh and could be picked up by the plateful or ordered hot for delivery to your nearby table. The seasoned and spiced aromas coming from the catering dishes were perfectly paired with the smoky smell of bread dough on the flat skillet cookers that crisped the bread to perfect texture and consistency for gathering the sauced foods on your plate. The naan and roti breads took a while to prepare just right for everyone wanting it, so this station was often the most crowded with hungry, waiting people.

I decided not to eat right away because I still had a lot of photographic work to do and there were more people pouring in as the night went on. By 10:30, I could see and hear the full scale of everyone that was invited—easily hundreds of people. The turnout was remarkable and like no other wedding attendance I've seen. I began to wonder how many people were related to the bride and groom apart from all the friends that must have been invited. Given I was there as a friend of the aunt of the bride, the invitations must have stretched far and wide, but the general feeling was that all were welcome to celebrate this sacred day.

After I covered as much of the grounds as I could, I went back to the table to check-in with Neena. As soon as I sat down, I began to hear distant drumbeats coming from the road where Parkash dropped me off. I realised that this was the beginning of *baraat*, or the groom's procession to the wedding venue. I quickly grabbed my camera and was on my feet again, wading through the crowd to get to the entrance gate and down the cement drive to the dirt road where the *baraati*, or those joining the procession, were gathering. Since *baraat* is usually reserved for the groom's side of the family, Neena's family stayed in the venue while I ventured out to watch the excitement.

When I reached the main road, I saw a crowd of people illuminated by headlights of cars of guests who were still arriving and looking for parking. Before I joined the crowd, I saw members of the brass band toward the front who were dressed in red velvet costumes with gold trimmings and matching turbans that had pieces coming out the top that looked like paper fans folded like xylophones and held pinched at one end to form a 'V'. Behind their turbans hung lengths of red-and-gold velvet cloth that reached down to their waists. They wore white boots that reached up past their calves and had thick, black, horizontal stripes around them. The first of these band members held a black, rectangular sign with gold lettering that read, 'INDIA FAMOUS MAHARAJA BAND® TAGORE GARDEN' followed by phone numbers. Hovering over the crowd was a drone that was whizzing back and forth just feet above everyone which must have been video-recording everything on the ground.

The band began to play procession beats on their trumpets, tubas, and drums in a rapid cacophony of sounds. I was delighted to find that I instantly recognised the tune; it was the same one that was being played in Tulsi's wedding in *Eat Pray Love* under the canopy of marigold garlands as Liz looked on retrospectively, thinking back on her own wedding. I lit up instantly when I remembered this because I found it catchy in the movie, but never thought I would hear it played in real life.

Looking over the crowd and between the lines of parked cars on each side of the road, there were brightly-lit bulb lanterns that looked like carousels of light with one large round bulb at their tops, beneath which was a smaller ring of light, then another larger one below that, each with smaller bulbs lighting their undersides.

Attached all around the base of each ring of light were long strands of clear and pearlescent beads that ebbed and flowed with the lanterns' movement like tentacles of jellyfish. The circular rings of light were affixed to gold columns about six or seven feet high that sat on small red pushcarts manned by red-coat-clad members of the *baraati*. They held strands of extension cords that powered these giant ornaments at their grasp of the handlebars of the pushcarts. The extension cords ran down along the procession to the other lanterns in an interconnected festival of electrical light. There was one row of these intricate lanterns on each side of the procession, each one lumbering along slowly like parade floats. They struck me as enchanting but also having a ghostly quality to them in the way they swayed like strange, veiled entities.

I decided to skirt the edges of the procession behind the row of parked cars to the left so I could get suitable vantage points for photos as I watched the procession move slowly in the direction of the entrance to the venue. The band played their instruments with tremendous force to the point I felt vibrations rise and fall against my skin as they passed by with dancing, jeering followers behind them. Sometimes there were shouts and celebratory hollering that went with the beats; other times, there would just be the hum of voices in Hindi as the band played on.

Toward the end of the procession was Ashish, the groom, who sat proudly on the seat of a chariot under an umbrella of white and yellow flowers. The seat looked more like a throne with a wreath of more yellow, white, and red flowers and fans of palm fronds. The sides of the chariot were similarly adored with garlands of these same flowers and greenery, under which hung strands of sparkling beads like those on the lanterns. Ashish wore a crimson-red kurta with gold pajamas, a white-gold sash, and studded khussa shoes. His shimmering, bronze-coloured turban was decorated with clusters of white flowers around his forehead, and longer, delicate strands on each side of his face. Against his short black beard, pointed moustache, and stoic gaze, he looked like a handsome, imposing maharaja. I felt like I wasn't just watching a groom on his wedding night but royalty arriving for coronation.

Pulling his chariot were two white horses decorated with thick garlands around their necks, fluffy tassels in primary colours at their harnesses, and white, pointed, feathered headdresses between their ears. They also wore sparkling silver saddle blankets over their backs that extended down each side of them to cover their flanks. At the front of the chariot sat a driver who handled the reigns and wore a black suit with gold and red trim. Occasionally, he would stop the chariot so photographers could take photographs and members of the *baraati* could share their blessings with Ashish.

After walking the length of the procession back and forth a couple times to get as many photos as I could, I walked ahead to a length of the road the procession had not yet reached. I stood to the side where others were waiting for the crowd to reach the point where they would have to turn right onto the cement drive that led down to the entrance of the venue. I just marvelled in surreal amazement that I was there, in the moment, watching a custom that I had only seen in the movies and acknowledged that the real thing was so much better.

There was a time to analyse everyone's expressions, hear the side conversations (even though I didn't understand a word), smell the air of the wide expanse of Dwarka I now could not see under the cloak of darkness, broken only by the comparably small sphere of piercing light of the *baraat* lanterns and the billowing instruments of the band that carried far beyond that sphere. Against the beating of the drums and trumpeting of the horns, I wondered what my friends and family were doing at that moment on the other side of the world as they were starting their day, about 13 hours behind the present time.

When the procession reached the final stretch to the venue entrance, I walked down to the end of the drive to join other guests from both sides of the family who were slowly assembling under the decorated arch to welcome Ashish and his family. For a while, there was a delay at the end of the drive for the procession to continue, so I went back in to share with Neena some of the photos I had taken. While I was out watching the procession, Neena found some of her other relatives who joined the group. I was introduced to them and engaged in some light conversation about being in India on holiday and having never been to an Indian wedding before. An overall buzz of anticipation started to grow among the crowd now that the procession was within sight.

Studying the slow movement of the procession making its way down the drive, I realised that it would take just as long to officially arrive as it did to change direction toward the entrance parallel to the venue. I was asked to take portraits of Neena's immediate family and relatives before I started making my way back to the entrance where more and more people were gathering, as if a tide was carrying everyone ambling about the venue to the entrance gate.

Catering staff dressed in long-sleeved white shirts, grey woven vests, and black trousers began to line up at the entrance with round, silver trays of drinks: bottles of water, juices, and mango lassis, with upright arrangements of pastel-coloured straws in the middle. Others carried rectangular trays with napkins and finger foods for those who might like a snack in passing. The servers stood in postured, dutiful poses with expressionless faces of event workers. It wasn't until one of them playfully motioned for me to take their picture that I began to see smiles and even some shy laughter out of them; suddenly, they all wanted their pictures taken. To me, everyone here was interesting and important, so I gladly obliged, taking a series of photos, then showing all of them for their amusement. Though I don't recall any words exchanged, it was the simple presence of my camera and a moment of idling that initiated a jovial exchange between these strangers and me. It made *me* smile, too.

Once the procession started moving slowly down the drive toward the entrance, more and more people began to make their way under the arches and outside of them onto the drive, amassing to await the arrival of the groom. The drums and horns of the band echoed off the cement and filled the venue, drowning out the music coming from the speakers. The whole of the procession was a party all its own and gave one a great sense of anticipation to stand there at the entrance to wait and watch for the convergence of the groom's side of the wedding with the bride's—a ceremonious joining of two people by two separate crowds of many.

When Ashish's procession arrived, the *baraati* joined with those waiting and became a jeering mass of costumes, saris, suits, and lights. Photographers (including myself) were waiting with everyone. I waited under the pergola where I stood on a raised foundation of one of its pillars to gain some height over the crowd just behind everyone else. There was a row of giant spotlights situated just over the hedge at the entrance which shone on the archway and illuminated Ashish's carriage that stopped right in front of it. Ashish sat there, high above in his carriage seat, featured prominently in front of those spotlights, with a sparkling array of camera flashes igniting in his direction.

For a while, Ashish remained in his carriage as, one by one, individuals stepped up to and on his carriage for photographs. At one point, the band stopped playing to reveal an uproar of voices that met with the sound of clapping and sight of excited gesticulation of some people's hands waving above the crowd. Members of the crowd—family, from what I could guess—also posed together around the carriage for photographs together. Some of the men in suits and red turbans also wore garlands of marigolds around their necks. The camera flashes sent light ricocheting off the carriage adornments, glittery saris of the women and their sparkling necklaces and earrings.

As more people filled the archway to greet Ashish, I found myself more and more in the middle of the crowd, even though I was off to the side of it. Eventually, I came down from my perch atop the pillar block and made my way to the back of the crowd where I could see the gathering more completely, revealing a new array of saris in all colours. How complete it all looked with the spotlights beaming behind Ashish between the floral curtain of the garlands and behind rows and rows of finely-dressed people all looking in the direction of the light and carriage.

After the photo-taking started to slow down, I went back inside with the expectation that Ashish and the *baraati* would be coming in soon, so I went to go sit with Neena's family again. I took more portraits of their family and we continued to talk until the drummers of the band began to sound for the entrance of the groom into the venue. The crowd outside started moving in toward the large stage canopy where white golden velvet and bejewelled wingback chairs were set for Ashish to sit and receive guests, family, and friends for photographs. In front of the chairs was a similar ottoman where a silver tray of food sat as a sort of appetising offering to the groom before he could finally sit and have a proper meal.

Ashish's family seemed to convene here in one final celebratory gathering before Shruti's arrival. The band came in with the *baraati* and began playing again, the drummers forming a circle under the canopy once Ashish had taken a seat and encouraged dancing among some of the *baraati* men to announce arrival of the groom. I stood on the platform just outside the dancing with and behind the other photographers and idlers to get what photos I could before everyone started to disperse for Shruti's procession. People began taking their seats at tables, but most sat at the iridescent covered seating arranged in rows like a theatre in front of the canopy.

Farther back in the venue between the pavilion where the canopy was set up for the vows ceremony that would take place later, and the pavilion where the food was set out, family members on Shruti's side—Sohrab and Saumya included—began assembling around her. The men held above her a square frame that was elaborately and diagonally strung with small white flowers and red roses.

Before long, everyone in the venue began to turn their attention to Shruti's procession as it began to slowly make its way toward the canopy where Ashish sat in waiting. At first, I watched off to the side, but as other photographers began following the procession, I too followed to photograph this like I had the *baraat*.

Shruti wore a bridal gown, a *lehenga choli*, in deep red, intricately decorated with gold, organic brocade along the base and in large ornamentals and small accents throughout the open lengths of red in the entire garment. The veil was similarly coloured and decorated, running from around the crown of her head to her back that covered a long, black braid of her hair. A set of beads was worn around her head with a strand going down the centre part of her hair that ended with a circular jewel resting on her forehead. Below that, she wore a *bindi* about the size of a pearl between her eyebrows. Her makeup was beautifully done: bold, dark eyeliner and eyeshadow around her eyes with just a dusting of gold above her upper eyelids; elongated eyelashes; and deep red lipstick that surpassed the depth of red of her gown. Around her neck she wore an elaborate beaded and jewelled necklace of tiny gold rings and pearls that covered her chest. Along her forearms and hands could be seen the henna designs from the night before and many bangles hanging at her wrists. With her she carried a small box which I imagined was a ceremonial gift to her soon-to-be husband. In all, she was a walking masterpiece.

Upon their joining under the canopy, the best part about being witness to the moment Shruti and Ashish saw one another in their wedding attire was to see the expressions on their faces: you could see that there was love there and an outpouring of excitement that they were about to embark on a new part of their lives together. When they came together, there was applause and photographs before each were handed long garlands strung with purple orchids. Each then took turns to place the garland over the other's head and around their neck in the tradition of *varmala* where each presents the other with a symbolic proposal of marriage in the form of the garland. Shruti first placed hers around Ashish, then Ashish placed his around Shruti. After each had presented the other with their garland, there was a rise of applause and whistling in celebratory exclaim before photographs were taken of them together, then with friends and family.

After *varmala*, I looked back out across the venue and noticed that the crowd had started to thin with the closest of friends and family near the canopy where Shruti and Ashish had joined together. The crowd was no longer in the hundreds of people like it was before and the remaining attendees had moved farther back into the venue where people were gathering to eat.

I joined Neena and Meera who went to fix themselves plates in the pavilion. It took me several moments of pacing back and forth along the tables to decide what I wanted and how much of it. My love of Indian food is deep and it's real; there's so much to like between the spices, textures, and intoxicating flavours. I've taken to many Indian dishes in the past just because of their smell—not necessarily knowing what exactly they were at first—but settling for trying them just because of their aromas alone. There were several new ones that I saw and ventured to try a little bit of but kept my fuller portions to what I was already familiar with: rice, vegetarian curries, and dahl. Once my plate was loaded, I had to go to the open station outside of the pavilion where they were preparing the naan and roti bread.

By the time I had gone back to the food to round my meal off with Indian sweets like gulab jamun, Shruti and Ashish had made their way with family members to a U-shaped table formation that was set up outside of the pavilion. The tables were covered with matte purple cloths and the chairs with the same iridescent purple and white cloths seen at other tables around the venue. The table settings at each seat had beautiful golden trays and cutlery. In front of each plate was a curved platter that held five small golden bowls for smaller foods or sauces. To the left of each place setting were golden goblets with precisely-folded napkins sticking out from the top, and bottled water. Around the edge of the insides of the tables were set various fruit drinks with straws and cut pieces of fruit like pineapple and watermelon wedged along the rims.

I learned that this dinner was a separate and private one from the rest of the dining. Only close family members of the bride and groom would eat at this dinner, apart from myself who was an invited guest. I had no knowledge of this private meal with the family, otherwise I wouldn't have gorged myself on all the dishes and delectable desserts just moments before. Judging by the elaborate place settings, this additional meal would by no means involve small portions.

Everyone sat outside the table formation so that all could see one another—especially Shruti and Ashish who sat near the centre of the bottom of the 'U'—and so the caterers could serve from within the opening of the tables. I sat at the right apex with Virender to my right with Neena to his right, and Shruti's father to my left. When most of the seats were filled, caterers came around with warm dishes of various foods including more curries, dahls, and breads to eat them with. There was also fresh fruit which I opted for instead since I had already finished a large meal. It was tempting to finish another round. I also felt a sense of guilt for refusing food at the table populated entirely by the bride, groom, and their intimate family members, so I ate only sparingly, wishing my stomach was larger. On top of the fruit I ate, there was chocolate mousse served in small glasses, and cake served on small plates.

I felt especially honoured having been seated next to the father of the bride, Virender's brother, whom I had yet to speak with until everyone settled in to eat. I was fascinated to learn that he was the executive chef and coordinator behind the ongoing catered feast of the night. Mahender Singh Pawar, Executive Chef of El Mountes Catering, was an incredibly kind and welcoming man but in observing his interactions with his staff, I could tell that he ran a tight ship. Occasionally our conversation would be broken by him giving orders to one or a few of the caterers who required some direction. I could only assume that he was always a sharp and professional manager, but this was his daughter's wedding, so everything had to be perfect. I guessed that there was also a great deal of added pressure to appeal to Ashish's family.

Mahender and I spoke a lot about his background in the culinary business and all the skilled training he had to go through to get to where he is now. He was very passionate in the way he talked about food and was like a shepherd of culinary delights. He spoke of the different roles he has had to play as both a manager and a chef and the challenges that come with balancing these responsibilities. His manner was friendly, warm, and disciplined; interacting with him for the short time that I did was clear evidence of the success of the quality of the dining experience and the food itself.

After Neena had finished eating her portions of this second dinner, she and I talked either in front of or behind Virender as he spoke with his brother to my left. Neena explained more about the tradition of the second dinner: Ashish's family adhered to an older, more formal version of Hinduism where the men are of a higher standing in marriage. Shruti's side, conversely, adhered to a more modern, progressive, and less formal Hinduism, but in getting married, they would essentially default to tradition of Ashish's family. The second, more intimate dinner took precedence over the general dining of the other guests in the belief that the groom's side must be shown the utmost respect and impressed by the bride's side of the family. I felt sharply struck by the inequality of how this sounded, but it was also different culture from what I knew. It may have all just sounded more archaic than it really was because, on the surface, it did not appear or feel as rigid as what I was hearing.

As people ate, the caterers came and went like bees among flowers. The lights above shone down brightly on the banquet that hummed with conversation in Hindi and English, and the clinking of cutlery and dishes. I occasionally glanced over at Shruti and Ashish who respectfully and lovingly helped one another eat. By now it was after midnight, so they both must have been hungry after the earlier festivities and formalities. They would need to eat because the wedding was not even close to being over yet. The venue had almost cleared out except for a few lingering guests, an active coffee and chai stand in the centre, and caterers ambling about who seemed to be doing initial picking up of food and drink stations around the perimeter of the venue. The music had long since stopped playing, and the night air had grown cooler and damper.

Between the end of the groom's dinner and the beginning of the vows ceremony, there seemed to be enough idling time for me to walk around the venue alone to see it all again as I had before the guests had arrived. It was just as it had been, but it showed signs of use and presence of hundreds that were there only a short time ago. It seemed that everyone had come and gone like a monsoon storm: suddenly and with great commotion and force, then dissipating as quickly as it had arrived. I watched some of the workers at their tasks for a few moments, then gravitated to where the only real noise and commotion was coming from now: the coffee and chai stand. An espresso machine hissed and a few people there talked at small tables set up in front of it. I had a chai which I finished quickly while standing in place, then another that I sipped slowly and took with me as I started wandering toward the decorated pavilion where the red-and-gold draped canopy stood in the centre of it in preparation for the vows.

Around the interior walls of this pavilion were mirrored arches set within shallow recesses painted in rich burgundy and bronze colours. These tall, rectangular spaces were bordered by golden, elaborate frames. All along the ceiling hung sparkling chandelier lights that illuminated all the regal colours below and sent light bouncing off the mirrored arches to ignite the entire space in a diamond-white light. The floor was covered in thin carpet mats and all around the walls were futons where people could sit. There was also a small collection of chairs near the vast opening to the pavilion where older family members could sit comfortably.

As everyone began assembling for the vow ceremony, younger family and friends seemed to take the futons on the right side of the space if you were to look at it from the outside. I took a seat in a chair near Neena while Shruti and Ashish's parents and close relatives like Virender and Mahender stayed near the edge of the canopy as they would be taking part in the ceremony. Shruti also sat off to the side near Neena while Ashish took a seat cross-legged on one of the four futon cushions that were set out around the canopy and covered in white sheets so that the square area between them created a sort of recessed sacred space. In the middle of this space was a display of various items that would be used during the ceremony: upon two bricks sat a shallow, round, silver dish filled with water that sparkled like a looking glass from the chandelier light above; a censer within the water holding a lit cone of incense; and at the centre of the dish, heads of marigold. Around the bricks sat smaller round dishes in silver, white, and gold that held what looked like various spices and other substances that I imagined all had their own individual religious significance. There was also a honey-coloured candle flickering in its own silver dish, and a pile of marigold heads that sat in the middle of all these other things and directly in front of a man whom I gathered was the religious figure officiating the wedding.

Across from Ashish sat this priest-like man who was preparing to start the final ceremony of the wedding. He wore a white-gold kurta, white pajamas, and a vertical red smudge for a *tilaka* on his forehead. He had a grey scruff of whiskers and black, receding hair on his head. He appeared to be middle-aged and was very solemn and expressionless, but he had a very important role to play in the long vow tradition that was about to begin.

The ceremony began with Ashish and next to him on the right, Shruti's parents sat on the cushion with Virender behind them. Mahender had since put on a white cloth over his head that covered his forehead and went back behind his ears like a bandana. He now also wore a similar *tilaka* as the priest. The beginning of the ceremony was very subtle and there was a lot of oration from the priest that Neena told me was being spoken in old Sanskrit. With the presence of Shruti's family and Ashish sitting together, it was as if a holy bond was being established between both families. Hands were clasped together by these family members as if in prayer and the priest would occasionally place one of the things from the bowls in their hands, then dab his index finger in something else and raise it in the direction of Ashish, all while chanting to supplement his actions. I didn't understand all the separate details of what was happening, but it was powerful to watch all the same.

The photographers were circling the canopy during the oration, so I joined them to capture each phase of the ceremony. They got as close as kneeling down on the cushions to take photos, but because I was not an official photographer for the wedding and merely a guest, I kept my distance and instead circled the canopy without feeling as though I was getting in the way of the other photographers or creating a distraction for the priest or the others sitting within the canopy in concentration.

Among the sea of strangers earlier and now in the presence of only the closest family members to the bride and groom, it was almost certain that I would commit an accidental blunder as the only Westerner guest that night, and it ended up happening at only the most important part of the wedding. While I was engrossed in taking photos, one of the photographers approached me to let me know that Shruti was motioning for me to go see her. It seemed like a very abrupt summoning, so I did so immediately. I walked over to where she sat and knelt down next to her. She smiled and asked me if I was having a good time to which I expressed my fascination and gratitude for being there. She then very kindly and sweetly mentioned that the area around the canopy was considered sacred and that my khussa shoes would need to come off. I instantly looked around at everyone else in the pavilion and noticed that all their shoes were off and that I was the only one wearing mine. I felt myself getting flustered with embarrassment and was only able to manage to say, "Oh! Of course!" I don't even remember if I apologised or not, but this sinking feeling of having just ruined the entire wedding flooded over me, even though I knew that that was irrational and that I couldn't possibly have ruined anything, but the feeling remained all the same.

I receded into a corner of the pavilion after that, sitting cross-legged, as I very casually slipped my shoes off my feet, hoping no one saw me do it. I had a feeling that everyone there already knew. I fumbled around with my camera to appear unaffected by the immense embarrassment I just caused myself but collected myself anyway and began taking more zoomed-in shots from where I sat.

I knew that I wouldn't be circling the canopy with the same curious vigour that I had before. I would need to just sit down where I was, let the professional photographers do their jobs, and let the ceremony continue without the ignorant interruption of the stupid American who didn't know to take his shoes off. I felt that it was a great calamity, but after I calmed down and felt brave enough to look out around the perimeter of the pavilion, everyone looked just as unaffected as I tried to appear earlier. No one seemed to care if they knew what I had done, except for Shruti, and if they did, they must have already dismissed my *faux pas* with forgiveness because the American didn't know and the vows would go on.

I think what made the whole embarrassing experience worse was that all the young people who had piled together on the futons across from me were laughing and carrying on as if they were in a dorm room. They were doing this before and after the oversight with my shoes, but I felt so injured from my own stupidity that I just assumed they were laughing at me because they knew I would eventually be called out for my mistake, then continued to laugh after because it must have been quality entertainment to see the American get called out by the bride herself. Honestly, in retrospect, if I was one of them, I think I would have been laughing too. However, I think their behaviour had little to do with me, if at all.

It wasn't until I noticed the younger adults were throwing marigolds at one another playfully like classmates might throw crumpled up wads of paper at one another in grade school that I realised they were engaging in their own strange sort of festivities during the vow ceremony. To me, it seemed inappropriate and disruptive during the stark contrast of the serious nature of what was happening under the canopy. I wondered if this was normal, but if anyone was going to draw unwanted attention, it was them. I felt less guilty for having forgotten to take my shoes off only moments before. Sometimes their ruckus would overpower the chanting of the priest, so I started to feel like I was in the right again. Their loud, playful behaviour continued into the early morning until they all started to become more subdued with exhaustion.

After a long while, Shruti joined Ashish on the cushion to his right. It took some time for family members to assist with the voluminous folds of her gown so that all the red-and-gold fabric lay presentably around her as she sat cross-legged. Behind them knelt Ashish's mother who wore a light green sari with gold trim and leafy gold designs throughout. Her hair was made up into an elaborate, curly up-do that showed off her earrings and gave her a regal look. Now, it appeared that all parents of the bride and groom were present as the priest continued with the ceremony.

As people got up and moved about the pavilion, I got up from my cross-legged position and took an empty seat next to Neena who seemed to be holding up well considering the late night was transitioning into early morning. I'd glance over at her sometimes and she would seem observantly reverent while the vows continued.

The commotion from the younger crowd began to wane on the other side of the pavilion as others began to lay down on the futons. Most of the adults, myself included, began to show signs of fatigue, but we remained upright and attentive in our seats. I felt myself fading, but I reminded myself that I may not have another opportunity to see an Indian wedding from start to finish, *So perk up and take in as much of this as you can!* I remained serious, curiously observant, and smiled with adoration when I was inspired to do so as the various ceremony rituals would change from time to time. Just as I started shaking one of my feet to keep myself awake, servers came in quietly to serve a selection of hot drinks to those of us who were awake. I was delighted that they had made fresh masala chai, so I drank a few of these during the end of the vows. This was exactly what I needed to remain alert through the rest of the ceremony.

When I started to feel a bit more awake, I repositioned myself in my chair and focused on the details of what movements and words were coming from the centre of the canopy. The priest murmured along in the words of the ancient script, seemingly unaffected by the early hour. I figured that he must have done many of these late night/early morning weddings, so he seemed physically prepared for the job. Ashish and Shruti remained seated next to one another on the cushion, now and then clasping their hands together in prayer, tossing various things into a small fire that had been built on a raised, rectangular firepit, then returning their hands to prayer. The timing of their actions seemed to match the rising and falling of the words of the priest. They must have understood what he was saying because I understood none of it and could only guess what vow gestures were being officiated by small actions and body language.

Dawn was approaching by the time the vows ended. Everyone in the canopy stood, some helping Shruti with the fabric of her gown in preparation for Ashish and Shruti to complete the final stage of their vows: to circle the fire together nine times in a clockwise motion to bind their union and mark a new stage of life as a married couple. Only then would Ashish and Shruti be officially husband and wife.

Once their ninth circle around the fire was complete, everyone clapped and the ceremony was officially over. Some slowly rose from their resting positions around the walls of the pavilion and shuffled toward the centre where they could talk to Ashish and Shruti after the many hours that were spent in observation. Others slowly strayed toward the exit to make their way home to get some sleep after saying their goodbyes and congratulations to Ashish and Shruti. I continued to sit and watch everyone greet one another and looked to Neena to try and determine when would be a good time to excuse myself to get back to Malti's to get some sleep myself.

I stepped off the pavilion platform onto the lawn that was now wet with dew. The morning air felt brisk and heavy with moisture. A faint twilight had begun to colour the sky with dark blues and purples. I could hear birds and see the caterers continue to pick up around the venue. I could also hear their chatter from across the lawn along with the occasional clanking of dishes. *What a tremendous amount of work*, I thought, considering they were here long before I was. I fumbled around on my phone to arrange for an *Uber* driver to take me home before I walked back into the pavilion to say farewell.

As everyone was dispersing, I went to tell Neena my driver would be there soon and to tell everyone I had met goodbye. I also had the opportunity to meet Ashish briefly and shake his hand. I think everyone was ready for sleep after a long night, especially Ashish and Shruti, so few words were exchanged apart from, "Nice to meet you" after our handshake. In a way, it was sort of surreal to meet Ashish after the grand display of his procession. He seemed princely before and still did in the way he was elaborately and handsomely dressed but seemed gentlemanly and human after meeting face-to-face.

Before I left, Neena made sure I took a white box of treats that were prepared for guests. It looked like a box of chocolates before opening it, but inside there was an assortment of different sweet and salty snacks. On the outside, 'Ashish & Shruti October 23, 2016' was inscribed to commemorate their wedding.

Dinesh, in a Suzuki Wagon, would be arriving shortly, so I made my way back down the cement drive—camera backpack slung over one shoulder with the box of treats in hand—to the dirt road where Parkash dropped me off the night before. I had to walk the dirt road out to the paved road where I would be picked up, so I tried not to drag my feet even though I had absolutely no energy left for physical exertion. I could see tracks in the beige dirt from where the wheels of Ashish's carriage made long, meandering impressions, along with a multitude of shoeprints around them.

The morning had brightened up more, revealing open acres of farmland all around me. As I approached the paved road, I could hear the occasional passing car and motorbike, and a rooster crowing somewhere in that big, wide-open agricultural expanse. The air smelled like sweet ash and the fertilised, cultivated soil of the fields around me. I started to feel awkward walking along that dirt road alone, all dressed up in my wedding outfit—khussa shoes and all. Walking through the fog seemed to complement my exhaustion. It felt like a veritable walk of shame, only I was just plain tired and walking along a dirt road through farmland in the middle of South West Delhi instead of city streets toward my car, hoping I hadn't parked it in a towaway zone overnight.

I came to the end of the road and took a seat on the end of a barrier to wait for Dinesh in his Suzuki. I wondered if he would be able to speak any English, but I didn't have the energy for conversation if he did. I waited there at the road as a few of the wedding attendees came down the road in their cars to leave. The rooster, wherever it was, kept crowing in intervals, and the sun tried burning through the fog as I saw its hazy, sienna sphere veiled behind it.

I figured a tall, kurta-clad American sitting along a country road would be hard to miss, but I kept my tired eyes peeled for this Suzuki. About 10 minutes later, Dinesh showed up. As I suspected he would, he spotted me immediately and pulled up alongside. There's always that initial rubbernecking through the passenger window first to make eye contact of confirmation that each one has found the right person, then I opened the rear passenger door. "Dinesh? *Aap kaise ho?*" He nodded and said, "*Chrees?*" I confirmed and immediately followed with "I'm sorry, I don't speak much Hindi," to which he just did the bobblehead nod thing and smiled in the rearview mirror. "Come from wedding?" was the only thing he said after that. Once we drove away, I nodded off now and then against the window until I was dropped off at the kerb in front of Malti's. I thanked Dinesh after paying and shuffled back in through the gate and to my room where I had just enough energy left to change and collapse in bed. I could hear

Delhi waking up, but I needed at least a nap before joining the rest of civilisation.

Living as an Honourary Citizen

I could only sleep until about 10:30 a.m. when I felt rested enough to get ready for another day. I could hear traffic whirring down August Kranti Marg, Raju shuffling about the courtyard doing his daily chores, and Scrappy Tom meowing outside my doors. I felt a little drowsy from the long night but nothing that coffee and a hearty breakfast couldn't remedy.

I sat up in bed, wondering if I should get just a couple more hours' sleep, asking myself the question, then firmly declaring, "Nope, get up!" like I do on workdays. When I got to the bathroom and took my shirt off to start washing up, I noticed large, red welts all over my back, and some on my arm. I ran my fingers across a few of them and knew immediately what they were: mosquito bites, and big ones at that. I must have been bitten at the wedding since I was out in the open all night. They must have bitten me through my kurta and undershirt, which I found remarkable. "What the *hell*? Were these *Jumanji* mosquitos?" I said angrily. I was a bit alarmed, hoping they weren't the malarial variety of vampire faeries because I never finished my malaria pills before my first trip due to the side effects from either those pills or the typhoid pills I was taking at the same time. As bad as the side effects were, I figured the real thing couldn't be much worse, so I never finished either vaccination. I decided not to worry about the bites, as agitating as they were, and continued getting ready for the day.

I chose Diggin again for breakfast, taking the same route through the colony: right-left-right after I had gone through the gate. The guards started to recognise me now and greeted me with an even more emphatic, "Good morning, sir!" and smiles. The guards were always the friendliest of chaps and a pleasant way to be greeted by the world whenever I would leave Malti's property for the sidewalk along the busy road.

When I sat down at a table in Diggin—this time at the end of the restaurant to the left of the entrance where I had a full view of the place—I realised I was extra hungry and had the appetite for a more wholesome meal than just the yogurt and coffee I had last time. I looked through the entire menu before deciding on herbed scrambled eggs, chicken sausage, and hash browns. By then, it was already getting warm, so instead of hot coffee, I tried their cold coffee, which was satisfyingly frothy and almost a smoothie-like drink over ice.

The coffee came first after I placed my order which I sipped to my delight until the food came moments later. Having ordered a pretty standard American breakfast, I imagined it would all come out on one plate, Denny's style. Surprisingly, each item came out on its own plate in hefty portions until the entire surface space of the table was filled with plates. There were a few other guests at the other end of the restaurant, so sitting there alone in front of a table full of food made me feel like a gluttonous American who was about to overeat like many of us do. I wasn't quite sure I could eat it all, but I got started anyway. I felt like Liz from *Eat Pray Love* when she was chowing down on her "large meal" in the mess hall at the ashram when Richard from Texas walks over and gives her the nickname Groceries. I looked at all the servings and thought, *Wow, I am Groceries.*

The cold coffee went much too fast, so I ordered a second so I could have more to drink while I shovelled through my food. It was delicious and, fortunately, just looked like more food than it really was. Shamelessly, I finished it all without feeling terribly full and continued sipping my second cold coffee daintily as if all that eating never happened. I took some notes and read a bit from the book I brought, occasionally glancing out at the bright day, pondering on what I would do with it since I didn't have any plans.

Back at Malti's, I sat out on the patio to read as Scrappy Tom came around to lounge in my lap while I held my book up over him. I learned to keep my arms occupied around him as loose limbs meant something to latch onto and attack if they weren't petting him. He was quite a pleasant cat when he wasn't treating me like his personal chew toy. He'd curl up with his head on my thigh, wincing his eyes open and shut according to whatever noises he could hear, and slowly flick the tip of his tail in contentment.

※ ※ ※

In the afternoon, I got a call from Rita, Neena's sister, asking if I'd like to go with she and her sister, Meera, to the India International Centre. They wanted to do some shopping at a craft market there, so I immediately agreed and we arranged a time. Rita would be picking me up outside of Malti's, so I let her know where she was to go. I continued reading before I decided to take another nap so I could be more rested for my outing with Rita and Meera. I hadn't seen Rita since my second trip, so I was anxious to see her again. Of course, I saw Meera at the wedding the night before, but I didn't want to look like I hadn't gotten any sleep.

Rita messaged me when she had arrived. She was parked on the opposite side of August Kranti Marg, so I had to leapfrog my way across in the thickening traffic. Meera was already in the front passenger seat, so I hopped in the back and expressed my excitement with Rita at seeing her again. Meera asked if I got enough sleep after the wedding and I told her I had hoped I did so I could make the most of the rest of the day. I also told her that I stayed all through the vow ceremony. She seemed surprised that I lasted that long.

When we arrived at the India International Centre, traffic was considerable but not overwhelming. We parked Rita's little car on a side street across from the Centre under the shade of enormous trees. When I got out, I felt the heat of the day envelope me and I began to sweat again. There was a long, stone wall in front of where we parked. I could see stray dogs running along the base of it sniffing noses-down through the garbage like they were looking for something to eat.

The India International Centre is an older, mid-century building with a circling driveway in front of it where guests could be picked up and dropped off at its entrance. Cement pathways cut through grassy lawns that lead up to it. There were also manicured lines of bushes and smaller plants and palms growing just outside its outer walls. Between the palms were plumeria trees with their white, swirling blossoms blooming in scattered patches between their long leaves. The heat seemed to disperse their fragrance that sat upon the air like incense smoke floats delicately in undisturbed air.

The craft market was in an open area between a road and the Centre with large, square flagstones laid throughout. There were just a few vendors in this space, maybe half a dozen or so, with sprawling assortments of goods laid out on blankets over the stone or on grass if they were set up near the lawn areas. There were a few people meandering from vendor to vendor, so this wasn't the bustling marketplace I thought it would be; rather, just a calm shopping experience like an outdoor giftshop. I much preferred this to throngs of people in a larger marketplace.

The first vendor I approached was a man selling terracotta goods such as pots, statues, figurines, and lanterns. He was a thin man wearing a modest button-down shirt with jeans. He crouched down while picking away at soft clay in his hand with a sharp utensil. The figurine he was working on resembled others that were clearly finished, dried, and set out for sale. Ahead of Diwali, I decided to buy Malti one of his terracotta lanterns with little shapes cut out of the top that fit over a circular base that was big enough to comfortably hold a votive or tealight candle. I knew it would be perfect for Malti's courtyard table.

Rita and Meera were across at another vendor who was selling jewellery and other trinkets. Holding the little lantern, I slowly perused the rest of the vendors' spots, respectfully gazing upon the craftsmanship of their goods. I stopped to look around too and could see large terracotta statues of horses and cows with elaborate designs sculpted and carved into them. One horse had this wild, somewhat comical face with wide eyes and its mouth gaping open to show its teeth and a tongue sticking partially out of its mouth. The decorative work on it made it look like one of the horses pulling Ashish's carriage the night before. There were also these two adorable little cow statues that were positioned so that they looked like they were about to touch noses in a kiss or were having a conversation about whatever cows talk about. They were set at the base of a rectangular, stone monument about my height that read, 'FOR US TODAY THERE CAN BE NO SACRIFICE HIGHER THAN TO FORGET DISTINCTIONS OF HIGH AND LOW AND TO REALISE THE EQUALITY OF ALL MEN. —MOHANDAS KARAMCHAND GANDHI'.

I saw a man crouching before a pottery wheel with two women sitting in chairs and another man crouching as his audience while the potter demonstrated his craft. In front of the wheel was a modest collection of pots in all different shapes and sizes on a rectangular slab of wood. Many of these could fit into a child's hands. There was also a piggy bank and a couple of other decorative pieces with slots in the tops for inserting coins. The bodies of many of the pots were bulbous and jowly with narrow necks that looked as if they had just enough room at their tops to hold the stem of a single flower.

The rotating potter's wheel—about the size of a steering wheel—was powered by a cylindrical motor affixed to the right of the metal frame the wheel sat on and was plugged into a flat power strip about the size of a standard hardcover book. One woman sat with one leg crossed over the other with a hand on her cheek and elbow on her knee in concentration. The other woman sat forward in her chair with the same placement of her hand and elbow as she too looked on. The man watching sat crouched down to the left of the finished pottery as he looked on at the potter with one hand on the wheel's frame to balance himself.

I approached to stand and watch the potter demonstrate work he was doing on a tall, conical piece of clay at the centre of the wheel with what looked like the form of a small pot taking shape. It didn't seem like the entire cone of wet clay was going into the making of this tiny pot. His hands were wet and caked with clay. He wore a white button-down shirt and white trousers—*Strange choice*, I thought, *for someone working with clay*. The potter massaged the clay to continue forming his new pot as he would occasionally dip his hands in a bowl of muddied water to his left while explaining the process in Hindi. I didn't understand what he was saying, but as he projected his voice over the sound of the small motor, it seemed to be an instructional tone that fit the action of his hands. It was fascinating to watch how delicate he could make his creations.

Rita and Meera were still at the jewellery vendor's table when I walked away to find out what was catching their interest. They had been holding up earrings, necklaces, and other items in examination while asking each other what they thought of the other's finds. Rita would occasionally say something to the vendor which I guessed was her asking what the price of each thing was. I approached Rita to ask her how to say, "How much is this?" She said, "You can say, *Kee-tah-neh-kah-hey?*—'How much is this?' or just *Kee-tah-neh?*—'How much?'"

After Rita and Meera finished buying what they wanted from the market, we noticed there was a small beverage stand in a shaded part of the market area. Rita was kind enough to buy us tea and we idled around a bit more until we finished our drinks.

While walking around with my tea, I saw another gentleman doing the same and greeted him. He looked Indian, was dressed casually but professionally, and spoke excellent English as he responded back. "Where are you from?" he asked. "The United States," I said. I always hate saying, "I'm from America" whenever I'm abroad and anyone asks me where I'm from because I've always felt it's disrespectful to South America to use "America" as a general name for The States despite South America being comprised of countries. I imagine South Americans commonly refer to themselves as nationals of whatever South American country they're from, but "I'm from America" has always felt too, "'MURICA!" to me.

The gentleman introduced himself as Nilanjan Gupta, a journalism and law professional who had just happened to transition to law from journalism—the exact opposite of my professional goals—so this became an instant topic of discussion. He was visiting the India International Centre for an event being held and was using his spare time to visit some of the local attractions. I was immediately fascinated with his career choices and the opposite order of them compared to mine. I asked him a great deal about the transition from one to the other, but he told me about how he still did some writing in addition to his work in law.

Given our presidential election in the United States was only weeks away, our journalistic minds naturally arrived at discussing the candidates and the impacts of what different presidencies would look like for both the U.S. and the world. Having just left a politically heated and increasingly divided United States to travel abroad, I was intensely curious about how foreigners viewed the contentious campaigns of Hillary Clinton and Donald Trump. Having a better sense of the Indians' take and general feelings about the election, Nilanjan illustrated his perception of a pro-Hillary consensus among Indians, many fearing a Trump presidency would be dangerous for foreign affairs.

This was a conversation I took seriously, almost forgetting that Rita and Meera were still wandering around until they finally joined Nilanjan and I to introduce themselves and find out more about this gentleman who had kept me in conversation longer than they seemed to want to linger. For a while, the four of us spoke together in a circle, a little on the remnants of the conversation Nilanjan and I were having before he enquired about what Rita and Meera did. Meera told him about her home-based baking business which Nilanjan seemed to take interest in and asked for her contact information in case he wanted to order something from her. Information was exchanged, including mine and Nilanjan's before Rita, Meera, and I set out to leave.

Before leaving, Nilanjan mentioned some sort of low-key concert playing near the Centre and asked if we wanted to join him. There was a part of me that wanted to go so I could continue our conversation to find out what I might learn from further journalism discussions, and see said concert on a whim in what was turning into a cooler and pleasant late afternoon. Rita and Meera declined but insisted I stay since I was the one on holiday. I didn't exactly know where I was in relation to Malti's anymore and wondered how I'd get back (even though, in hindsight, an *Uber* could have taken me straight there like they had done from both the *mehendi* party and the wedding). However, it was the fact that I came there with Rita and Meera that prompted me to leave with them.

After leaving the market, we needed to drop Meera off at her house where we could also pick up some boxes for Rita who was moving the next day. By now, the sun had dipped low in the sky that left it veiled in dusty twilight. By the time we reached Meera's neighbourhood, the houses started to look more distinct and prominent, some of the homes upscale.

As we got closer to Meera's we passed a large, stately, three-storey home partially hidden by large, overhanging trees that grew along the parkway. The architecture was modest, the entire home white, and it was surrounded by tall security fencing that reached as high as the roof. All along the top of the fence was coiled barbed wire that ran along the entire perimeter. There were also bright security lights all around the property. It struck me as looking almost like a small penitentiary rather than a home. It stood out among the rest of the homes in the area in such a way that it was obvious that someone important lived there. When I asked Rita and Meera who lived there, they told me it was the actor Amitabh Bachchan's New Delhi home.

When we arrived at Meera's, she went inside and began carrying flattened moving boxes out to the car. I helped load them vertically in the back seat until we couldn't fit any more. I wasn't sure when I might see Meera again on this trip, so I said farewell as if I might not and gave her a hug. It was nearly dark now and yellow lights of the street lamps were lit. I liked the area we were in because of all the trees that hung over the streets and opulent plant life of the residents' yards. Before leaving, I thought, *This is a neighbourhood I could see myself living in if I were to live in Delhi for a time.*

I got in the front seat of Rita's car as she got in the driver's side on the right to take me back to Malti's. On the way back, I asked Rita what 'GURUJI' meant as I kept seeing it as a decal on the back of people's cars. She explained that Guruji is the name of the human incarnation of Lord Shiva who had—when he was alive—and still has devotees who seek his divine blessing, very much like a saint. In a way, the decals serve as a sort of homage to the late guru, but his grace and divine light are considered eternal. "Ask Guruji for what you want," she said, "and it will come true."

When Rita dropped me off at Malti's, I suspected that I might not see her for the rest of the trip either, so I gave her a final farewell before opening the door to get out. The traffic had thickened on August Kranti Marg by this time, but she dropped me off on Malti's side of the road, so I didn't have to leapfrog my way back across. A little sad, I waved, thanked her for the invitation to the market, and shut the door. Rita rumbled off into the traffic where she turned at the median to go back in the other direction for home.

When I came through the gate, everyone was home—Malti, Monica, Raju, and Sharmeen, Monica's upstairs neighbour. Even Scrappy Tom was around, but I couldn't see him, only hear him meowing somewhere in the bushes. As I walked up the driveway, he too made an appearance and scampered out from the side bushes like a tiger with the energy and stamina for a night of hunting. Malti and Raju were in the house with smells of food coming from the kitchen window that overlooked the driveway. Monica came out from her apartment to greet me and Scrappy Tom, bending down to give him some pets on his back and meaty head. His body language signalled that he was irritated about something, so he took a few swats at both Monica and I before running off and returning like a cantankerous little beast of the jungle.

Malti, Monica, and I convened at the courtyard table for a while to catch up on what we each did with our day. I gave Malti the terracotta lantern I bought at the market and told her it was my Diwali gift to her for the table which was turning into our regular hangout spot while I was there. Before Malti had come out, Monica suggested that we light up the lantern to add some ambiance to the warm night. There was a slight breeze which made the flame flicker, causing little yellow shapes to dance from the lantern. Before I got too comfortable, I brought out some of the SULA wine I still had and shared it with Monica while Malti kept to tea that she had. Eventually, Sharmeen came down from her apartment over Monica's and joined us at the table.

Since it was just days before Diwali, Halloween (the first in my life that I'd miss because I was abroad), and Dia de los Muertos in Mexico, our conversation centred around the festivities of each. There was growing uproar of fireworks and firecrackers each night ahead of Diwali, so there were intermittent explosions since I returned to Malti's and while we all talked. We unanimously decided that the explosions were what was making Scrappy Tom agitated and unpredictable.

Diwali is a festival of light, so I drew parallels between Halloween's jack-o'-lanterns and the brightly-lit shrines in honour of the deceased I had seen in Mexico for Dia de los Muertos. Though Diwali has elements similar to Christmas with its spirit of giving and goodwill, all three celebrations felt so alike to me and appropriate that all three were back-to-back between three different cultures. I joked to say that I ought to find myself a pumpkin so I could have my jack-o'-lantern to go with my *diya* lights (oil lamps made from clay with cotton wicks dipped in vegetable oil) for Diwali. Since there are many charms seen around India for scaring away evil spirits, I thought a lit pumpkin face would fit right in. Unfortunately, I was never able to find any pumpkins at any of the produce markets for my jack-o'-lantern.

I didn't have any plans for the rest of the night, so I ended up having an impromptu dinner with Malti and Monica. Meals were not part of my Airbnb arrangement, but I often found myself included like a family member regardless which often included unexpected meals, inclusion in random outings, walks, events, and the occasional Indian dessert that either Raju or Malti would bring to my room. I don't remember any other time in my life when the careful interaction as a new guest dissipated so quickly into feeling like I had known my hosts for what seemed like years. It made me laugh to myself in wonderment because it took a trip around the world to experience this.

After dinner, Monica and I retreated outside to the courtyard for more SULA wine and Djarum clove cigarettes. It was nice enough of a night to stay out, so we decided to play Scrabble among the white faery lights that were strung in the courtyard just outside of Monica's apartment door. We dragged the table over to where the lights were so we could see what we were doing on the gameboard. As we got into our first game, the wine eventually ran out, so we switched to vodka that I had bought and some of Monica's soda. We took turns playing music on our phones to add some tunes to the voids of silence while we contemplated our next wordplays.

I was enjoying myself so much that my normal competitiveness during Scrabble games was completely nonexistent. Sitting there on a gorgeous night playing Scrabble—one of my favourite games—with a new friend, while sipping drinks in Delhi was such a delightful novelty to me. I was more casual about my word placement with an uncharacteristic lack of strategy. I didn't notice my own poor showmanship until Monica eventually caught on because she was the one keeping score. When she noticed that I was the one losing miserably, she started egging me on to essentially get my Scrabble shit together. She wanted competition and I wasn't giving it to her. The two games we played were probably my worst Scrabble performances ever, but I had fun nonetheless.

When it was getting close to midnight, we decided to call it a night and went to our own rooms to prepare for bed. The pre-Diwali explosions that echoed throughout the colony had died down, leaving Scrappy Tom in a far friendlier disposition. During the last Scrabble game, he would switch laps and rattle his purr motor which was like a massage in itself. He seemed calmer but vigilant as he was now on his nightly duty to protect the surround from intruding cats as master of his little kingdom.

※ ※ ※

The next day, Malti invited me to go shopping with her at the annual Diwali bazaar at the Blind Relief Association. This wasn't too far from her home, but we still had to hail a tuk-tuk to get there. Parkash was off driving around town and I would see him later anyway, so I didn't want to summon him from his other fares just for a special trip down the road.

The Blind Relief Association in New Delhi is sort of an imposing, light grey building with long, vertical, rectangular windows. It looked more like another penitentiary to me, but the surrounding area was vibrant with colour and alive with bustling crowds of shoppers going in and out of booths snugly arranged next to one another.

As soon as Malti and I walked into the bazaar, I immediately saw a sign for paper products, so I instantly gravitated to that area. If I wasn't going to take home a typewriter from Delhi, I was sure going to acquire as much unique paper as I could for letters and sharing with correspondent friends. What's unique about some of our letters is that we use our many different typewriters to compose them, but we also use a different kind of paper for each page. Carefully selected stationary always adds extra charm to correspondence with another.

The Paper Products booth was at a corner of a vendor arrangement and was set apart from the main foot traffic by processing tables and counters. Near the narrow entrance to the booth were perpendicular tables set up with computers and card machines wired to their surfaces. The amount of room to look at the merchandise was limited, especially with the many people coming and going. Fortunately, I'm tall, so I was able to stand back to survey all that was being offered for sale. There was artisan craft paper, wrapping paper sold on bolts, loose-leaf papers in every size, colour, and shape, and boxes full of journals, pads, and stationary sets. I was more interested in the sets of paper and envelopes that I could use for letters, so I settled for a few smaller sets that came with ornate, circular print designs with glitter on them over paper colours in blue, purple, teal, and Easter egg yellow. There were also sets of envelopes with gold print designs like those used for gifting money at Indian weddings (without the one-rupee coin), but I thought they would be perfect for sending letters in. The colours that I chose were rich red, turquoise, and orange.

Meanwhile, Malti was across from the Paper Products booth looking at clothing, textiles, and spices. It seemed like the crowd was growing quickly after we arrived because the walkways between the booths were becoming thicker with heads and the volume of voices rose higher as they echoed off the walls of the buildings. It didn't take me long to pick out what I wanted before I maneuvered my way through the people crowding in the booth. I made my way to the line at the counter for purchases which was really more of a tightly-packed gathering of people with armfuls of their paper shopping, raising their heads and looking from left to right and right to left behind the people standing in front of them to see if there was any progress.

After waiting about 15 minutes in this mess without any movement, Malti noticed I was still standing in the same spot and came over to find out what was taking so long. Malti, being the no-nonsense person she is, pushed her way through the crowd of waiting people to the counter and started speaking forcibly to the checker in Hindi. A few minutes later, things started moving again and I was placing my items on the counter. "Let me know if it takes any longer," she said before returning to peruse the booths across the walkway.

What was puzzling to me was the counter I went to first was only one step in the checkout process. They took my items, my name, and gave me a slip which I was to then take to another part of the counter. At this other counter, I was to give the cashier the slip with the name and list of items I was buying. She then took my cash, stamped the slip and handed it back to me. I was then directed to the end of the booth where I was supposed to show yet another checker my proof of purchase where they would then hand me a bag with the items I bought. All this took about 30 minutes. After experiencing this pattern at some of the handicraft shops I had been to, I wasn't terribly surprised by the strange process of buying basic things, but I was still annoyed by the inefficiency of it. I walked over to meet Malti after that and said, exasperated, "Jesus, all I wanted was some damn paper." "It's ridiculous," she said, "but you have to be forceful to get anywhere."

I wasn't particularly keen on stuffing myself in an overcrowded booth again, so Malti and I just wandered throughout the bazaar, stopping occasionally at booths where merchandise was within arm's reach like stands for incense, spices, dried produce, and teas. I could smell the spice stands before seeing them. Some of the spice samples were unique, like the silver sugar-coated anise seed that erupted with the flavour of licorice as soon as you cracked it between your teeth.

At the centre of the bazaar was a food court where many Indian fried foods and snacks were being sold, sort of like the Indian version of fair or carnival food in The States. Above the tables where people sat to eat were colourful canopy covers to block out some of the sun, but it was no less cool there than being in the direct sunshine. I was wearing a light kurta but was sweating profusely anyway. I was always self-conscious about that because everyone else—besides any other tourists I might see—never seemed fazed by the heat. I'd even get a bit jealous and mutter, "Damn you all and your acclimation to this godforsaken heat," as I'd constantly wipe the sweat from my forehead and try to air out my back by wafting the back of my kurta with my right index finger and thumb to try and get the sweat from dripping down my back. I had to strategically wear colours that were complementary to pink because I was just about always a bright pink whenever I was out during the day.

After passing the food court, I saw various goods in different directions that caught my attention, so I told Malti that I would walk about on my own in the general vicinity but that I would look for her when I was done. Really, that meant that I would just walk out into the crowd when I was done to make myself known like a giraffe in the grass because I was probably the tallest person there and brilliantly pink. "It's not like you'll miss me in the crowd," I quipped. Malti snickered and said, "No, there's no way *you'll* get lost."

There was just about everything one could expect to see at the tourist markets, but the prices at the bazaar were much more reasonable. I was not in a touristy area and I hardly saw any other tourists at the bazaar. Many of the booths had fixed prices, so I didn't have to go through the stress of having to haggle for decent prices because most of everything was priced below my expectations. All the usual merchandise—kurtas, scarves, religious trinkets, textiles, etc.—were things I really didn't need, so I stuck with my paper purchases and a few other small items. There was a sandalwood incense I couldn't pass up (I love sandalwood), and something I hadn't seen before: Greenbrrew® Green Coffee, a natural instant coffee that looks like green tea, smells like coffee, and tastes like something in between. I had one of their samples out of a paper cup and was instantly sold. I wasn't able to have my usual coffee in the mornings unless I went to Diggin for breakfast, so I thought a Greenbrrew® would be an excellent start to my days while there. I bought a box which contained packets of this instant green coffee in powder form that I just needed to pour into boiling water—easy to do with the kettle I had.

As expected, Malti found me first after I started to look around for her when I finished my shopping. It was just after midday and I was too hot and sweaty to want to do anything more, so I followed Malti around at different booths until she was ready to leave too.

I was glad I learned the two new market phrases from Rita because I was going around everywhere at the bazaar going, *"Kee-tah-neh-kah-hey?"* or just *"Kee-tah-neh?"* when I wanted to know how much something was if it didn't have a price tag on it. Of course, I remembered my *"Namaste"* before asking about prices and *"Shukriya"* that Parkash taught me. If one is to live as an honourary citizen for even a brief period of time, it's a minimal gesture of kindness to know one's basic phrases of salutation and gratitude in the language of the country one is visiting. This simple etiquette may seem insignificant, but it goes a long way.

I wasn't used to taking tuk-tuks that weren't driven by Parkash. When Malti and I were trying to hail one back to her house, I witnessed the art of negotiating your own fare to get to a particular place. This was so novel to me since the fare rate for taxis in The States (and very likely elsewhere in the world) is always set by the driver. I let Malti handle this after we crossed the street from the bazaar and waved down the first tuk-tuk. There was a lot of quick back-and-forth in Hindi between Malti and the driver before he waved his dismissal and drove off, leaving Malti looking miffed. I was getting too hot to stand out in the sun any longer, so I almost didn't care how much it cost. We waited for a few more minutes before another tuk-tuk pulled up and the negotiating between Malti and the driver began again. The driver nodded in agreement and we got in.

On the ride back, we stopped at a wild intersection I had been through a few times already with Parkash. It was a crossroads with streets going in a variety of directions underneath an overpass. Because of the shelter the overpass provided, many of the poor camped here and would beg at the idling vehicles. Parkash and I normally drove right through this intersection without having to stop, so there was never any opportunity to be approached by the beggars. This time, however, we were stopped for the light. A young woman carrying a child that looked to be about two years old approached Malti's side of the tuk-tuk and began doing the hand-to-mouth motion. The child wore soiled clothes and was eating from a packet of Oreo® cookies and had black crumbs collecting around its mouth. I couldn't tell if the child was a boy or a girl. Cookies certainly aren't good nutrition for a child, but it was something. Malti opened her pocketbook and handed the woman some cash before the woman receded back to the side of the road where she came from. Malti then said, "Diwali is the season for giving, so we give more than usual." After that, I made sure to be more generous to those in need.

❊ ❊ ❊

Not long after Malti and I got back from the bazaar, Parkash picked me up and took me to the Nepal Embassy to obtain a visa application. I had decided that I would make an effort to go see Nepal while I was visiting because, after all, it seemed so close in relation to Delhi. There was never any way I could go off to see Nepal on my own during my business trips, so I knew I would have to save such a side journey for a trip taken on my own.

The Nepal Embassy was a large, white, stately building with a separate, dull-looking building reserved for administration. Parkash stopped the tuk-tuk in a long parking area just outside the wall to the Embassy. We walked down along it where a few people were loitering and through a gate that was heavily guarded by men in uniform. Parkash said something to them in Hindi and the guards let us both through. Just within a short walking distance from the administration building was the white building with a brick driveway that wrapped around a botanical roundabout. This space was filled with plants and made for a charming presentation to the formal government building, creating a sense of welcome. Flying from the edge of the second storey was the flag of Nepal. This place looked like one where they would receive presidents and other international dignitaries. I wanted to go there for a tour, but I had business to attend to.

The administration building was dark and unwelcoming unlike its neighbouring building, and entering it felt more like going to the principal's office. The short hall we walked through to get to the counter had announcement boards on the walls with a lot of material on visiting Nepal, much of it in Nepali or Hindi. The waiting room just outside of the counter had a table in the centre with loose-leaf pamphlets and other reading material strewn upon it. There was also linked metal chairs around the perimeter of the room. It was uninviting and I wouldn't have wanted to wait there, but for my purposes, I was only there for pickup and drop-off.

We went to the window at the counter and waited for someone to appear. I could hear some commotion in the back of the room somewhere beyond that window and tried to peek around to see if anyone was coming back. Parkash said, "Hello?" a couple times before someone finally appeared. In Hindi, Parkash then asked the clerk about visa applications and the clerk handed me one. I asked for another in case I made any mistakes on the first. There was more conversation between Parkash and the clerk before we left. Parkash explained to me the specific times for dropping off my application and picking up my visa before we noticed they were posted:

Document submission: 9:30 a.m. to 11:00 a.m.

Visa collection: 12:30 p.m. to 1:00 p.m. or 4:00 p.m. to 4:45 p.m.

I was also required to get my photo taken for the application, so that was another errand I would have to run before returning to the Embassy the next day. I had brought a printout about obtaining a Nepal visa that I packed before the trip, so I had that on-hand and wrote down the submission and collection details so I could make sure I was back in time and had everything necessary for the application before I dropped everything off. The administrative hours seemed especially short and oddly specific.

On the way back to Malti's, Parkash and I passed between

India Gate and the Presidential Palace—familiar sights from my previous trips with grassy expanses on each side of the road. The lawns going toward the Presidential Palace are like a vast park with bins for picnickers to dispose of their garbage. There were also people strolling up and down the sidewalks along the road, many in large and small groups out on the grass. Trees grew tall and fluffy with leaves all the way down to the palace. With all the trees, it was no surprise that there were also troops of rhesus macaques either running across the lawns from left to right with their tails high in the air, or slowly sauntering on all fours toward the garbage bins to see what they might find to eat.

The public services that manage those garbage bins must have known the macaques roam that area because the bins are closed at the top where garbage can be securely placed in them without the possibility of coming out. The cans also swivel around vertically on bars affixed to the ground to thwart monkey business. As we drove by, I watched as one macaque tried getting onto the bin but took off in a hurry after making it tip over in the opposite direction.

Parkash and I decided to stop at a street-side chai café where we had a couple glasses of hot chai each and spoke about some of the logistics of travelling to and throughout Nepal. Being a Nepal national, Parkash was the best person to talk to about this. He also travelled back to Nepal regularly to visit family. Getting the Nepal visa was the easy part, but if I was to go, I still needed to decide how I was going to get there and when I would go. Back in The States, this whole idea seemed like just a possibility I'd look into when I got back to Delhi, but now that I was there, figuring out how to get there seemed a little more daunting than I imagined. Would I go by train for the full authentic experience, or would I fly to save myself time getting there? I would go back to the Embassy the next day to submit my visa application with my passport (and hopefully get it all back in the same day), but the getting-to-Nepal part (and *where* in Nepal) would require more consideration.

When Parkash dropped me off at Malti's, I had no plans for the rest of the afternoon and evening. I decided to relax with some reading out in my little patio garden, catch up on notes from the day, and see if Scrappy Tom might pay me a visit like he had done each day. I also intended to fill out my visa application to have it ready for drop-off at the Embassy the next day.

When Malti noticed that I was back, I received an unexpected invitation to join her and Monica for the Bolshoi production of *The Nutcracker* on a pass that they had in addition to their tickets. The production was being coordinated by the Indian Council for Cultural Relations under the Cultural Festival of Russia in India at the Siri Fort Auditorium which was just walking distance from Malti's along August Kranti Marg.

With Diwali approaching, it made sense that there would be an arrangement for *The Nutcracker* given Diwali's similarities to Christmas celebrations. I accepted Malti's invitation emphatically, anxious to have the opportunity to see a production I've often seen in The States near Christmastime. To see it before celebrating Diwali at a time I would normally be celebrating Halloween was new and unusual—throwing me for a cultural loop—especially since the heat of New Delhi was so incongruous to what I was used to feeling when I saw *The Nutcracker* during wintertime.

The production was supposed to begin at 6:30, so we started walking down August Kranti Marg around 6:00. The day was still warm to dress too formally, so I wore my light beige khaki trousers with one of my short, custom-made kurtas that I ordered from Nirula Handicrafts Bazar, which I frequented on my prior trips. This time, I chose the fabric and requested the length of kurtas I wanted before they took my measurements, took my payment, and sent me on my way with a delivery guarantee at Malti's for the next day. For the ballet, I chose the one with a base colour of warm beige with a faint print design of marble veins under bold, black, intersecting lines of various widths. The entire design made a statement but was still tasteful. When I first saw it and the version with red lines instead of black, I immediately thought that each could easily be fabric designs one might see in Africa.

Joining us were a couple of friends of Malti's who arrived and met us on the sidewalk outside her home. By the time all of us started walking down August Kranti Marg, the road was thick with traffic, honking, exhaust, and dust. The sun was setting in the west, making the horizon that I could see through the trees that lined the road look like variegated sienna: a darker, almost yellowish brown higher in the sky, and a lighter, orangish blend closer to our line of sight through the accumulated dust and pollution. That sky and the remnant heat from the day made it seem almost impossible that I was about to go see *The Nutcracker*. It felt like the late afternoon on an autumn day in Southern California where Santa Ana winds can churn vast wildfires that char the landscape in the east, and all you know of the inferno is the smoky air and a sunset that glows of brownish orange.

When we got to the Siri Fort Auditorium, there was already a crowd outside and many were heading indoors to take their seats. I don't think I've ever seen so many Russians mixed with Indians in one place before; it was fascinating to see the contrast. A lot of the Russian men looked dapper in their formal wear while the women looked almost like pale dolls, something like porcelain china dolls that came to life. Indian men and women were all dressed accordingly for the event: the men either in dress shirts, trousers, and ties, or in kurtas; many of the women wore saris or kurtis and scarves. Malti and Monica wore kurtis. After examining what other men were wearing, I felt a little underdressed, but I was at least festive and felt comfortable in the warm evening.

Monica and I smoked Djarums before going in as we stood apart from the crowd and people-watched. Being as there was this wonderful, unexpected end to the day, I was glad I was there rather than alone in the quiet of the garden with a book. *I could do that anytime*, I thought, but when special invitations like this are extended, one must accept the opportunity. There should be a limit on plans and scheduling while on holiday in a faraway place because oftentimes, the unplanned, impromptu stuff is the best stuff.

Monica and I went to find Malti before heading inside. We had remarkably good seats just behind the cordoned-off section that was reserved for Russian dignitaries and visiting friends and family of the Russian performers. We sat in the central part of the auditorium just several rows from the stage, so the performance would be slightly below our line of sight. The auditorium itself was made up of rich colours with cream-white walls, red cloth seats, and red curtains. Monica sat to my left and Malti to her left. We briefly chatted amongst ourselves as more and more people filed into the auditorium and down aisles to take their seats. The Indian women in their glittering saris lit up the carpeted aisles while the Russian women, in their own standard of formal wear, created a fascinating cultural contrast.

The Russian woman who sat in front of me in the sectioned-off area must have been one of the performers' mothers because she carried a stoic mother's pride. With her was a man who must have been her husband, and their younger daughter who was dressed like a china doll with her hair immaculately curled and in ribbons, and ruffles on the sleeves and bottom of her dress. Her mother looked strikingly like an American from the 1950s in that she wore a fluffy, cocktail-style dress in a rich and shimmery purple with a fitted, buckled belt worn around her waist. Her auburn hair was also perfectly curled and styled just above her neck. She wore modest jewellery and had smoothly-manicured red nails. After getting her daughter situated in her seat, she sat next to her husband and they began to speak in Russian. I watched, fascinated by the meticulous pursing of their lips, as they conversed in what seemed like a completely unknowable language.

Before long, an Indian woman in her sari came out to a podium from the left of the stage. As the audience noticed her presence on the stage, people quieted down until the auditorium was silent enough for this presenter to speak. In a thick Hindi accent, she began to introduce the Bolshoi production of *The Nutcracker* in English as it was being arranged in collaboration with the Indian Council for Cultural Relations under the Cultural Festival of Russia in India.

Following the first round of applause after this introduction, the speaker then continued by introducing a yet-to-be-seen "Russian president" to appear for a lamp-lighting ceremony for Diwali before the ballet began. I leaned over to Monica and whispered, "What the hell is Putin doing here?" There was a pause, and everyone started looking around, dumbfounded. Even the Russians seemed confused, looking around or shifting their eyes in wonderment at why their president was there. Finally, the man who appeared wasn't, in fact, Vladimir Putin, but the Russian *ambassador*. There was no formal correction made, so the lamp-lighting ceremony commenced, leaving everyone to realise for themselves that there was just a lost-in-translation moment in the introduction. I was, I admit, a little anxious to see Putin himself pop out from behind that curtain.

The actual production of *The Nutcracker* was, of course, spectacular. This version didn't have the live orchestra like the shows I had seen when I was younger and on my holiday visits to see friends and family in California, but the performances brought the story to life exactly as I always remember it. Many times throughout the ballet—both before and after intermission—I would take a moment to think how peculiar it was that I was seeing *The Nutcracker* again but for the first time in India during a time of year when I would never normally see it, and with actual Russians in the production and the audience. It really shouldn't have been all that mind-blowing, but it was.

After the ballet was over, Monica, Malti, Malti's friends, and I met outside to leave the Siri Fort Auditorium together. Just outside the exit gate were brightly-lit stands of street food where we all stopped for a bite. I was still a little leery of eating any street food. I had had a wonderful day and evening, so I didn't want to chance ruining it by eating something I shouldn't and land on the pot for an undetermined number of hours. Ultimately, I decided not to be the prudish visitor and got something to eat. Of the selection, I figured that *vada pav*—friend potato patty between two buns—was probably the safest option. It was hot, cooked, and had basic ingredients, so I couldn't see how that could possibly go wrong. It was, however, surprisingly flavourful despite being starchy, and curbed a bit of appetite I had after the ballet. There were also fried *puri* cups with some sort of spicy liquid that everyone else was getting, but after Monica seemed too affected by the spiciness, I avoided any. I was content with my plain little potato burger that wouldn't sear my innards.

※ ※ ※

The next morning, I filled out my visa application over cups of my new Greenbrrew® and handfuls of some of the dried foods I brought from The States. I didn't get the application done the night before since Monica, Malti, and I decided to visit in the courtyard after the ballet. I needed to get it done because Parkash was picking me up early to take me back to the Embassy to drop it off along with my photos we had stopped to have taken after picking up the application. I would be required to leave the completed application, a photo, my passport, and pay the fee.

Parkash arrived early enough to get us through the city without getting stuck in morning traffic. The day was still cool with residual morning mist around the city as we drove along the *margs* and circled the roundabouts again along the same route we took the day before to get to the Embassy.

Once we got to the Embassy, it was quick business to submit the application, my photo, passport, and pay the fee of 1,500 rupees (roughly $25). I was given a token which I was supposed to give back to them when I picked up my passport with the affixed visa for Nepal, but I didn't quite understand the point of the token. I wondered why I couldn't just give them my name and/or show them my identification to pick up my passport. I had never been without my passport while travelling abroad, nor had I ever left it with a government agency before, so being without my passport was a little unnerving. I made note of the time for pickup and left.

It was nearing 11:00 a.m. and I would have to be back at the Embassy around 4:00. It didn't make any sense to make the long tuk-tuk drive back to Malti's just to have Parkash pick me back up again a few hours later, so we decided to spend the extra time together. Any extra time spent with Parkash is always wonderful, but I often wondered how many fares I was depriving him of when he would graciously spend many hours with me throughout the city.

Our first stop was at Regal Theatre in Connaught Place, but what was showing didn't seem to be of interest to either of us, so Parkash took us to Old Delhi where we instead went to the grand, old, Imperial-style Delite Cinema to see the new Amitabh Bachchan movie *Pink*. The interior of the cinema itself was very posh with dark-wood bevelled edge panels, mirrors, and opulent marble. It smelled and felt as though it had been there longer than its original opening on April 30th, 1954 but felt almost out-of-place now.

After we got our tickets, we went to an upstairs concession area where we got sodas and took a seat. We spoke more about what I had been doing with my time back home since my last visit to India. It felt strange to describe it because it seemed so long ago despite being only a matter of months since I was last in Delhi. I was disappointed because there really wasn't much to say aside from what I had been doing at work. Being on holiday in Delhi and to do all the things I wanted to do when I was there on business trips was the wealth of discussion. I introspectively knew at that point that travelling was what I lived for. Everything else I did with my time in between trips seemed trivial.

When the movie was about to start, Parkash and I went to take our seats in the assigned theatre. When I walked in, it was probably the largest movie theatre I had ever seen. The technology was completely state-of-the-art and billowed and rumbled an audio quality I have never experienced.

The theatre was already dark and playing previews when we walked in, but there was just enough light projecting from the screen that I could see the slight decline in the floor leading down to it. This massive theatre seemed as though it could easily fit a couple hundred people. There were other movie-goers seated throughout the theatre, occupying just a small percentage of the available seats. Parkash and I sat near the back where the air conditioning seemed to be strongest.

Pink was primarily in Hindi, but I noticed that there were a lot of English words and phrases used. I wondered if this was just done in movies to reach a broader audience, or if the adoption of some English into Hindi was becoming more mainstream. With

English being widely spoken in Delhi, I just attributed it to the blending of the two languages given their interchangeable use. There were also English subtitles, so I was able to follow along. At one point, Parkash leaned over and asked me if I knew what was going on. I told him the occasional spoken English helped me more than having to read the subtitles.

After the movie, Parkash and I went to eat lunch since we still had a couple of hours left before I needed to be back at the Embassy. We ate at a pan-Asian restaurant near Connaught Place that I hadn't been to before. Between the theatre and the restaurant, I was already hot and sweaty again, so I opted for a mango lassi before we ordered food. These are, by far, the most satisfying non-alcoholic drinks to indulge in on hot days in India with their smoothie-like consistency and fruity flavour.

I had been craving butter chicken all day, so that's what I ordered. Butter chicken is one of those dishes that I don't trust myself to stop eating, even long after I've realised I'm full. The eating stops when the portion I was given is all gone, and even then, I might order more to take home for later. To date, I haven't had a butter chicken dish I didn't like, both in India and in The States.

Over lunch, I asked Parkash about the little goblin-like faces I kept seeing on the backs of vehicles as decals. These were often black or white depending on the colour of the vehicle, had intense eyes with disturbingly penetrating gazes, and bore sharp teeth. Some also had serpentine tongues sticking out in mockery. Parkash said that these were just another form of charm to thwart the Evil Eye. This also applied to the charms I saw everywhere—the *nimbu-mirchi totka*—where a lemon is strung at the base of a string with chili peppers on top of it. I'd see these charms hung in tuk-tuks (including Parkash's at times), over doorways, in shops, and under the overhangs of food carts along the streets. I was reminded that Hindu culture has many superstitions about the presence of the Evil Eye and malevolent spirits.

We returned to the Embassy around 4:00 and in time to pick up my passport with the Nepal visa affixed inside. I dug out the token from my pocket to hand to the clerk in exchange for my passport book and turned to leave. I don't think we were there even five minutes; there was no one else in the office so it was a quick exchange. I wondered what would have happened if I somehow lost that token. Would my passport be confiscated forever? The token looked like something you'd exchange for prizes at a fun centre, so it couldn't have been too terribly valuable, but I decided to dismiss the idea and just go. I got what I needed and now it was time to figure out how I was going to get to Nepal considering it was now October 26th and I wanted to go for a few days right after Diwali, so the day of my departure would have to be October 31st — Halloween.

Before going back to Malti's, I suggested we stop for a chai. This time, Parkash chose a different roadside chai café where we could sit and discuss what he knew of the logistics for travelling east to Nepal. Initially, I wanted the journey there to be as much of an authentic adventure as it could possibly be, but I was also having to consider that the most authentic journey would also take a bigger chunk out of my actual visiting time within the country. First, we discussed the possibility of going to the Gorakhpur Junction by train. This would take me closer to the border of

Nepal but would necessitate taking a jeep from there to the Nepal frontier at Sunauli. After that, I would still have to take a bus or jeep once I walked across the border to Bhairawa. At this stage in the planning, I just wanted to be able to cross the border, explore border towns to say I've been in the country, stay a night if there was a hotel nearby, then travel back to Delhi the next day.

Before even addressing all the travel time it would take for just the one-way trip across the India-Nepal border into the unknown, there was the part of the discussion about the different classes and costs of those fares if I were to take the train. Having seen the movies *Slumdog Millionaire* and *The Darjeeling Limited*, I thought I was sure to get my authentic journey to this new and mysterious country, but Parkash gave me the rundown on what to expect of a train ride to Nepal, especially for a Westerner.

Parkash said, "If an authentic experience is what you want, then you can take the train, but there are different classes." I remembered that I had printed a document about travelling to Nepal by land that I got online before travelling to Delhi. I pulled it out of the packet of information I brought with me and went over the details with Parkash.

Of these available classes, AC1 and AC2 were, of course, the better choices. AC3 was getting more into the Economy category and not a tremendous leap from Sleeper Class. While AC1 and AC2 would have been the most comfortable, the higher the class, the less authenticity I would experience. The journey would be a good part of a day to the border, so I had to ask myself how much comfort I was willing to sacrifice for hours of travelling just for the sake of authenticity. Sleeper Class—the cheapest of the fares—

would indeed be easy on the travel budget, but as Parkash advised (and I could sense in his tone that he was warning me), I would be in a crowded space with a diverse cornucopia of Indian locals that may or may not consist of pick-pockets, incessant salespeople—many likely children—that would try to make me their number one customer the entire way. The Sleeper Class began to sound more and more like the dregs of society. I remembered Jamal and Salim from *Slumdog Millionaire* when they were trying to make their way by selling a miscellany of things to the passengers in Sleeper Class. Yes, this would be the most authentic experience, but I wanted to spend more time *in* Nepal rather than on the train rides there and back again.

I carefully considered all the details surrounding a train ride to Nepal, but the possibility was seeming less and less likely. I took the information that I had and Parkash's advice and decided that I would confer with Malti to see what her thoughts were. I considered that she could also ask Raju since he is another Nepali.

I began to consider that if I'm making the trip to Nepal, why not try to make the journey down to Kathmandu where there would be more to see and the greater certainty of having comfortable lodging once I got there. Taking the train was still on my mind, but I would be losing much more time trying to make it that far, spend some quality time, then head back to Delhi in the mere three days I had reserved for this side trip. The information in my printout from the site of "The Man in Seat Sixty-One" about taking the train to Kathmandu didn't sound very promising given my window of time:

India to Nepal overland…

Delhi to Kathmandu by train + bus…

It's quite easy, cheap, and an adventure to do this journey overland.

• *Day 1:* Take a train from Delhi to Gorakhpur. The Vaishali Express leaves New Delhi at around 19:50 and arrives at Gorakhpur Junction around 09:00 next morning, or there are plenty of other trains. The fare is around Rs 2761 (£30 or $46) in AC1, Rs 1656 (£17 or $26) in AC2, Rs 1181 (£12 or $18) in AC3 or Rs 458 in Sleeper Class – check current times and fares at www.indiarail.gov.in or www.cleartrip.com.

> You can buy the train ticket online, see this advice on how to register & book on the Indian Railways website. For an explanation of the different classes on Indian trains, see the India page.

• *Day 2:* Take a local bus or jeep from Gorakhpur to the Nepalese frontier at Sunauli (Indian side) and Bhairawa (Nepalese side, often also called Sunauli). Journey time about 3 hours, Rs 55 (£1 or $2).

• *Walk across the border,* it's then a few minutes' walk to the Bhairawa bus station. Then take a bus or keep on to Kathmandu. Buses take 9 to 12 hours and cost about 120 Nepalese Rupees or 130 Indian Rupees (£1 or $2). There are many buses daily, either daytime buses leaving regularly until about 11:00 or overnight buses leaving regularly from about 16:00 until 19:00. Indian rupees may be accepted here in Bhairawa, but not always further into Nepal.

If you travel this route and get any information or photos that would help improve this page for future travellers, please e-mail me. It's also possible to travel via Varanasi. An overnight train links Delhi & Varanasi, then buses link Varanasi with the Nepalese border…

After reading all this, I knew the travel time would have eaten up my trip. Parkash gave me great insight into the different classes on Indian trains, but I began to despair over the timing issue and being wanton for authenticity. I began to realise that I would need to get to Kathmandu by a quicker means and save more authentic time in Nepal than on the journey to and from. I decided I also wanted to see Kathmandu rather than just border towns. It made daring sense to go deep into the heart of this new country or not go at all. Border towns were probably just tourist traps.

Parkash and I finished our chai and he took me back to Malti's for the night. I felt a little heavy-hearted when I realised that there was a lot more planning to do beyond just getting my visa. Getting the visa to enter Nepal was the easy part. I was confident, though, that I would figure out a way. I would seek more advice from Malti and Raju on how best to go about it. Flying was the obvious choice, but I wanted to find out if there were domestic commuters given the relatively short flying distance. The day I wanted to leave was also just a few days away, so I wondered much it would cost me to book a last-minute flight to Kathmandu.

When I got back to Malti's, the sun had set, leaving a twilight glow in the sky. Faery lights were on along the wall to the right of the driveway between Malti's property and that of the complex next door. I could also hear more pre-Diwali fireworks explosions start to rise throughout the colony and beyond. It was still warm, and I began to work up another sweat now that I was out of the constant breeze of the moving tuk-tuk. Monica was home, so she and I enjoyed drinks in the courtyard and caught up on our days. Scrappy Tom eventually appeared between the explosions and looked agitated as he had been before with the barrage of firecrackers both near and fear. We must have been enough of an invitation to him to come out from wherever he was hiding.

I asked Monica more about Raju when I told her I might need Malti to ask him for his advice about travelling to Nepal. Raju, as it turned out, was married, but his wife lived back in Nepal. He was one of the many people who worked outside of his native country to earn higher wages than he might earn in his own country, then would send money home. It sounded like an awful sacrifice to earn a living for one's family but a necessity. I felt sad for Raju, especially since he was just as gracious to me as Malti and Monica were, but this was a kind of arrangement I knew nothing about since all my efforts to earn a living are for me alone. I wish I could know how he felt, but there was the language barrier, and I considered it far too awkward to ask Malti or Monica to translate for Raju if I were to have a separate discussion with him.

Raju was very humble, quietly friendly, and dutiful about his daily chores and responsibilities. I am not accustomed to being looked after, so I would tidy my room daily and go as long as I could in the clothes that I had so there would be less laundry I would have to ask him to do for me. Sometimes he would catch me sweeping the outside of my space—the patio and flagstone leading up to it—so there would be less he would need to do for me during my stay, but he'd often come over and take over, despite whatever he was doing. I couldn't adequately explain that I could clean up after myself, including my room and space around it, but I could also sense that it was important for him to do these things because they were all part of his livelihood.

❊ ❊ ❊

During the next couple days, the only solid plans I had were to figure out how I was going to get to Nepal (and where in Nepal) as cheaply and quickly as possible. I was also to meet a new weaver friend whom I met through *Facebook* prior to leaving for India. The connection was made through one of the fibre artist or weaving pages I joined on *Facebook*. Once we began chatting, I learned that my new friend, Pradeep Kumar, was within the vicinity of where I was going in India. Given our mutual ability to meet during my visit, we made plans to do so and talk textiles.

❊ ❊ ❊

As with my previous two trips to India, I realised how clean water could sometimes be taken for granted in the U.S. When I brushed my teeth in the morning and evening, I would always have to keep my mouth shut since the shower water was the same as the tap water. I often worried about getting it in my eyes and ears, but there was just no way I wasn't going to wash my head. I figured I'd take my chances, but consciously making the choice to drink any water other than filtered bottled water wasn't an option. If they can help it, even the locals don't drink the tap water. Malti kept a dispenser of Kinley® water in the kitchen from which I would refill water bottles for my tea, brushing my teeth, and pouring into a glass to drink from. It takes some getting used to the first few days to not run your toothbrush under the running faucet, or keep your mouth open during a shower, but to rule out ways for getting the dreaded Delhi Belly, you gain awareness of your daily habits with water very quickly.

※ ※ ※

During some of my outings with Parkash where we'd stop to eat at sit-down places, even if they were just little roadside eateries, I started to notice a common placement at tables. They were small red onions sprinkled with lemon juice, served with a small dish of what looked, smelled, and tasted like a cilantro pesto. It was as common as being served chips and salsa at Mexican restaurants. I thought this was unusual, but not too unusual since I'm a lover of anything onion, so I would often find myself eating these red onions with the dip whenever I found them out to eat. The lemon over the onions seemed to soften their potency and added a tanginess that I found appetising. I began to wonder if the meeting of red onions with lemon and cilantro (or coriander) might have not only been a strange appetiser but also a culinary remedy to prevent food sickness.

※ ※ ※

Whenever I was back at Malti's just lounging away in the hottest parts of the day, I noticed that I rarely heard any of the munitions that would start firing off in the evenings. I imagined that most people with said munitions were at work and waited until they got home to set them off. The same could be said for the Fourth of July's explosive festivities before the day arrived. However, whatever they were lighting off in Delhi weren't the same explosives that I am accustomed to hearing during the U.S.'s Independence Day. India, I think, takes the cake for blowing things up for holiday festivities. With the possibility of becoming a foreign correspondent one day including, but not limited to, war correspondence, the randomness and shuddering impact of explosives felt, to some degree, like a preparatory primer. They would start around dusk and continue long into the night along with the varied cacophony of the horns of the autos along August Kranti Marg. It wasn't even Diwali yet.

※ ※ ※

When I was out and about in the city, I would often notice the slender, delicate physiques of many Indian men. Those who appeared to be around my age were often lanky, slim, and had almost poetic limbs in the way they moved. They dressed decently enough; trousers and button-down shirts were common outfits, along with jeans and t-shirts, name-brand or locally-tailored dress shirts. I'd consider myself slender, but being of European descent, I felt more like a large, stocky giant among them, with the possibility of ever obtaining their tiny waist measurements completely unobtainable.

I began to see how some Indian men could easily become supermodels. Many of these men worked in the most ordinary jobs—chaiwalas, labourers, shopkeepers, and even tuk-tuk drivers. I wondered if they even realised their own stunning beauty, or if it was just my Western perspective and attraction to dark-skinned men. Very few seemed capable of vanity, even those in their over-the-top Western wear, but most of them seemed humble and completely unaware of their beauty. Looks, of course, aren't everything, but I'd find myself a little weak in the knees whenever I'd be served hot chai by one of these Indian men who looked like they belonged in a photoshoot on glossy print.

In contrast, I couldn't ignore the aesthetic beauty of women as I spent my time in and around the city. I was fascinated by the steadfast way women go about their day—dressed in colourful saris or kurtis, hair braided, tied in a bun, or neatly brushed in a cascade of black down their backs—as they marched and floated about the filthy conditions of the city in the dust, heat, and overwhelming pollution. The preparation of their appearances against the conditions around them seemed almost effortless and, in a way, remarkable.

* * *

After much deliberation and advice from Malti and Raju, I decided to make Kathmandu my destination in Nepal and fly there. I figured that if I'm going to all the trouble to see another country, I might as well go deep into the heart of it rather than just going to the border where it may not even be that interesting. I would be going on October 31st—Halloween to me, and the day after Diwali—and coming back to Delhi on November 2nd. It was just enough time to get acquainted with Kathmandu before returning to Delhi where I would spend another couple of days before returning to the U.S.

Rather than booking the flight directly through an airline, Malti suggested I use a travel agency she was familiar with and had used: AirCruise Travels Pvt. Ltd. I was surprised that I could book the trip and pay when I got back. So, very kindly, Malti called the agency for me and arranged the trip. I would be leaving the Indira Gandhi International Airport on IndiGo, an airline I hadn't flown before. Within minutes, the trip was decided, planned, and booked. I was very content on the outside, but on the inside, I was full of childlike elation. I kept repeating "Nepal" and "Kathmandu" over and over to myself to make these places seem more real and within reach so I could begin preparing myself mentally before actually going. When I had left for India, the idea of going to Nepal was just a thought I casually entertained, not knowing then what would be involved in getting myself there when I got myself to Delhi. I wanted to go, so I told myself that it's possible with a sly "perhaps." Nepal was another one of those faraway places I dreamed of visiting, and within mere moments, it was a realised dream that was now just days away from becoming reality.

Right after booking the flight, my initial thought about lodging was to find a place in the heart of Kathmandu by taxi from the airport to the centre of the city. A bit risky perhaps, but I thought that it would add to the adventure. Fortunately, however, this would not be the case. Right after announcing my Nepal side trip on *Facebook* (mainly because I was dying to say, "What do crazy cat men do? They go to Kathmandu!"), my fibre artist friend and a gentleman of many other creative talents, Justin Bullard, commented on my post to say that he knew a family there that he stayed with during a short-term residency in the country. He also mentioned that he would be getting in touch with his friend and member of this family, Rajkumari ("Mari") Lama, to find out if they might be able to host me during my short visit. It felt like this trip was meant to be because everything seemed to be falling into place.

❈ ❈ ❈

On the afternoon of October 27th, I met with my new weaver friend, Pradeep Kumar, at Coffee Home, opposite Hanuman Mandir near the Maharashtra Emporium in Connaught Place. I got a ride there with Parkash before he drove home for the day, and I would get an *Uber* ride back to Malti's once my meeting with Pradeep was over. After Parkash dropped me off in Connaught Place, there was some confusion over which café I was to meet Pradeep at, so I found myself wandering around a bit. I was more worried about my running late as Pradeep was already there and trying to direct me where to go via *Facebook Messenger*. It was more embarrassing than anything since I had been to Connaught Place so many times before and thought I was familiar enough with it to know most places of business by heart. Eventually, I did find Coffee Home after confusing it with Indian Coffee House.

Coffee Home is a large coffeehouse on Baba Kharak Singh Marg with a high ceiling and fans whirring above. It was a plain, nondescript building inside and out, with tables and chairs set out over the entire floorspace. It reminded me of what a mess hall in a state penitentiary might look like with its neutral paint colours and bright fluorescent lights. When I walked in, it was filled with patrons who were already seated over their hot drinks and conversing loudly with their company. You had to speak loudly because of the number of people and the collective echo of everyone's voices in this place. There were also lines of people in front of counters where you had to first order your drink before taking a seat.

I only had Pradeep's *Facebook* profile picture for reference, so I had just a vague idea of what he looked like. Once I had walked in, I stopped near the entrance to look around in the crowd to see if I could find him. I quickly spotted him sitting at a table near the entrance and across from the counter where they served chai and coffee. With him was another gentleman who introduced himself as Dharbalilal, Pradeep's associate who handles marketing and manufacturing for their weaving studio. Pradeep resembled his photo but was dressed in casual business attire and had his black hair slicked back. The photo of Pradeep showed him wearing a white kurta and casual trousers while he sat at his floor loom in their studio space. Dharbalilal was also dressed nicely and was much taller than Pradeep and of a stockier build. Both were very welcoming and invited me to have a seat across from them at their table. I noticed that they had already been sipping chai before I arrived, so before taking a seat, I went to the counter to order a chai for myself.

The first thing I noticed about our interaction was that verbally, it seemed laboured and slow in that we'd often get lost in translation. It seemed like Pradeep spoke stronger English than Dharbalilal, so after I would say something—perhaps too fast at times—they would confer together so they both understood what I said. Sometimes, I wouldn't quite understand them and would request repeats of what one or both said so I could decipher the meaning. One thing I learned was that their studio was about 530 miles away in the next state of Uttar Pradesh. This was disappointing because one of my hopes for this trip was to see their weaving work first-hand at their studio and to do a separate written piece on their whole operation and learn more about their weaving processes. I was of the understanding that their studio was within Delhi and that I could make it there easily by tuk-tuk. I also learned that they had other business ties in Delhi, so I was happy to find out that they didn't make the journey from Uttar Pradesh just for a conversation over chai. I would have felt terrible.

Because of the weaving work I had shown Pradeep through links to listings of my own finished garments in my Etsy shop, I began to make some sense out of why he brought Dharbalilal. I had assumed this it was just going to be Pradeep and I having a casual conversation about our weaving techniques, but I sensed that they also wanted to see more visuals of what I do to make a possible business connection. Pradeep and I fiddled with our smartphones to share photos of our work—each of us handing the other our phone for further examination—before commenting and making mental notes by evidence of all the nodding that was going on, especially from Dharbalilal. They were fabric producers from which clothes were custom-tailored while mine were individual accessories that could supplement an outfit.

The weaving work that came from Pradeep's studio was truly exquisite—much of it made from cotton-based fibre content. It was cloth I could see shirts made from that one might wear in the tropics to stay cool. The region I was presently in was indeed such a climate, so it made perfect sense that the cloth was climate-appropriate. To keep the conversation simple and my use of descriptors basic and essential, I found myself repeating some of those adjectives ad nauseum, but they both seemed to appreciate my complimentary nature nonetheless. I could also sense that they had genuine intentions about doing business together, but as a sole proprietor, I doubted my ability to meet or keep up with any sort of wholesale demand that might have been required of me in a business deal with a foreign entrepreneur.

My meeting with Pradeep and Dharbalilal was short, lasting all of 30 minutes or so before I had to decline doing business with them. The idea appealed to me on some level, but I didn't go there in the spirit of striking any sort of business deal. I knew I was too small of an operation to do so given all the garments I make are handmade by me, and often in minimal amounts of spare time just to keep up some degree of inventory for my shop. The language barrier also made it challenging to discuss anything that was substantive, so it was more of a sharing experience of the work we do as fellow weavers. Before we left the coffeehouse to go our separate ways, I agreed to pay their weaving studio a visit should I return for another stay in India for an equal length of time as this trip. With Diwali fast approaching, I wanted to stay within Delhi and watch the burgeoning of the festival season.

After bidding farewell to Pradeep and Dharbalilal until our next meeting, I lingered in Connaught Place for a while. It was approaching dusk and the streets were becoming wilder with autos and foot traffic. I watched the familiar ripening of the orange, dusty sky above me and between the buildings of Connaught Place, especially westward where the saturation of the sunset's glow was richest. I wasn't ready to go back, so I meandered throughout the streets, first walking through the open area outside Pracheen Hanuman Mandir, across Baba Kharak Singh Marg from Coffee Home.

The tunnel I took under Baba Kharak Singh Marg to get to Pracheen Hanuman Mandir was well-lit with yellow lights above and harboured street vendors against its walls who sold tourist trinkets and things for Diwali like clay, teardrop-shaped *diyas*, fresh marigolds, and incense. It felt like a small piece of an underground world as I walked through it. I declined offers to buy something on my way through, but as I felt (and probably looked) worn from the day, I was left alone by most.

In the park-like expanse outside and around Pracheen Hanuman Mandir, it was more of the same, only in greater numbers. There were clusters of vendors set up under tarps or just the open sky. Because I was now more street-side, there were more food vendors, so the smell in the air was not only the constant exhaust, but laced with a thick, ethereal fog of incense and fried foods. I wasn't hungry enough yet to eat here, so I kept walking, weaving my way up and down aisles of vendors where I drew attention but blended in enough. Locals were here tonight, so either the tourists were few or they had decided to retreat to the comfortable confines of their hotels now that it was nearing dark. The lingering heat was the only thing that made me uncomfortable, and perhaps even the dust accumulating on my feet between my sandals, but in India, I opted for dusty feet rather than hot ones confined in shoes.

Arranged in free-flowing spaces in this bustling area were shrines where people stopped to pray and pay respects to the deities. Shrines were colourful, adorned with marigold garlands or heads sprinkled here and there. Incense burned from sticks and cones in their respective censers and throngs that gathered paid utmost attention to their central figures, chanting or simply placing their hands together respectfully when greeting with "Namaste".

The *Uber* ride with Sumit was about 15 minutes away, so I walked to my pickup point within that time. I came across a group of beggar children that began as three, then two others arrived, following me along the road. They were the usual types dressed in soiled clothes, wearing flip-flops or went barefoot. I knew if I gave them money, more would come, so I kept walking this time, looking for a shop to duck into quickly so they would go away. One tugged on my kurta holding his palms out, and I responded with a firm, *"Na-hin!"* ("No!") which sent the tugger and his friends to move along in their own directions.

On my walk back to the designated spot where Sumit, in his Maruti Suzuki Swift Dzire, was to pick me up, drivers in tuk-tuks offered me a ride like others incessantly had on previous trips, but I declined. I was met with the same faces of frustration of tuk-tuk drivers on prior trips. *Only in Connaught Place*, I thought, the tourist trap mecca. Trying to hail a ride in non-tourist areas as a tourist is as difficult as it would be for locals. I could stand along the street outside of tourist zones, exasperated, for 15 minutes before an available tuk-tuk would finally pull over. Having this to contend with, Parkash had not only become my dear friend but my transportation saviour.

Once Sumit and I found one another along the busy Baba Kharak Singh Marg, I lept in after we made that yes-you're-my-ride/yes-you're-my-fare eye contact of confirmation through the driver-side window. Sumit spoke limited English but he said, "August Kranti Marg?" to which I answered, *"Haan"* ("Yes") before he did the bobblehead thing and drove off. In place of the language barrier that would have resulted in another long, awkward drive back to Malti's, Sumit happened to be playing his choice of Indian dance, techno, and electronica music. Before long, I was doing the bobblehead thing too.

※ ※ ※

In talking with my *Facebook* friend, Justin, about possibly lodging with the Lama family in Kathmandu, I learned that due to upcoming holidays in Nepal, the Lama family would be hosting other family for the celebrations, so there wouldn't be any room for me at their home. However, there was a nearby lodge called The Alliance Hotel that the Lamas suggested I stay in, because it was within walking distance of their home and reasonably priced. Mari would be expecting me the afternoon of the 31st and get me to the hotel where I could check-in first before being shown around. This seemed best so that I could have my space and so there wouldn't be any awkwardness with this American stranger in their house. I also liked the idea of being able to come and go on my own so that I could explore Kathmandu on foot and immerse myself at my own pace.

Before going to Kathmandu, I began to formulate some ideas of what I wanted to try and see while I was there but leave room for spontaneity. Because I was going to stay in the heart of Kathmandu, Justin said one must-see sight is the Bauddha Stupa where I might get the opportunity to see monks chanting. Seeing the stupa is considered one of the quintessential Nepal Buddhist experiences. After checking to see where this Alliance Hotel was, I located the stupa within walking distance, and designated that part of my Kathmandu itinerary.

From a journalistic perspective, I wanted to see as much of Kathmandu as possible to find out what had been rebuilt and what hadn't since the earthquake that devastated the city on April 25, 2015, along with severe aftershocks that followed thereafter. I wanted to find out how much relief had been received since then, how much reconstruction had taken place, and damage that remained. Damaged and intact landmarks were of some interest but most importantly, I wanted to find out more about Kathmandu's citizens since the disaster. This, to me, was more an assignment I wanted to dedicate myself to before touristing around. Earthquakes in third-world countries and their aftermath sometimes seem like mere blips in Western media reports, then quickly leave the collective consciousness as domestic news reports take precedence. I recall there being little follow-up on the earthquake, so now at a year-and-a-half later, I wanted to see for myself what transpired.

※ ※ ※

The day before Diwali, Malti and I went to the National Handicrafts and Handlooms Museum in Pragati Maidan. Knowing of my love for textiles, Malti knew that it would be a great place for me to visit during one of my last free days before Diwali and my trip to Nepal. It didn't take long to arrive at the museum from Malti's house by tuk-tuk, but as it was getting into the middle of the afternoon, roads were becoming more congested. Workers were getting off early from their jobs to do last-minute Diwali shopping.

At the sidewalk, the museum was walled off from the bustle of the city around it, contained in its own peaceful confines. We walked through a colourful stone archway to reach the interior courtyards. Once inside, it was a world apart from what we came from on the streets: noticeably calm, quiet, and filled with large, overhanging trees scattered in and around brick walkways that meandered all over. Many of the trees were large, whimsical jungle trees like ones I remember seeing in *The Jungle Book*. There was one banyan tree that grew partially over a small brick wall between it and a brick pathway that caught my attention. Its vines cascaded down its trunk, spilled around its base, over the wall, and onto the pathway like liquid. The top of the tree was wild with thick, intricate branches and vines. I imagined monkeys living up there somewhere and remember thinking to myself, *If I was a monkey, this would be my home tree.*

Malti and I followed the brick pathway around the outside of the museum to large, open huts with angled, thatched roofs finished with red clay, semi-circular tiles. Beneath these structures sat a variety of handicraft vendors. One sold woven rugs, another *papier-mâché* figurines, and another sat among stacks of textile accessories like scarves and shawls in every possible colour. Outside these huts were other vendors who sat in their own separate covered areas. Some sold kurtas, others more accessories, and another selling paintings on old, brown manuscript paper. Adjacent to the vendor stalls, there was another vendor that Malti and I thought especially unique because he was selling colourfully- and intricately-painted parrot ornaments that looked to be of *papier-mâché*. They came in all sizes, some individually, while others were part of larger group-displays of parrots on hanging wires. These parrots were comical to me, even though artfully made. I wasn't sure what I'd do with them, or whom to give ornamental parrots, so I passed them up. Malti, on the other hand, bought several.

I took keen interest in the vendors: a rug weaver and a man selling a miscellany of *papier-mâché* figurines and boxes. There were several cat figurines in different sizes, colours, shapes, and even expressions. One of these would be a perfect gift for the neighbour-girl back home who was taking care of my cats. A cat lover herself, I made a point to purchase a cat-related souvenir to give as a thank-you, in addition to her fee.

The woven rugs also caught my attention, and I spent time perusing these while Malti was still picking out parrots. What I found unusual about these rugs was that the designs more closely resembled those of Native American textiles than the ornate, organic designs I was accustomed to seeing in the rugs of India. The designs involved simpler geometrics in stripes, triangles, and rhombi. When I showed interest in the stock of wovens, the vendor kindly rolled out different designs to display the variety. I always feel bad when vendors do this because of the work they'll have to go to rolling them up again after I've bought one or none at all. However, this time, I did want a rug to place my large, traditional-style spinning wheel on, back home. After inspecting several rugs and practising my Hindi, I settled on one measuring about two feet by three feet—just big enough for all three legs of the spinning wheel. The vendor rolled it up, tied with a twine at both ends to form a string handle, and thanked me.

Vendors outside the hut area—the accessories vendor and the painting vendor—were more aggressive selling their products. I looked at and ran my hand through a few scarves, but it was a lot of what I had already seen before. I enquired about prices and learned that they were much more expensive than some of the local bazaars, but expected, since they were selling outside of a museum. Seeing scarves in different materials and a plethora of brilliant colours day after day, I grew desensitised to any got-to-have-it visual appeal. The same applied to the paintings I would see in nearly every craft bazaar and shop. Still, I indulged the vendor and let him flip through the display of pieces for sale. I looked upon them inquisitively, considered and remarked on their beauty, then moved along as Malti joined me with a giant, crinkly bag full of parrots carefully wrapped in newspaper. Shopping had become an unexpectedly long distraction before I realised that there was still the entire museum to see.

We entered the museum through an empty, white-washed room that echoed with our footsteps and voices. Materials lying around indicated this space was being staged for another exhibit. We walked up a flight of stairs reaching the large floorspace of a room with a ceiling high like that of a white, square ballroom. Light filtered in from windows high along the walls and the only sounds heard in this room came from us. Given the size of the museum, I expected more people, but Diwali preparations must have been keeping people from leisurely activities like touring a museum.

The first of the many exhibits were rows of glass cases that held a variety of aged silk saris in colours that still radiated under the floodlights above them. Their visual beauty was overwhelming when staring at them head-on because the museum was quiet except for the footsteps and whispers of a few others who were walking around and marvelling. There was a powerful voice to these garments in their stillness behind the glass, much in the same way being in a place of deep historical significance for the first time has a silent narrative in its energy. I wondered about the hands that made the woven cloth for these saris, then the person or people who created the saris out of cut cloth, then finally the woman or women who had worn these saris. Each display made me wonder the same things.

The clothing and costumes were impressive, but the tapestries left me without adequate words beyond repeated exclamations of "amazing," "incredible," and "phenomenal." Sometimes the details of handmade artistry can leave one without words because the brain is trying to keep up with and process the imagery that is flooding through the eyes. The trouble I faced—especially as a fibre artist myself—was giving each piece due attention to sufficiently appreciate all the work that went into each creation. It wasn't just that there were so many textiles, but that each was a representation of textile design from all over India, including block printing, embroidery, and a variety of weaving styles that embodied many cultures and hundreds of years of one country.

While there are mechanical elements to weaving cloth, it's still a very manual craft that requires skilled hand-and-eye coordination. What captured my interest most was the detailed handwork of block printing, embroidery, and sewing. While so many of the textiles and clothes that we buy today are mass-produced, it's extraordinary to the modern mind that every minute detail of the craftmanship I saw was painstakingly done with the effort of someone's hands. I wanted to imagine where the creators of these pieces knelt, sat, or stood while they did this work. Were they indoors or outdoors? Who were they doing this work with? What were the sounds heard and scents smelled while they concentrated on their task? What were they talking about while they worked and in which language of the country did they use? I also wondered what they must have been thinking about while they focused on the precision of their work.

When I crochet, knit, spin, and weave, my mind tends to drift off to all sorts of places because of the calm, centred, quiet, dedicated balance of creative productivity that I have created for myself. It's a form of meditation that simultaneously taps into the mind, body, and soul. Knowing how this affects me and enhances my quality of life, I wondered how spiritually involved the creators of these works of art were, especially without the distraction of all the technology we have today that seems to be altering how we value the importance of creating something tangible with our hands.

After viewing all the museum had to offer, Malti and I stepped back outside to a garden of terracotta statues ranging from knee-high to human-height, to taller than my highest reach. They were figures of dogs, robust moustached men, decorated horses, bulls, and elephants. These statues of men and animals all stood proud and stoic—like giant pieces to a chessboard—looking poised for a battle or procession. They were all placed together in a large, rectangular space that was sectioned off by chains that hung from waist-high posts in the ground. The statues all faced one another from all sides of this space, creating a quiet intensity in the empty space between them that was paved with diagonal bricks. This space was clearly off-limits to foot traffic, but Malti suggested we step in individually so we could take photos of one another. We were able to get a few photos of each of us with the statues before one of the museum guards spotted us and told Malti in Hindi that we weren't supposed to be in there. We were just lightly reprimanded before we continued to where we had first come in.

* * *

That night, Malti and Monica invited me to go with them on a walk to Lodi Gardens. Lodi Gardens is a park-like, manicured setting around tombs from the 15th century, therefore protected by the Archeological Survey of India (ASI). While the scattered, prominent structures—tombs of Muhammad Shah, Sikandar Lodi, Shisha Gumbad, and Bara Gumbad—were preserved by the ASI, visitors of the gardens could walk around them and through them, regardless of the time of day. I thought it strange that one would be allowed to walk among the tombs of these former Lodi and Sayyid rulers, but even without any visible security, I could sense by the gardens' upkeep that both its caretakers and visitors paid the site utmost respect.

Before entering Lodi Gardens, Malti, Monica, and I meandered around the India International Centre just beyond the gardens' entrance. There were some smaller buildings around it that were lit with lights for Diwali that glowed a calming and complementary yellow against the blue twilight. It was still warm and the fragrance from clusters of plumeria flowers in nearby trees fused with the cooling air. Many spent plumeria blossoms had fallen to the ground, so scent came from above and below. Malti and Monica picked some of them up—many still holding their shape—and placed them in their hair. I gathered a couple myself and stuck them in one of my chest pockets. I had never seen so many plumeria trees in such a concentrated area, let alone the proliferation of their flowers. They were the largest plumeria trees I had ever seen, the flowers large enough to fit in the cup of your hand.

We walked through a long parking lot—now empty of cars—

before reaching the entrance to Lodi Gardens. A pathway cut through shrubs and under thick trees before opening to rolling green lawns surrounding each tomb that claimed its own generous plot of acreage. Spotlights on the ground near each tomb illuminated details of the architecture in a ghostly way. Along wide dirt pathways through the gardens were lamp posts that created a beautiful outdoor ambiance and a feeling of safety for those walking the grounds at night. Gardenia bushes proliferated and I saw more plumeria trees. The pale, cream-white gardenias were full like the plumeria flowers and seemed to emerge from the glossy green foliage of the mother plants like little benevolent ghosts among the tombs that blew kisses with their rich scent as you walked by.

I'd occasionally let Malti and Monica walk off on their own while I strayed off the path and onto the lawns to get a closer look at the tombs. It had grown so quiet here, with only the sound of far-off autos humming along the roads, occasionally sounding their horns. The gardens felt buffered from the outside world and eerily calm under the descension of night. I approached the Bara Gumbad tomb at the base of its steps that led to an open courtyard space. Through the tomb's central archway that led to the other side of the towering, dome-topped structure shone beaming rays of light from one of the spotlights that caught the moisture in the air. The contrast of piercing light took the shape of the archway and shone through brilliantly against the darkness of the enclosure of the courtyard at the top of the steps. It appeared like a portal to another world.

I had reservations about climbing up to that dark expanse, so

I instead remained there at the base, peering at this spectacle with awe. I was stuck to the ground there, instantly absorbing the enormity of years between its construction and my brief years here on Earth. The weight of energy in those centuries between it and myself was palpable. Malti and Monica might have had to come retrieve me if I had decided to get lost in exploration of this place—tomb by tomb—but we visited on this night for just a brisk walk. If not on this trip, I will have to return to Lodi Gardens for more thorough exploration, perhaps spending prolonged seated time at each magnificent tomb to absorb and marvel at the energy.

We left the realm of the Moghul tombs and inserted ourselves back into the now and walked back to the India International Centre where an indoor food court was open late. Being an international centre, there was an array of foods at small restaurant fronts like the food courts found in U.S. malls. The space was long and rectangular with fixed tables and chairs between the high windows and the line of walk-up food counters. I had had my fill of spicy foods in previous days, so I opted for fish-and-chips while Malti and Monica ordered an assortment of Indian foods. We ended up treating all our orders as a tapas-style meal and took bits and pieces from each of our meals to share the variety. My fish-and-chips weren't half bad. After having ordered Mithapur's version of a club sandwich back in Anand Lok, I was skeptical, but they must do better culinary research at the International Centre. Of all the food we ate, I was impressed. There also stood a confections counter of glass cases full of delectable sweets. I couldn't leave without a slice of chocolate cake (with a name that had "mud" in it, so I knew it would be delightfully rich), and I ordered my favourite gulab jamun.

There was something so other-worldly about Lodi Gardens that I felt awash in the influence of another era of a country not even my own; a deep and humbling feeling because the history of my nation is so short in comparison. The effects of spending time among tombs of the Old World after being present for my short years in the New World is impactful, potent, and permanent. You realise how small your own existence really is and how short your own time is in this world. It reminds you to make the most of your life and to do your best to make it meaningful so you won't be forgotten after you're gone. Centuries are but a blink of an eye to the universe, and a human lifetime is but a swift passing within a procession of centuries.

Diwali

The day before Diwali, people clean their homes frantically and with dedicated vigour. This is done with the belief that Lakshmi is coming, much in the same way Christian observers of Christmas anticipate and prepare for the coming of Christ. Lakshmi comes to bestow blessings upon households during this festival of light, fertility, and prosperity. If a deity comes to impart such blessings, you'd want your home to be as presentable as possible. Additionally, it is also a time of generosity and selflessness, so one must make their home presentable and welcoming for friends, family, and neighbours. General tidying of one's home may begin even days before Diwali where larger projects may take place like repainting one's home and putting strings of lights up. To a Westerner, Diwali is like preparing for Christmas, mixed with spring cleaning, and Fourth of July with resounding munitions late in the day and into the night, all rolled into one.

On my morning walk through the Anand Lok colony to get breakfast at Diggin, domestic help of the affluent residents were busy washing luxury vehicles that belonged to those residents, yardwork was being done, driveways were washed clean, rugs shaken out from balconies, and I could hear the hum of running vacuums inside homes. Many houses were already adorned with strings of lights around the edges of roofs or cascading down to the ground. Sweeping and general tidying up of properties included repainting as large or small projects on facades of homes.

When I got back to Malti's, she was in the process of going

through storage to pull out woolens. Like we do in the U.S. in autumn, it is a tradition before Diwali to pull woolens out of storage and air them out in preparation for the colder winter months of December, January, and February in Delhi. Given how warm it already was after breakfast, I thought this highly peculiar. I was already working up my first good sweat for the day just from walking through the colony and longed for lounging at a poolside, but Malti was unpacking sweaters for cold weather I didn't think was possible in this part of the world. When Malti told me what she was doing, I said, "I pulled out my woolens in Seattle almost two months ago!" She quickly reminded me that what was warm to me was cool weather for the locals. I had to do my best to put it in perspective because in the Pacific Northwest, we, of course, don't experience temperatures upwards of 100 degrees in a veritable sauna nearly half the year.

Of the many garments Malti took out of storage, she also brought out a beautiful red-and-gold headscarf that belonged to her late mother. She mentioned having no use for it anymore and asked if I wanted it for decoration. I gladly accepted. Handling it myself, I could tell that it was an old heirloom as it felt as delicate as cobweb. Having cats at home, it's difficult to say when I might actually use it for display but having someone gift such an item—especially as a guest—was certainly an honour.

Of gifts typically given during Diwali, sweets are common, as are money handouts to those who would not expect it. While I was at Diggin for breakfast, I noticed the shop down below, House of Chocolate, was opening and already attracting customers. Before I walked back to Malti's, I stopped in to see what kinds of sweet treats they were offering for the holiday. I walked in to an open floor plan with beautiful display cases all around the walls of the patisserie. Among the many sweets available were, of course, chocolates that you could buy individually, or in assortments to go in gift boxes similar to See's Candies® in the U.S. There was also all manner of Indian sweets that you could purchase in similar fashion. Many were the same sweets I saw at Shruti and Ashish's wedding. Near the front of the shop were stacks of pre-packaged and beautifully-wrapped boxes that came in different sizes and shapes. The whole shop smelled of sweet things, an impressive olfactory experience and spectacle for those with a sweet tooth.

Buying something new, especially for the home, is another Diwali custom. There is an element of renewal to Diwali much in the same way people make their New Year's resolutions. There is a frantic shopping for and buying of things at markets and shops everywhere to find gifts for friends and family, but also preparation for the festival with new, often more practical items, like dishware (especially auspicious silver), clothes, and furnishings for the home. I found all this activity complementary to people cleaning their homes and making ready for the arrival of Lakshmi.

When visiting brick-and-mortar shops around the city, the outside of them looked as if they had exploded with merchandise. The many wonderful things to buy were set out on tables and in stacks if boxed, and often extended far beyond the entrance in two rows on each side of the main walkway to enter the shop itself. People busily handled trinkets and treasures to examine their quality as their collective voices hummed over the clinking and clattering of dishware. I found all the sounds at the silver shops particularly amusing as different-sized pieces resounded their own unique gong or clank as tops were pulled off and put back on, or pieces bumped up against others during the examination process, then set down on top of or next to others if pieces didn't meet the shopper's approval.

Inside one fluorescent-lit shop that Monica and I stopped in one night felt like a claustrophobic nightmare. We had to squeeze to the back where we found shelves of small silver dishes and containers. We decided to buy one another the same of two little cylindrical containers with tops much like ointment jars. The silver was thin, not much thicker than aluminum, but sturdy, and perfect for storing coins or other small items. In the spirit of Diwali and friendship, we were buying each other something new, and something identical to show that no matter how far away across the world we were, we would both have matching trinkets as a symbol of friendship.

❊ ❊ ❊

Puja, or prayers, begin around sundown. Malti had set out a small altar space on the countertop in the kitchen which included figures of the deities Hanuman, Vishnu, and Ganesh. A central, circular *diya* was filled with oil and a wick that was lit, along with money for prosperity, rice, sweets, and milk as offerings, and marigolds. Malti and Monica were dressed in kurtis of warm pinks and oranges, while Sharmeen joined us in her own multi-coloured kurti. Raju also joined us for *puja* in one of his usual button-down shirts and trousers that he wore around the house. I wore my forest-green kurta with embroidery around the collar and down the front. We were all given the traditional red *tilaka* smear on the forehead for the occasion, which Malti applied.

All throughout the outside of Malti's home and courtyard were set teardrop-shaped *diyas* that were lit among their own little gatherings of marigold heads. Two *diyas* were also placed on each side of the double doors of my room. The *diyas* made it beautiful and serene and, together with the strings of lights on the neighbouring buildings and their own *diyas*, it was celebratory. The sight reminded me of the quiet, exciting preparation of early Halloween evening when jack-o'-lanterns are set out around the porch and yard in anticipation of trick-or-treaters. But this was a different kind of anticipation with the arrival of Lakshmi and the ushering in of good energy for another prosperous year. The candlelight felt akin to that of Halloween, but we were attracting blessings rather than thwarting evil spirits as is the traditional custom of jack-o'-lanterns. By the time we assembled for *puja*, I could hear others in the apartment complex next to us chanting in their own *puja* ceremonies over bells being rung. Other residents around the colony must have finished *puja* early as the explosions began sounding off in isolated places just as we were getting started.

When our *puja* ceremony began, Malti, Monica, Sharmeen, and Raju gathered around closest to the altar arrangement on the counter. Malti led the chanting off a script while all of them joined in unison. Monica held one bell while Sharmeen held another; one was brass and the other was glass. They each swivelled their hands that held the bells in loud chimes with the rhythm of their chanting. I did not know what they were chanting, so I remained silent and stood just behind them all with my hands held in front of me in reverence. I felt extremely honoured to be present for *puja*.

The *puja* ceremony lasted 15 or 20 minutes. I knew the ceremony was complete when I could sense their chanting coming to a close and the bells were set down. All of us, smiling, wished one another a happy Diwali, and let the *diyas* remain burning among the deities with their offerings. I wasn't sure when and if I might attend another *puja* ceremony, so I asked Malti if it would be appropriate to take photos of the altar so I could visually memorialise the occasion. "Yes, of course," she said, as she stepped aside to let me get closer so I could photograph it all at various angles and in detail. Malti did the same, capturing memories of another year's *puja*.

After *puja*, Malti also wanted photos of the various *diyas* that were lit around the property, so I walked the perimeter around her home and yard to photograph those as well. As I did so, I could still hear neighbours either continuing or starting their *puja* ceremonies. I could hear autos out on the road and the frequency of firecrackers and other explosions increase. The night, now fully upon us, was warm and sultry. I wondered if all the *diyas* being lit around the city inside and out might have made the air warmer than it would have been without them. The smell of smoke from the collective explosives began to infiltrate the air and even mask the smell of fumes from the traffic going up and down August Kranti Marg. I had a feeling of having completed a religious duty like evening mass on Christmas Eve before the real fun began.

We all assembled in the dining room for photos after capturing a sufficient number of photos of the outside. We felt happy in the spirit of celebration, and even a bit silly now. Malti brought out her colourful *papier-mâché* parrots she got at the National Handicrafts and Handlooms Museum so we could use them for props. The parrots ended up being held on our shoulders by someone else as photos were taken with an outburst of laughter as we tried taking photos without capturing the person holding them up from behind. I even got to see a rare and sillier side of Raju as he let me photograph him holding a giant grapefruit next to his head.

Similar to the American tradition of driving around to look at other people's Christmas lights, Monica, Sharmeen, and I decided to take a walk around the colony to see the spectacle of the decorated homes, warm flickering of *diyas*, and firecracker festivities in the streets. I was fascinated by the different ways people decorated for Diwali. The types of decorations were usually similar, but the way in which people decorated was unique. Most houses were strung simply or elaborately with lights, *diyas* were set out in fiery rows or individually placed throughout front yards or walls, and marigolds were either strung and hung down the length of walls and fences or clustered around the scattered *diyas*. Electric lights varied in colour but were more often warm in the form of yellow faery lights or strung bulb lighting along fences, eves, and railings of patios and porches.

We walked along the streets in Anand Lok, stopping to take photos of one another in front of decorated houses that we thought most spectacular. You might walk past a few houses with nothing happening outside them, then approach a large gathering of people in the street lighting off a veritable armory of sparklers, firecrackers, and other explosive incendiaries. Men, women, and children were all out surrounding the spot at some distance where they would light these explosives and laugh and cheer wildly when they went off. My camera slung and ready over my shoulder, these gatherings of family and friends are what I'd capture most. Some noticed me with my camera and must have realised I was a visitor for the festival and invited me over to their decorative displays and even some outdoor *puja* altars they gave me permission to photograph. I was again deeply honoured by these gestures and wished all whom I'd met a very happy Diwali. I thought, *The kindness of strangers is certainly not lost in this country, both in times of celebration and in everyday life.*

Back at Malti's I spent time out front in the driveway watching the young neighbours outside the apartment complex light their sparklers and firecrackers in the small parking lot just outside the wall. Most of the population must have been at non-local Diwali celebrations because the traffic on August Kranti Marg had thinned considerably. This allowed neighbours to take their larger explosives out into the street to light between the passing cars. They would watch the road and as soon as there was an opportunity, set up their firework, light it quickly, then run back to the sidewalk to watch it sizzle, crackle, then explode into glittering embers above the ground. Raju came out occasionally to watch the festivities and stand at the gate smiling before going back inside. Even the colony guards that sat outside each residence had looks of glee on their faces. I caught their glances now and then and we'd exchange a shared feeling of wonder and celebration.

When I walked back into the courtyard to enjoy a drink at the picnic table and listen to the booms of explosives and cries of excitement resounding throughout the colony, Monica came out to join me. She told me that she had seen bats flying around and that I ought to go to the roof of her building to see if I could catch a glimpse of them and to get a better view of the fireworks lighting up the skies all over. I ascended the stairs and reached the top where my laundry had been hung on the strung lines to be dried. I did, in fact, see little winged things flittering and diving about, seeming undeterred by all the noise. It gave me a great peripheral view of the colony and an easier way to absorb all the sounds and collective voices from neighbouring homes. I stood there quietly, reflecting on the moment like one does when wanting to experience something totally, as if it might be the last time doing so.

I stayed awake long enough to get my fill of celebration before I heeded the call of exhaustion. The next day was October 31st — Halloween back in The States — and the day I was flying out to Kathmandu. I lingered outside with Monica until she called it a night herself. Scrappy Tom was nowhere in sight as we sat there, so I imagined he took refuge somewhere to escape the blasts. I wouldn't have minded seeing him before I left for a few days, but he probably would not have been in an affectionate way; rather, agitated given his perceived threat from the noises all around him.

The booms and thuds of explosives continued long into the night and might have ended sometime in the early morning hours. I was still somehow able to sleep soundly enough to be rested for the next day. Before drifting off to sleep, I wondered if this is what it must be like for war correspondents in active bombing zones. I'm sure sleep would not be much of an option, not with the threat of bombs ripping into structures from above rather than simply making noise. The cracks and rumblings ripped into the night, but I knew they were merely sounds of celebration. I surrendered to sleep wondering what the arrival of Lakshmi is like when she comes to bestow blessings on the people of India.

Journey to a Neighbouring Country

My flight to Kathmandu wasn't until 11:45 in the morning, but check-in closed at 10:30 and the Anand Lok colony was roughly an hour away as the tuk-tuk drives. By car it would have been half that time, but because we found that tuk-tuks are not allowed to pull up kerb-side to pick up and drop off passengers at the airport, Parkash decided we would instead take the nearby metro. This would also buy us some time.

Parkash picked me up from Malti's just after 7:00 a.m. I had been up earlier in anticipation of my journey. I packed only a knapsack to tide me over for the next few days and intended to bring my backpack full of camera equipment. After the night of explosions in the colony and throughout Delhi, the morning air was murky with haze and moisture that stuck like carbon fog. It was cool though, the most comfortable time of day.

I said a temporary farewell to Malti the night before as she tended to sleep in, but Monica asked that I check-in with her before I left. Monica was a night owl, but she wanted to see me before I headed to the airport. Parkash arrived and it was time for me to go. It was strange to be leaving a place I was staying in in one foreign country to go stay in a neighbouring country. I thought, *Soon, evidence of my existence will be scattered between three different countries.* It was an unusual feeling to have the effects of my existence in three different parts of the world at once. It was a feeling I liked better than setting roots, so I knew my wandering around the world in this life was nowhere near over.

The drive to the metro took roughly half-an-hour, and we rode the rest of the leg to Indira Gandhi International Airport. Before we reached the metro, we chugged along through the waking city fast and slow depending on the kind of road we were on. We passed through the same blanket of haze that settled upon the city everywhere and saw ashy remnants of firecrackers on the ground where people had congregated the night before. It was an almost ghostly transition from the festive commotion I could envision was there the night before, to the present day which was business as usual.

When we got to the metro, Parkash left his tuk-tuk in an alley before we walked to the station to buy tickets for the metro ride to the airport. This Monday morning was still gloomy and people from all different walks of life assembled to take the metro to their destinations. Many were dressed in business attire, likely off to their corporate jobs in cubicles or offices. The Delhi Metro was clean and swift, riding high on tracks supported by cement pylons, and sped over the city below. Men slouched in their business attire—more casual than formal—resting their heads against windows with eyes shut, or upright with earbuds in, wearily flicking or tapping the screens of their devices. Fluorescent light shined down from the ceiling, making the dreary morning feeling of obligation even worse. I saw not one happy face and could empathise with disappointment that the festival was over and life again was back to normal.

After the metro, a short bus ride dropped us off at the airport. Parkash went with me all the way to the entrance doors where I would then check-in. He helped me check my flight status on the screen—which showed it to be on time—before we parted. For this trip to the airport and all other excursions I took, Parkash would always personally see me to my destinations and be there upon my return. I never worried about getting to where I needed to be while in Parkash's reliable companionship. Not just a companion, Parkash's friendship is one of the most genuine, something one seldom finds in this world.

Parkash and I hugged and said our bye-for-nows before I headed into the airport. There are always guards waiting at the entrances to check that people have their tickets and verify them against their passports, so Parkash stood there waiting until I got through. Once I was handed my papers, I turned around to wave to Parkash before I joined the crowds that were assembling to line up at check-in desks. My next destination was Kathmandu's Tribhuvan International Airport.

When I boarded the flight, I was the first to take my assigned seat in a row of three halfway down the aisle. One of the flight attendants announced that it would be a full flight, so I got comfortable in my aisle seat and waited to see who would take the two seats next to me. Eventually, a middle-aged couple arrived, greeted me kindly, and took the seats—the lady next to the window, and the gentleman in the seat to my left. Once they got comfortable, I introduced myself and we exchanged conversation. Upon asking where they were from, I learned that the wife was a Scot and the husband a Welshman, both residing in Glasgow. Both were very kind, cheerful people, agreeable to conversation during our hour-long flight. Like me, the couple was travelling to Kathmandu on a side trip before they would return to Delhi. They had also never been to Kathmandu and planned to meet friends upon their arrival.

With the U.S. presidential election just over a week away, my conversation—mainly with the gentleman—turned to politics. It was an election the entire world was watching, so to hear other foreigners' views on the event piqued my interest. Both the man and woman, it seemed, kept themselves well-informed of the Democratic and Republication campaigns throughout their duration. I told them that it was a relief to have left the country for two weeks of travel abroad to escape the rhetoric and growing tensions over the past several months. Even as foreigners, they empathised. However, I expressed anticipation in returning to The States in time to perform my duty to vote.

There were many lulls and continuations in our conversation around the intermittent flight staff announcements and flight takeoff. Once in the air, the lady transitioned away from the conversation to rest her head against the window and drifted to sleep after what seemed to be a busy time for them in Delhi. The gentleman and I continued chatting. After all the surprising and shocking rhetoric out of the Republican campaign, I felt a strange duty as an American to tell foreigners who found the campaign equally shocking that *Please, if you could, understand that not all Americans think this way and that not all Americans are this disillusioned; many of us are as concerned over what a Trump administration could mean for the nation and the world as you are, a foreigner, looking at the state of our affairs from the outside.* The Welshman understood that this Trump character was an anomaly and wished me and the rest of the nation the best of circumstances, as he reflected on the impact of such an administration on the global community.

Conversing with the Scotch and Welsh couple seemed to expedite the time spent in the air as we were soon descending into Kathmandu. Judging by the light that shone in through the open windows, the air over Nepal was much clearer than Delhi. Extending my neck to get a glimpse of what lay below from all available vantage points, I saw green mountains set against blue skies. On those mountains were homes of all sorts, and at the base of those mountain lowlands lay clusters of villages and fields of lush agriculture. I had done no prior research on the terrain of Kathmandu; I wanted to be surprised and held no expectations. What I could see through the windows as the plane tilted left, then right, poised for landing, the sights were what I hoped this new place would be.

We landed and parked on the tarmac of what was the smallest international airport I had ever seen. There were no passenger corridors at which the airplanes could park, so it seemed that all incoming flights would simply land and find an open spot on large cement areas off the runway. As passengers stood up to get their things and line up in the aisle, I saw airport ground crew wheeling over mobile stairs to position against the exit door of the plane. When the line of passengers moved forward at my position, I bid the kind Scotch and Welsh couple farewell and went on my way.

I followed those ahead of me as we exited and took the flight of stairs to the tarmac where everyone filed toward the entrance of Tribhuvan International Airport just a couple hundred feet beyond the plane. The weather was as pleasant as it appeared through the windows before landing; brilliant blue sky above us, green mountains surrounding us, bright sunshine bathing us, and a steady breeze to temper the sun's warmth. Even at the airport, the air smelled cleaner than Delhi's yet had a mixed aroma of city and natural, open land.

Upon arrival to Kathmandu, visitors can apply and receive Nepal visas right there in the airport. I suspect many passengers on my flight knew this already as many made their way to long counters against the walls and windows where they could fill out the requisite forms. I'm sure it was easy enough to get one upon arrival, but I'm one for timeliness when I travel, so I was relieved that I made the effort to get my visa ahead of time.

In our exchanges via *Facebook Messenger* after providing one another's contact information, Mari Lama said she would be at the airport to collect me at the time my plane landed, so I was glad to not have to face additional delays beyond customs. I don't know how long the visa process takes upon entry into Nepal, but for those who wish to travel there, I would recommend getting one beforehand as I enjoyed breezing through the rest of the airport operations to leave and get on with my visit.

As I made my way toward the exit—light-handed with just my knapsack and photography kit on my back—I messaged Mari that I was soon to appear outside, not knowing what the passenger arrival area looked like. I hoped to be recognised easily as I imagined I would stand out the most as a Westerner. I had just a few *Facebook* photos of Mari, so I hoped to recognise her too. Fortunately, we seemed to find one another almost immediately after I walked out the exit doors to a crowd of others looking for their arrivals. Just to my right was Mari and a young lady who introduced herself as

Tanya, Mari's niece. Once we all knew we had the right people, Mari came up to present me with what I later learned was a *khata* scarf, a symbol of goodwill bestowed upon the recipient. It was a golden yellow, very light, silky, and had markings that looked like Tolkien's Elvish, and other ornamental designs. Mari put it around my neck with a smile and said, "Welcome."

After introductions, we walked past a parking lot to a street where small taxis lined up waiting for fares. Mari spoke limited English and would often say things to Tanya in her language for Tanya to translate to me. Tanya was all smiles and full of enthusiasm whenever she spoke to me. I told her that she spoke wonderful English to which she responded by saying that English was part of her regular school curriculum, so it had become almost another fluent language for her. I was very impressed with her bilingual ability but began to feel guilty for coming without knowing a word of Nepali.

The three of us got into an available taxi. Mari and Tanya climbed into the back while I got into the front passenger seat on the left. The driver was a kind, smiling Nepali man who may have been somewhere between his thirties and his fifties. The headroom in this tiny vehicle was plentiful for Mari, Tanya, and the driver, but I had to laugh at how it barely accommodated my height, and I had to slouch the duration of the ride to my hotel. I felt like a giant, hunched ogre in that car, but the quick immersion into the streets and wild presentation of new sights of Kathmandu made me forget any discomfort.

The streets were tightly packed with the bustle of autos and pedestrians much like Delhi. Taxi cars were all as tiny as the one we were riding in and there didn't seem to be tuk-tuks here. Shops and businesses lined each side of the road beneath three-, four-, and sometimes five-storey masonry buildings that were often painted in warm neutrals. Dust and smog rose from the streets, but it didn't seem to linger; the sky was clearer and bluer than Delhi. Looking up, I saw a vast network of electrical cables that ran along and across the road almost haphazardly and bunched in tangles at the poles and connection points on sides of buildings.

We took Bauddhanath Sadak/Bauddha-Jorpati Road which brought us past the Bauddha Stupa and closer to the hotel where I'd be staying. This stretch of road was precarious to drive over, especially in such a small car, because of the unevenness of the pavement, cracks, and holes that were dirt patches that one could expect a car this small to get stuck in. We bounced along, my head occasionally bopping the roof of the car. Sidewalks were narrow, so people overflowed into the gutters, around parked cars, and sometimes out into the middle of streets where they trailed between moving autos to get to where they were going. Now and then I'd see policemen in blue and black uniforms with masks over their mouths, standing along the road to help direct this herd of traffic around colourful mandala artwork drawn on the streets and cordoned off by cones and barriers. Nothing on the roads moved very fast.

I looked at people more closely after taking in landscape and city surroundings. There were fewer Indian faces and more Asian-looking facial features like their Tibetan and Chinese neighbours. Pedestrians on sidewalks and in the streets seemed lighter in spirit and more carefree than their Indian neighbours. I don't know if this was because it was a time for festivals, but smiles seemed more prevalent, even in the everyday attendance to one's business.

We rumbled over uneven ground to take a narrow side street that broke off Bauddha Road and led us past carts and stands where people sold produce and other street-side goods, resembling a farmers' market. We had to stop frequently because of the congestion weaving in and out of streets; there were now more people riding motorbikes and bicycles. Sometimes another car would come from the opposite direction, catching us in a pinch, so either we or the other vehicle would have to squeeze over to the side as far as possible without bumping into vendors before one of us could safely pass. The traffic wasn't much different from Delhi, but it was slower and drivers seemed more considerate. I just sat there in the front seat trying to absorb as much detail as possible while holding onto the grab handle to steady myself as we bounced along.

The hotel I would stay in for the next two nights was called Alliance Hotel Pvt. Ltd. It was situated above and away from the busy city streets we came from and sat in a quiet residential area. We pulled up to a gate where we stopped, paid the driver, and were let in to walk through a stone lot that was a large, sheltered rectangle between the walls of other properties. Manicured shrubbery grew against the walls between tall, thick trees reaching high above them. There was a tourist van parked at the farthest wall near the entrance to the garden courtyard just outside the hotel's entrance. As Mari, Tanya, and I walked from the lot to the courtyard, I saw a small grey cat near the van, watching us. I crouched down to see if it was agreeable to approach for petting, but it scuttled under the van and into the shrubs in disagreement.

We walked under a brick archway to enter the hotel's small lobby, the front desk was to the right. A kind-looking middle-aged man appeared to greet us and Mari began speaking with him in her language—presumably about this visitor of hers who needed a place to stay. The man, in excellent English, welcomed me to Nepal and began the check-in process. It wasn't much of a process though. I merely confirmed the length of my stay before I had a room key in my hand. I enquired about the cost of staying for each night and payment, but I was told to wait and pay when I checked-out. The USD equivalent for each day's stay was roughly $20, so my entire stay would be about $60. This seemed almost too good to be true given it was such a lovely, yet small luxury hotel. I was surprised I didn't even need to provide a credit card. It was welcome-with-a-handshake and here's-your-key-sir.

Before ascending the stairs to my room, the front desk man invited us to enjoy some green tea. For me, it had already been a long day, so an afternoon tea was appreciated before going about the rest of the day. There was no one else there in the lobby, so the gentleman came out from behind the counter to chat. He asked me where I was from and if I had come directly from The States. I told him I had come from Washington State—not to be confused with Washington D.C.—and explained that my coming to Kathmandu was a side trip to a longer stay in Delhi. Mari leaned over to say something to Tanya after which Tanya translated that they would be taking me to their nearby home to meet their entire family before we would go venturing around Kathmandu on foot. Excited at the prospect, I chugged the rest of my tea—probably offensive to any other self-respecting tea drinker—and gathered my things.

Mari and Tanya followed me up to my room where I could drop my things off and have a look at my accommodations. Mari said that they would let me get comfortable while they went to the rooftop and I was to meet them there when I was ready. They asked if I was too tired to walk about the rest of the day, but despite being up early that morning, I had a surge of energy explained only by being in an entirely different, wild, and attractive country. Just as I did when I first arrived in India, I wanted to *get out there*.

My room was a lovely white-washed space with a large, duvet-covered bed in the left alcove, a quaint little desk against the wall where I knew I would be writing my notes in the evenings, and a raised shower room in the right alcove. I had to take a step up to the bathroom which was tiled throughout like a steam room and had a sink, toilet, and showerhead all in the same space with a drain in the middle. It was a unique setup and I liked the utility of it, for an adventurer only needs a hotel room for the four s's. The best and most unexpected feature of the room was my own cement and marble balcony that overlooked the city below. There were mountains within sight in the distance, and I was high up enough to catch a pleasant breeze that seemed to come from their direction. The balcony was small—perhaps only big enough to seat two people with cozy proximity to one another—but I was delighted to have this private lookout all to myself. Between the bathroom and door to the balcony were tall windows, so I decided to leave those open so my room could catch the mountain breeze while I was gone. This was a perfect, well-lit place.

When I reached the roof with my camera, all the magnificence of this new and exotic place revealed itself to me. Mari and Tanya were there waiting, standing at the edge of the enclosed roof to gaze out upon their city. They too must have appreciated the view like I did, even though they lived here. I was frozen in place at the overwhelming sight of elegant clusters of dwellings as far as the eye could see. Beyond the doorway to the roof, I had a 180-degree view. A light, warm breeze blew through a crystalline sky scattered with fluffy clouds. I walked to the edge, looked out to absorb every measure of detail, and quietly mused at the fact that I was there.

A vast array of colour was everywhere. Multi-storey dwellings abutted pagoda-style buildings that I guessed were temples. In and around buildings surrounding the hotel, I could hear voices chattering in a language I didn't recognise. Laundry hung between buildings farther out. I saw recognisable prayer flags in vibrant primary colours fluttering in the wind. From my vantage point, this was a happy, cheerful place in cleaner air, embraced by mountains, and rich with enduring spirit. From here, there was little evidence of destruction and turmoil the earthquake in April 2015 had brought.

Mari and Tanya were patient as I walked the perimeter of the roof, capturing images with my camera. Images, I knew, would be forever emblazoned on my memory, but it seemed criminal not to memorialise all that lay before me. In almost every structure, windows were left wide open, inviting the magical mountain air ebbing and flowing throughout the city. Kathmandu was immensely welcoming—the pleasant nature of its people reflected in the ambient nature of the wind over the rooftops and in proud flags of this place. I thought to myself, *I can't believe I'm here.*

We descended the rooftop to walk a short distance to Mari and Tanya's home so they could introduce me to the rest of the Lama family. We meandered along paved and dirt roads between other dwellings of all shapes, sizes, and colours until we reached their house, a multi-level building like many I saw from the rooftop of the hotel. Guarding it was a large metal gate with a small courtyard just beyond. We ascended a narrow flight of stairs to reach the floor where they all lived together. The entrance was covered by curtains and an assortment of shoes sat outside where I proceeded to remove mine before entering.

Mari and Tanya invited me in to the sight of small children wandering here and there; they looked at me inquisitively, smiling, and excited by a new visitor in their home. I was shown to the living area where I took a seat on their sofa. Mari and Tanya went off to fetch everyone else. Looking around the room, white walls were full of framed certificates of family accomplishments; there was a desk with office equipment and materials to my left; a bubbling fish tank above the desk; another, longer sofa against the wall to my left; shelved books; and a small television with cartoons, speaking in what may have been Nepali.

The first to come greet me was Mari's mother, Lakshmi-Durga, or just Durga, the matriarch of the family. She was a meek, yet cheerful woman, warm in her welcome as she shook my hand. After that, the small children of the family—Mari's nieces and nephews and Tanya's siblings—began to wander in to greet me in their own ways. I wondered what they all thought of this tall American in their home; I even felt large sitting, my height still well-exceeding all the children.

Mari's father and patriarch of the family, Krishna Bahadur Lama, followed the children and greeted me enthusiastically. I could instantly tell he was an extrovert and seemed to take great pride in my visiting their home. Krishna and his wife spoke little English—Krishna spoke the most out of the two—but we were able to exchange enough words to maintain sufficient conversation. I also met Mari's teenage son, Pranil, Mari's sister, Situ, and Situ's husband, Tsering. The collective warmth and welcome from the Lama family was tremendous.

After a few moments, Mari came out with some green tea, followed by her mother who brought some unexpected snacks and arranged them at the table in front of me. This was a real treat because they were all Nepali snacks—including *sel roti*, a sweet, ring-shaped rice bread—enough to be a late lunch. Between the welcome and the refreshments, I felt gratitude I almost didn't know how to sufficiently express. I ate and drank in as polite of intervals as I could muster while I continued to speak with Krishna, who sat on the sofa across from me.

Tanya and Pranil stayed nearby as they were the most proficient with English from their schooling and often had to fill in when there were translation gaps. Krishna was intrigued by my background and origin. We spent a great deal of time talking about our mutual friend Justin who made our meeting possible. After Krishna exhausted all questions to get to know more about me, he was very proud to share a chronology of all his accomplishments as a social worker. He showed me his award certificates that decorated the walls, and photo albums that chronicled all the events he had been to, and people of importance that he had met throughout his career. By this time, he had taken a seat next to me on the right as we had large photo albums spread out across our laps. It was all a little difficult to keep up with, but of what I learned of his professional history, he had had an incredible tenure.

When I had eaten about as much as I could of the copious snack portions, I finished my tea and waited for Mari to come back into the living room and I continued chatting with Krishna. When Mari returned, it was time to go see the sights of Kathmandu on foot. By now, it was in the late afternoon, the sun low in the sky. The food had given me enough energy fuel the rest of the day, wherever we might go. I would see the Lama family again the next two days, so when we left, it was simply *bye-for-now*.

When we went out, Tanya stayed behind and Pranil came with us instead. We walked down streets and through alleyways that often squeezed between different properties and yards where I could see children out playing and adults tending to chores like laundry-hanging and general pottering around the home. It was mostly women I saw doing domestic activities and I seldom saw men except for when we passed little corner shops selling displays of packaged snacks and household items. The pathways were often dirt, usually littered with loose garbage on each side, and stray mutts with their tails bouncing around as long curls above their backs. Sometimes I would stop long enough to stretch out my hand to one that might come up to sniff my fingertips before scampering off when it realised I had only affection to offer.

The first of our many stops was at a large, grassy field with patches of dirt here and there. It was a sort of open playing area between homes up against short, terracotta or cinder block walls that separated residents' backyards. Laundry lines hung, banana trees grew, squash vines rambled, and floral vines clung to walls and climbed the height of entire buildings. Two cows—one the colour of maple syrup and the other a dark, golden honey—were tethered to ropes and grazed on tall grass to one side of the field. The honey-coloured one had marigold garlands around its neck.

The most prominent feature set in the middle of the field was a large swing made from thick bamboo shoots, hand-bound with rope in two sets of large 'X' formations set apart and joined at the top by a crossbeam also of bamboo. Hanging from the crossbeam was a long rope, its ends tied up at the crossbeam so that it hung down in a long 'U' shape. The whole swing structure must have reached at least 20 feet in the air. Children and young adults took turns swinging on this rope as others stood by and cheered the higher the one on the swing would go. Rather than taking a seat like one might on a traditional swing, they were swinging standing up, feet firmly planted in the curve of the rope as they held on to the rope lengths on each side, using their undulating bodies to increase the inertia of their motion. Some got high enough to reach a full 180 degrees back-and-forth; these swing champions, of course, received the most applause.

After standing around a while, Pranil took a turn on the swing and was one of those who could reach an astounding height that made me hope the rope bindings held together. The whole bamboo structure creaked and groaned every time gravity took him back down. It was clear that he had plenty of practice at the swing; he was also one of the taller young adults, so he was able to make a more impressive show out of swinging, far more than I knew I could accomplish.

After Pranil's turn, everyone seemed to want to see me try the swing. Mari and Pranil encouraged me to give it a try and the diverse gathering of age groups motioned for me to get on. I felt a little silly after literally arriving in the country only hours before and just moments before to that very spot. As a new group of people to my eyes, I considered it an endearing gesture of join-the-crowd, and a show of welcome. *Why not be a little silly and a good sport*, I thought. I handed my camera to Mari, walked over to take my footing on the rope and started to swing. As I gained momentum, I heard the structure creak louder than it did for Pranil. I was bigger than everyone else there, so I was already self-conscious. I reached only enough height to make everyone giggle with delight but didn't go any higher than 45 degrees or so each way in fear of breaking the structure (and how awful I would have felt if I had done so). It was high enough, however, to at least have an exhilarating go of it.

When I slowed down to get off the swing, one of the children came up to take over the rope for his turn. Mari and Pranil seemed amused that I gave it a try and asked if I had fun. Before we left the field, I slung my camera back over my shoulder and proceeded to take some photos to memorialise the bit of recreation I had with the locals. I started walking around to capture photos of the swing in action, surrounding buildings, and the cows. A little girl, maybe five- or six-years-old, noticed me and ran over excitedly to greet me. She wore a pink pullover dress with a pink bow on a white band around her waist. On the front of her dress was the image of a white cat that wore a plaid bowtie that looked as big as the cat's head. The little girl had short black hair with clips at the top of her head to hold wisps of her hair in place. She started to tug at my camera strap to indicate that she wanted to see what photos I had taken. I knelt down to show her the digital screen which thrilled her. She then pointed to herself, so I asked, "Would you like your picture taken?" She smiled and ran a short distance in front of me to pose with her feet together and arms at her sides. It was one of those moments where I wished I had a Polaroid camera so I could gift her with the photo I had taken. It was the most adorable moment I had that day.

I walked back over to Mari and Pranil to signal that I was ready to continue. We walked along similar alleyways and dirt paths that cut through grass knolls between homes until we got closer to a broader thoroughfare. I began to hear music projected on speakers that echoed between large, cheerful, multi-storey homes that appeared when we came out from one of the alleys. These buildings looked newly-constructed, painted in bright, warm colours. Like the Lamas' home, ornate metal gates secured the areas of the first floors, many adorned with marigold garlands, signifying auspiciousness. Each storey of these buildings had prominent balconies with potted marigolds and other plants set out on their edges. Windows and doors were open and there were residents standing outside to watch the activities below.

The song playing through tall, black speakers set out in the street was Justin Bieber's "Sorry". One young lady wearing black leggings, a grey top, and sneakers was dancing on the sidewalk while a crowd of people of all ages watched and sometimes cheered.

Her choreography seemed to be that of her own—zig-zagging her feet back and forth as her arms swung around in all directions—but it was an attempt to mimic the choreography of the dancers in the music video. She was having fun and it was impossible not to smile. A lot of the crowd was young adults—teenagers—who, judging by their enthusiasm for the music, were probably more in the know about Western pop hits than even I was.

As the young lady danced, an older woman brought out a platter with what looked like religious offerings displayed on it. She set it down in front of the dancer and arranged the contents a little. The offerings clearly weren't for the dancer, so I anticipated learning their purpose after the song was over.

When Justin Bieber's song ended, what followed was more traditional Nepali music with flutes, drums, and string instruments that I didn't have the ear to properly identify, in a very slow, melodic pace, but with enough beat to dance to. Immediately after it started, several young people gathered on the sidewalk around the platter, dancing around it in a circle, swaying their hips, hands, and arms in the way that a Hawaiian dancer would hula. I liked this music better than Justin Bieber's and was glad to see and hear something more traditional to the region. I stood and watched, wanting to get up and dance too, but I elected to observe.

Walking farther down the road, pavement turned into dirt again—white and chalky in places—dwellings were smaller, sometimes shoddy, and farther apart. The sun now hovered just above the mountains in the west, sending brilliant orange light rays across the sky. Houses were now just one-storey, perhaps one- or two-rooms, made from red brick with corrugated tin roofs. Some had what might have been covered patio or outdoor storage spaces next to the home, also covered with corrugated tin, plywood, and tarps.

Beyond this, I began to see foundations where homes used to be—some clean slates, some with rubble around them—as evidence of the earthquake. There were sites where rebuilding with the same kind of clay brick had begun again as walls rose around foundations or cleared lots, with freshly-laid bricks and drying mortar or cement between them. Next to higher walls was bamboo scaffolding in similar 'X's and crossbeams like the swing. I thought it strange to use material that could easily come tumbling down again in another earthquake, but perhaps that's all the owners of these properties had to build with. I stood at a site with larger three-storey buildings, the setting sun silhouetting the brick construction in the foreground as it beamed like a fireball between buildings in the background. A year-and-a-half after the quake, rebuilding was still underway.

Faint sounds of the Nepali music at the street gathering was replaced by sounds of new music coming from a different location. In an outskirt neighbourhood between smaller homes and brick ones being rebuilt, we came upon another crowd of young people who had a sophisticated setup of audio equipment, complete with speaker and laptop. They looked like teenagers, some perhaps in their early 20s. Most of the boys wore Western clothing while most of the girls wore skirts and dresses in a variety of colours with organic prints. They danced and socialised together while we passed by. I was so enamoured with people randomly dancing in the street, I smiled and waved, which drew reciprocal responses from some. My own spirits were lifted from all the colourful festivity and happiness spilling out in the most usual of places, the street. Tremendous beauty and life permeated the city.

I also wanted to see relief efforts since the Gorkha earthquake that killed nearly 9,000 people and injured 22,000. The earthquake occurred at 11:56 Nepal Standard Time on April 25, 2015, with a magnitude somewhere between 7.8 and 8.1. When I was visiting, most of the population had moved back into rebuilt homes, but many still remained displaced in camps.

Earlier in the day, Tanya told me that, following the quake that hit Kathmandu, it took non-government organisations (NGOs) two to three weeks to arrive with any aid, and locals were so angry with the late response that many drove them off upon arrival. The largest evacuation site in Kathmandu was the airport. Tanya and her family had to live in a tent until it was safe for them to go home, taking aftershocks into account, of which there was a 6.7-magnitude quake the day after on April 26, followed by a stronger one on May 12, measuring 7.3, near the Chinese border between Kathmandu and Mt. Everest. This aftershock alone killed more than 200 people and injured over 2,500. Of the situation in Kathmandu, Tanya said, optimistically, "It was scary, but it was different and a lot like camping."

It wasn't difficult to find a remaining camp. Nestled between standing buildings on a large dirt lot about the size of a city block, and cordoned off by chain-link fence, I insisted we stop to visit so I could have a look around. The camp entrance was a wide stretch of dirt road. Chickens wandered free and along the fence separating the camp from the rest of the neighbourhood. This camp dirt road was flanked by shelters constructed from bamboo frames with arched roofs and covered with corrugated tin panels. The sides of these shelters were closed off with horizontally-placed panels of more corrugated tin and blue or brown tarps. Cutting across this main road were trenches about a foot wide and six or so inches deep. I couldn't immediately determine what their purpose was, but they were clearly manmade and led between the structures. Above us was dusty sky, and long, diagonal strands of colour-faded and frayed prayer flags tied to high-reaching poles of the shelters.

Toward the centre of the camp was a covered common area where a row of elderly Nepali women sat in chairs knitting what looked like socks on double-pointed needles. Across from them were two other adults: one a woman who resembled a Nepali Eartha Kitt who had her hair tied back tightly in a neat bun and held a child in her lap. To her right was a stout American-looking man with a dress shirt tucked into his trousers and had the bearing of an official overseer of the camp. Children gathered at their feet on the floor on an arrangement of wooden slats; all were conversing together.

Mari and Pranil waited outside while I approached these camp residents slowly, first with special fascination with the knitters, being a fibre crafter myself, and then introduced myself to the lady and gentleman. I was wary at first because I felt I perhaps ought not to have been there in case it was restricted, but it seemed the camp was open enough as people came and went about it freely. The man and woman were warm and welcoming, even though I caught a hint of what might have been suspicion from the man. I was dressed in my Western clothing, camera around my neck, so I didn't want to be perceived as an intrusive or disrespectful disaster looky-loo. I mentioned that I was visiting from the United States, did some freelance journalism work, and wanted to see what the relief efforts were like after the Gorkha earthquake. The man, who said he was based in Massachusetts, worked with humanitarian aid to deliver necessities—shoes, clothes, soap, food—to people displaced after the quake. Donations were gathered in The States, then he would bring them with him on routine trips to this camp as a continuous humanitarian operation until the residents could move into permanent housing. When I asked how long that might be, he said that this was one of the last camps due to be dismantled at the end of November 2016 (a little over a month's time from that point) when permanent housing would be ready for those who had called the camp home for so many months.

The woman—with a child on her lap—detailed the activities they do with the children in the camp, including teaching them English and keeping their minds and bodies occupied and active with educational and extracurricular activities. I was also briefed on the layout of the camp and all provisions that were provided to the residents. Among the dwellings were separate structures that served as a school; storage for food stock; a clinic with first aid supplies; and a shrine for religious studies and worship. The camp was primitive in appearance, but it was organised. I understood supplies to be at least sufficient, and the residents were all clothed, and had something to wear on their feet, even if just sandals or flip-flops. There was a strong sense of high morale, and in my short time there, I couldn't see one sad soul; the entire operation appeared to be an interim living success, despite the long wait for a normalised life. But who knows what tales of human loss and injury dwelled in these peoples' experience and future moving forward.

I was welcomed to take a tour of the camp while the man and woman continued with songs and conversation with the children. They asked two of the older children—either pre-teen or young teenage girls—to walk with me to show me the camp. Both were nicely clothed in black jeans and blue and white jackets—one of them with a large white watch on her wrist. They seemed a little shy but were willing to lead the way. "This is a good opportunity to practise your English," the woman said to the girls, before sending us off to walk about. Mari, Pranil, and I followed the girls as they meekly showed us each of the tents or structures and used what English they knew to tell me what purpose each served.

I peeked through the entrance covers to each tent or structure to see details of interiors. It wasn't until I started looking that I realised there was electricity running to each so that lamps and other light sources could be powered; lighting was tethered to the top-centre where fly tape also hung. The school was obvious as it was open in the front and had small desks set in a U-shape. The supply room had sacks of nonperishable foods. The clinic had a small bookcase where medical supplies and binders were kept, across from which was a table for administering, and next to it were little plastic benches set side-by-side to serve as small beds or seating. The shrine was the most elaborate with ornate furniture set at the far end with framed images of Buddha and other deities. In the centre was a statue of Buddha and a bright yellow light before him. Covering the floor in the shrine were woven rugs set vertically and horizontally where residents could sit as they meditated or prayed. Across one of the beams above the centre of the shrine hung lengthwise, was one of the yellow *khata* scarves like the one Mari welcomed me with at the airport. Each of these utility structures were an average of 10 feet by 10 feet.

As I headed back to the entrance of the camp, I saw a group of young boys kicking around a football just outside of a covered space where one of them was sitting. This space too, was covered at the sides with corrugated tin and had a tarp over the top of it to provide minimal sun shelter, but it wasn't necessarily a dwelling. One of the boys wore a blue and dark grey sweater with 'CHRISTIANO RONALDO 7 PORTUGAL' written by hand on the back in black marker.

Mari, Pranil, and I headed back to the common area where I thanked the man and woman for their hospitality in allowing me to speak with them and survey the camp. I was later disappointed that I had forgotten their names, especially since they were doing such important work for the people living there. I left with a new perspective on what it's like to live as a displaced person after a natural disaster—one example in a third-world country—but it was a heartwarming look at the resiliency of the Nepali people, especially their children. The good news was that these people would be in permanent homes in a matter of weeks and the site of this camp would be cleared of all that stood there, a site memory of life after tremendous upheaval, death, injury, and loss.

It was approaching dusk and the sky had turned into a hazy cyan, trees and bushes on the hills into silhouettes. Before we headed back to the hotel and Mari and Pranil back to their home, we walked farther south where we crossed a bridge over the tranquil flow of the Bagmati River where Buddhist and Hindu temples stood. As we reached the end of the bridge lit by yellow lamp posts, I could see and hear rhesus macaques both at the end of the bridge and climbing atop the temples just beyond it. A few larger adults sat on their haunches on the edge of the bridge, just feet away from us. They must have been used to pedestrians because they were mostly still, quiet, and unafraid, watching curiously as we passed.

Atop the roof of the first temple, I counted at least 20 rhesus macaques that ranged in size from small babies that clung to their mothers, to adolescents, and adults. Those on the roof were more active, scuttling from tier to tier, some sitting at the roof's edge, watching us with curiosity. This temple looked ancient, constructed mostly of stone, but the downward-sloping parts of the roof were fitted with corrugated tin that these macaques somehow had the dexterity and balance to cling to and move about on with ease. I stood watching them under the yellow glow of street lamps with the silhouettes of trees in the background of a twilight sky.

We took a roundabout route back over the Bagmati River through the dimly-lit streets toward the Bauddha Stupa. Along the river edges stood peculiar structures made of what looked like long bamboo shoots tied together like long stretches of jungle gym. I couldn't immediately determine their purpose, but when I looked closer, moving silhouettes of monkeys leapt between these bars. These were literally *monkey bars* that the monkeys seemed to get as much enjoyment out of as child classmates and I did on the playground in elementary school.

At night, Tihar festivities (Nepal's version of Diwali) could be seen in the streets with people lighting candles, playing music, and shooting off firecrackers and sparklers. Isolated areas lit up on the narrow stone streets as white and yellow explosions of fireworks illuminated the darkness. Fireworks popped off in all directions as the city was coming alive in a night of celebration, the air becoming damp and smelling of sulfur.

Some stores remained open, and I mentioned wanting to find some wine to bring back to the hotel with me. I still had enough energy to stay up at least until midnight to listen to and watch festivities from my hotel room balcony. These small markets were tightly-packed with goods, little rooms pushed out to the edge of the street. Above were floors where people lived. Finally, I came across a little shop where I had to duck under a doorway to enter and found some white wines with screw-tops for a reasonable 700 Nepali rupees (about $6.50) and took a bottle with me.

Mari and Pranil dropped me off at the gate outside of Alliance Hotel and bid me goodnight, and I bid them my many thanks. I was reminded that the next day was the final day of Tihar, Bhai Tika, which celebrates and honours brothers of the family. The Lama family would be celebrating at their home and I was extended the invitation to partake later in the morning as honourary "Chris Brother". We waved to each other and they slipped off into the darkness broken only by spots of yellow glow of street lamps.

That night, I sat on my little balcony over a sparkling 180-degree view of Kathmandu. The night livened up even more. Thuds of bass rose from pockets of neighbourhoods as Western and Nepali music blared. Firecrackers continued to shoot off in the streets but rarely went skyward. I could, however, see where they were being lit as ground flashes erupted behind buildings and walls. The air smelled of sweet smoke and there was enough of a breeze coming from the mountains that smoke didn't linger as in Delhi's festivities.

Mixed with the sounds of music were many voices as people celebrated together in large groups. In some areas just beyond where I was, it sounded like outdoor summer bars or clubs in The States. It made me want to get dressed up to go out, but I only brought a couple non-dressy outfits for trekking around in. If I was able to find my way out and back to the hotel, I wondered how I might be received if I was to just crash a party. But it was already late, so I enjoyed it all from afar, sipped my wine (which, unfortunately, tasted more like sweet vinegar), and took in the mountain breezes that swept gently over the city.

Bhai Tika

The next morning before Bhai Tika at the Lamas', I was up early to enjoy a continental breakfast in the gardens of The Alliance Hotel. Though their coffee probably delighted me more than breakfast, their food was delicious and consisted of eggs, toast, and fruit. I sat at my own table just outside the hotel next to a wall where I had a view of a neighbouring residential building with prayer flags fluttering above it, and a lush, manicured garden. There was a gazebo in the centre of the lawn with latticework all around it; stone pathways leading to seating under trees; pots of flowers; and brilliant *Brugmansia* (Angel's Trumpet) with a scent that filled the entire garden space with sweet fragrance.

Guest check-ins were nil that morning, so the concierge and I spoke together at my table as he waited on me. I enjoyed the exchange we had about his and my backgrounds, his narrative of the earthquake, and the Tihar festivities in the city. "You came at a very good time," he told me, as I would be seeing a more decorated, illuminated, and celebratory Kathmandu for the holidays. What I had seen already the night before and knowing I would be seeing the Lamas a bit later for Bhai Tika was exciting because it was like celebrating Diwali all over again.

After breakfast, I took my camera pack and ventured out into the streets of Kathmandu on my own. I specifically headed for the Bauddha Stupa—the Buddhist stupa of Bauddhanath—a landmark feature of Kathmandu that sits over a massive mandala-shaped platform. The stupa is surrounded by a colourful array of shops and architecture that attracts tourists. I'm not particularly fond of traditional tourist areas, but the stupa was one I had to see while also doing some requisite shopping.

The brilliant collective colours of the three- and four-storey buildings, their storefronts at ground level, and marigold garlands hanging in doorways, was stunning. Merchandise from stores—scarves, shawls, tunics, bags, rolls of prayer flags, and all manner of trinkets and treasures—were overflowing in displays outside the many shops and onto the wide brick and stone path that circled the stupa. The most detailed and intricate colour I saw was a bead shop where thousands of strands of beads in all rounded shapes and sizes were hung along walls and doors—the majority of which, as far as I could tell, were semi-precious stones. I personally know a few beaders who would have gone hog-wild in a shop like this. The glittering, pearlescent colours were a reflection of the colourful city itself.

It was a clear, warm morning—too warm, in fact, while walking to wear more than a single layer—that felt like a fresh, vibrant morning in spring. Throngs of people were walking around the stupa: Hindu, Buddhist, all sorts of Asians I couldn't necessarily place, and a few Caucasians that could have been from anywhere as I never caught any vocal distinctions. Pigeons gathered on rooftops and ambled around on the ground between people. In the white wall surrounding the stupa, incense burned in rectangular niches, and in many of the shops, giving the air a sweet and sacred smell.

I circled the stupa more than once to take in every minute detail. I marvelled at grand displays of tealights lit in clusters, with censers emitting fragrances that wafted far and wide. An old monk sat alone on the bricks near the stupa wearing canary yellow and crimson red robes. He sat cross-legged before a small table no bigger than a breakfast tray with nearly every inch of its surface covered with little bowls of powders and other substances; censers, images of Buddha, marigold heads, and tealights. Bent forward, eyes closed, with his hands clasped in prayer, he chanted quietly in meditative prayer, undisturbed by foot traffic around him, enveloped in his own spiritual world.

I had some Nepali rupees on hand, but not enough for shopping and picking out of gifts for friends and family back home. Most merchants only accepted cash, so I had to find an ATM outside of the periphery of the stupa which led down one of the shaded alley veins between buildings to get to the bustling street. The closest ATM was found not because of a sign, but because of the line of people waiting to use it. I waited there in the sun, my back sweating underneath my pack, for about 20 minutes before it was my turn. I ended up taking out more Nepali rupees than I thought I needed because I didn't want to wait for the ATM again if I was to do more shopping before I left Nepal.

Aside from assorted gifts I picked up for folks back home—figurines, prayer flags, incense, etc.—I spent most of my time in a shop with an almost overwhelming selection of handmade stationary. Being an enthusiast of typewritten letters, I wanted stationary for both my own collection, and to send some to my most prolific and regular correspondent friends. Browsing through the many selections eventually had me sitting cross-legged on the floor, sorting through stacks of loose-leaf papers, smaller pads of paper—all in different colours, thicknesses, and insignias printed in images of tigers, lions, mandalas, and yogic symbols. The coarseness of some papers were a tactile delight between my fingertips, yet smooth enough to be typewriter-fed.

All this time, two women were chatting together behind the front counter in Nepali while I had my back turned to them as I rifled through their paper inventory. I had to remember that I had very little pack room to bring things back from Kathmandu to Delhi, so once I selected enough of a haul, I brought the armful to the ladies to pay. The three of us began speaking together in English, mostly about where I was visiting from and how long I would be staying in Kathmandu. I told them that this was my second day there out of three, and immediately felt disappointment just in saying the words; I wanted to stay longer. I told them why I was buying the papers which they seemed to find fascinating. We spoke of the beautiful weather and, as I was about to leave with my large package of artisan papers, they told me that I would have to come back. "There is much more to see here than three days can offer," one said, cheerfully.

I had already come to own a number of kurtas from all my trips to India, and I wanted to find something authentic from Nepal to wear. Down one of the alleyways leading away from the stupa was a clothing shop run by a couple of young Indian men. One of them, with whom I exchanged the most conversation, was a student named Narendra Singh who was based in Delhi but often came to Kathmandu where he worked and spent a great deal of time. He was extremely helpful as I flicked through stacks of tunics and drawstring trousers for men. I favour warm colours anyway, but the festive nature of Kathmandu during my stay made me gravitate toward warm, rich hues even more.

After trying on a few outfits in a dressing room, which also served as their stock room filled with cellophane-wrapped garments, I decided on crimson red and blood orange for tunics, and matching trousers with thin, vertical stripes. The texture and casual nature of these outfits could almost serve as pajamas but still wear nicely to celebratory events. Narendra and I spoke at length after my shopping and exchanged contact information, and we agreed to meet again should we be in either Delhi or Kathmandu at the same time.

Now with a bag of clothes and a weighty bag of paper, I did another walkabout around the stupa to make sure I didn't miss anything of interest. I then meandered up and down the alleyways where some smaller storefronts were open for business. In doing so, I found a chic-looking café one might happen upon in Paris with tables outside on the stone path and colourful umbrellas set out to shade patrons from the sun that beamed down between the buildings. I ordered a coffee, this time a very rich one, and sat to look through my purchases. Another café patron sat at another table, quietly eating a pastry and sipping coffee, while I made loud bag crinkle noises, going through my stack of papers and folded garments. It was near 11:00 a.m. and I soon received a message from Mari that the Bhai Tika ceremony would be starting soon, so I finished the rest of my coffee and hurried back to the hotel to change into my new orange tunic.

I reached the Lamas' home just before 11:30 to find that they had set out a spread of various items for Bhai Tika on the floor of their balcony. Surrounding this arrangement were cushions for Pranil, Phurba (the youngest brother in the family), Mari's brother-in-law, Tsering, and myself. Set out were fruits, sweets, nuts, *sel roti*, juice, white wine, tealights, sticks of incense, a bouquet of tall grass, and flower garlands of marigold and fuchsia-coloured amaranth. There was also a tray with several smaller dishes, one holding white glue, and the others held pigments in vibrant primary and secondary colours.

As the ceremony began, Pranil, Phurba, Tsering, and myself sat together around the arrangement and were each given garlands of flowers around our necks. We were then circled by the ladies of the house, with oil that was dispersed using the bouquet of long grass, and we were then sprinkled with marigold petals. After this, we were given colourful *tikas* by having a strip of glue applied to the middle of our foreheads that were then dabbed with each pigment to form a line of colour. The significance of this ritual was for sisters to wish their brothers happiness, protection, and a long, prosperous life.

The Bhai Tika ceremony was concluded with the boys and men sitting together at a low table in the kitchen where a veritable feast had been prepared. Much of this consisted of rice, dhal, stew, and a vegetable and chicken dish. There was also sweet white wine. All of this looked and tasted like a fusion of Indian and Chinese cuisine. I sat on the floor with the others to eat cross-legged at the table while the girls and women served themselves and ate in the other room. I thought this was a little strange as I expected us all to dine together, but I sensed it was customary for the men to eat separately.

By this time, the sun was high in the sky and I could see to my right a grand view of Kathmandu from where I sat in the kitchen. Through the doorway which led to another porch, the sun shone in brightly, and prayer flags and flags of Nepal rippled in the gentle wind. I was still full from breakfast at the hotel, but my senses of smell and taste encouraged me to eat more than my fill as I wasn't sure when I'd again eat home-cooked, authentic cuisine of a Nepali household.

After we finished the meal, Mari, Situ, and Durga returned to the kitchen where they cleared the table and washed dishes. They had all been so gracious to welcome me and feed me, so I naturally asked to help, at the very least, with the dishes. I was refused, at which point Tsering had a little chuckle and told me that, "Women do the dishes." I didn't want to challenge what was customary but having been raised to believe that both men and women of the house contribute to the domestic chores, this was a cultural difference I wasn't comfortable with. Instead, I nodded in acknowledgement and continued drinking my wine as the ladies tinkered away at the sink. The subject of dishwashing was probably the biggest culture deviation I had while in Nepal.

After everyone had eaten and the kitchen was clean, it was decided that Mari would take the children and myself to Kathmandu's Funpark which is an amusement park nestled in the middle of Kathmandu. To get there from the Lamas' home, we had to walk a distance to find a taxi that we all piled into—I sat in the front seat on the left while the smaller children took the laps of Mari, Pranil, and Tanya in the back—to be driven a short distance to the park. When we got there, the entrance to the park was crowded with people who were out to celebrate the last day of Tihar. I saw boys and men all donned with colourful *tikas* on their foreheads, and some still wearing their marigold and amaranth garlands around their necks. Some people were finely dressed as if going to temple or church while others were dressed more casually.

I waited on a bench with Pranil, Tanya, and the other children while Mari got the tickets at the box office, which was a small building painted turquoise and had leafed branches painted all around the windows where tickets were purchased. The entrance to the park itself had a brightly-painted cobbled wall to the left painted pastel colours like Lucky Charms cereal, and an archway with statues of various characters from animated films such as *Winnie the Pooh*, *Alvin and the Chipmunks*, *Ice Age*, and *Kung Fu Panda*. The day had heated up considerably, the sun beating down as we waited there.

Once we all entered the park, Mari and I took the smaller children to age-appropriate rides where we watched them have fun, as evidenced by their beaming smiles. Either Tanya or Pranil would occasionally stay with Mari and I in case there were any language gaps to fill, but we enjoyed sufficient small talk that we could both understand. The area for the smaller rides was organised in patches of grass with different barriers around each, separated by wide walkways of hexagonal cement blocks that fit together to form grey mosaics. There were also tall trees with thick foliage scattered throughout the park. I enjoyed being there to help keep an eye on the kids, but I did join everyone for a ride on the bumper cars.

When we moved on to bigger rides, our first stop was at one

of those large Viking-style ships that sways back and forth in an almost 180-degree motion. I felt a little queasy just looking at it, mostly because the ride was jam-packed with sweaty people. Pranil, Tanya, and I decided to go on this one, but as it seemed to be one of the more popular rides, we had to wait an awfully long time, confined in packed switchback line rows of adolescents. Mari stayed behind with the little ones to wait, as they were too small for this ride.

I was just about the tallest person in the line, so I had a nice vantage point, especially when I started to notice that some of these teenagers were sneakily cutting in front of others in line. A couple of them got ahead of us before I realised that more were trying to do the same, so I went into instant protector mode of my two young friends, stretching my arms out to rest on the rails to my left and right so no one else could pass us while we waited. I also turned back to a few still trying to push their way through, leaned back, and gave them the stink eye. "Not today, you little shits," I muttered.

About an hour passed before we could board the ship to enjoy a ride that appeared to last about five minutes for the previous group. I didn't think it was worth it—especially while trying to be vigilant over the obnoxious teenagers who might dare challenge me to cut their way through the line—but I had fun because Pranil and Tanya were having fun. At the height of the pendulous swinging of the ship, we could see more of the park and all the additional patrons who had arrived after us.

Before we moved on, Mari and I decided to ride the Ferris wheel. The last time I remember riding a Ferris wheel was the Seattle

Great Wheel two years prior. The Ferris wheel at the Kathmandu Funpark was much smaller than Seattle's, but I thought, *What better way to see the surrounding area of Kathmandu?* Pranil and Tanya stayed with the children while Mari and I waited in line to board our car on the wheel; it took much less time than the swinging Viking ship. It was beginning to approach dusk, and the air was slowly cooling as the sun sank toward the mountains in the west.

When we boarded, the wheel began a slow stop-and-go motion as the wheel operators let off the passengers who had already ridden to let on new ones. Once all the new passengers were latched into their cars, the wheel began a slow rotation at first. It was a calm, breezy ride that allowed me to marvel at Kathmandu with every rise and crest of the wheel. Mari, who was sitting across from me with her tote bag over her lap, looked around with a pleased expression on her face. I imagined that she was aware of and appreciated the beauty of her city.

While Mari and I enjoyed the ride, the operators thought it amusing to turn the speed way up to the point we were spinning around at a speed I don't remember any Ferris wheel ever going. At the height of the speed of our ride, Mari and I stopped having as much fun and I became concerned over whether this wheel was ever going to slow down. Maybe it was because we were two of the older passengers on the ride, but I began to hope the wheel wouldn't fall off and take us rolling through the park. The rest of the young people on the wheel seemed to love it, but I was relieved when the damn thing finally started to slow down. The quick descents were the worst because it felt like my organs were about to fly out of my throat. Mari and I were quick to exit when the wheel came to a halt.

The last amusement park adventure we went on was through the House of Horror (or Horror House, as letters affixed to its overhang read) which was an elongated shanty with a wraparound porch separated from the dirt road, with a waist-high fence and windows completely boarded up. It was probably closer in appearance to something the Clampetts might have lived in than a Hooverville, but it looked the part for a place you wouldn't want to happen upon in the woods. It seemed oddly placed, nestled under jacaranda trees and had bougainvillea growing up one side.

We all decided to go through this last thrill together, so we got in line and entered faster than any of the rides. Even the little ones wanted to try it but were suspicious of what was inside as they clung to both Tanya and I and let out little shrieks of excitement before even entering the darkness. Judging by the size of the building itself, I considered it would be a short walk-through of mild thrills. Pranil went first and led the way with an unimpressed attitude, as if he'd gone through this before and was too old for this nonsense.

As most amusement park haunted houses are, it was set up like a maze, but rather than having live actors jumping out at you, there was an arrangement of rooms separated by walls and curtains with various scary scenes, but not too terrifying that it would upset the children. As an adult, it felt awkwardly foolsome, but the kids seemed to get a kick out of it, so much so that they wanted to go through again. Mari stayed behind the second time with one of the children while the rest of us went through again. There were no new thrills the second time, but the kids were just as jittery over all the things they might see this time that they missed before.

After the House of Horror, it was nearing the end of the day as the sun had dipped well below the mountains, leaving dusty blues and greens in the sky. Mari led us toward the park exit where we walked along a road next to the walls and fences that separated Kathmandu Funpark from the outside. We looked for a taxi to take us nearer to the Lamas' house and where I was lodged, but Mari had another surprise in store. Eventually, a small taxi we frantically hailed pulled over. Again, I took the front seat so my gazelle legs could have a place to go while everyone else piled into the back, the smallest of the children on laps. Mari said something to the driver in her language, but I assumed it was directions to get back home.

The taxi headed west through the city on streets that were not as congested. The mental map I had created from the Lamas' to the fun park had already faded from memory, so I had no idea where in Kathmandu we were, and just assumed we were heading back for the night. I didn't ask as I was already exhausted from walking through the city in the morning, and around the stupa before all the activities at the fun park. I just sat there quietly as I often do as a passenger in a foreign country and looked at all that we passed by. The city was a great big lovely mystery to me that left me curious, despite my fatigue. Mari had proven herself a remarkable steward of guests in her city, so I trusted her lead.

After a short ride—10 minutes at the most—we were dropped off in front of an area where there were large buildings, almost like a collection of museums. We paid the driver and got out for what looked like another excursion on foot through this centre of magnificent edifices. I quickly learned that this was the

Kathmandu Durbar Square—one of three Durbar Squares and UNESCO World Heritage Sites. It was a collection of old earthen-coloured buildings and pagoda-style architecture. Strangely, these buildings were surrounded by newer-but-still-old buildings in what looked like Classical Roman Composite-style architecture with smooth cylindrical columns on their bases, plain capitals with volutes, blank friezes, and square dentils nearer the rooftops. In contrast to the darker pagoda temples, the Classical buildings were white with patches of grey discolouration in places and dark smears running down where water flowed down over the years.

The most haunting part of walking through the square was that many of these buildings were flanked by scaffolding—both of industrial and bamboo construction—against sides that suffered the most damage during the 2015 earthquake. I don't know if Mari intended for me to see this because of the damage or not, but I felt that it was an important sight after witnessing how some of the displaced had been living since the disaster. In Kathmandu Durbar Square, people bustled about as normal while, surrounding them, were magnificent buildings from different times in history. Many were either mostly destroyed, with piles of brick and dirt laying at their foundations with patches of their facades broken or torn away to reveal brick construction; or, as was the case with the Classical-style buildings reaching three- or four-storeys high, they were split with cracks reaching from their roofs down to the first or second storeys, as if a giant had pounded them with a clenched fist. These appeared to be the most dangerous areas, cracked-looking to the point that the tiniest jolt might send chunks crumbling to the ground or disintegrating into powder.

The damaged pagoda temples were the oldest edifices of the square. Many were constructed out of rustic brick and other earthen matter as evidenced by the plants growing comfortably in their nooks and thick on their roofs. It wasn't difficult to understand why these were susceptible to the tremendous force of the earthquake. Many had piles of rubble around them, pieces of detailed carvings broken away, and whole areas of siding ripped down to reveal jagged protrusions of brick. Those that had not been completely destroyed had long, wooden beams propped against their lower levels in an attempt to fortify what was left standing. I wondered how effective these would be with the great weight of masonry just above them that could send those beams cracking like toothpicks, should more material come down. It was a brave and honourable attempt to save what was left of centuries of history.

In the centre of the square where many temples remained intact, beams were also placed against them on all sides as a precautionary measure, but there were no barricades surrounding them to prevent visitors from sitting on the steps or platforms leading up to the temples themselves. These too, were constructed out of brick and left me wondering why these didn't suffer the same damage as neighbouring buildings. It was a curious sight how it seemed that the energy of the quake destroyed some buildings of the same design and construction, but spared others in a way that a tornado might pick and choose what to destroy. There were several couples that sat among some of these intact temples, flashing photos or just talking. I decided to look from a distance. The only sign of modern additions to these temples were bright lights affixed around the perimeter of their rooftops and above the detailed niches around their sides. At the base of one of these such temples were two giant moustached lion statues that sat on their haunches atop tiered pedestals on each side of the stairway. They looked comically angry and intense like the heads on dragon floats seen in Chinese New Year parades.

Night descended on Durbar Square and the lights on the temples shone brightly, revealing detailed carvings around the diagonal edges of the roofs. The sky turned to richer blues and greens that could be seen between and above these old edifices and the giant trees growing randomly throughout the square. While there, it seemed like more people had come, and the sound of voices in various languages grew louder. We made our way through the gathering crowd as one collected group without getting separated. The little ones stayed closest to their Aunt Mari while Pranil, Tanya, and I stayed in front and behind to keep us all herded together.

Our direction took us down narrow streets lined in stone and cement. There were carts with street foods where Mari stopped to get the little ones some snacks as they had grown hungry since our Bhai Tika feast earlier in the day. Lights were strung in places but it was the bright yellow streetlamps that provided the best visibility. High above one street, I heard a high-pitched meowing. As we got closer, a young black cat made its presence known from a balcony above the street. Others noticed the meowing and stopped to look up, either pointing, expressing concern, or chuckling a little before walking on. I was genuinely concerned for it, but I could see nothing wrong from my limited vantage point and thought that maybe it just really wanted to get down. Tanya wondered about it too and showed the kids where the cat was so they could see it was not hurt. We had to keep walking, but it pulled at my heartstrings to hear the poor thing howl its mighty little cat roar from up above as we walked on. Soon the meowing slowly faded away into the sounds of people in the streets.

At a vendor's stand, I bought incense—in stick form and the rope incense that looks like grey gemelli pasta—for myself and my friend Justin, who had asked that I pick some up for him while there. There was also another stationary store I had to step into. It was small, compact, and brightly lit with fluorescent lamps attached to the low ceiling. It was nearly blinding with all the white light, like I had died and gone to handmade paper heaven but illuminated the colours and textures perfectly.

There were so many paper choices, I realised I was taking a selfishly long time to pick out what I wanted while Mari waited outside with the kids. Tanya and Pranil eventually came in to look around themselves and found something to buy. I settled on a ream of handmade, sand-coloured A4 paper and some smaller pads of different sizes and colours. All choices would be great additions to my collection of typewriter papers. My belief is that if you're going to take the time to write letters to people, whether handwritten or typewritten, the paper ought to be of good quality, a unique tactile experience for the fingertips, and obtained from interesting places.

Before heading back to the hotel, I wanted to get another (hopefully better) bottle of wine to bring back with me. Along the way, I saw a dimly-lit wine shop with an array of wines made there in Nepal. I ran inside to quickly peruse their selection while everyone else waited outside. It felt like it could have been a suitable wine bar atmosphere, but only bottles were for sale, some beers, and a small selection of liquors. While browsing, I was introduced to the wines of Nepa Valley (historically known as Kathmandu Valley or Nepal Valley, thinking at first, that it was a clever wordplay on California's Napa Valley) and chose a sweet white wine from this region. Another mild evening, I looked forward to enjoying wine and snacks on the balcony again while I looked out onto the city during my last night in Nepal.

As in Delhi, shops and vendors became one fluorescent-lit venue after another with folded and hanging clothes and textiles, a sea of trinkets, and plentiful incense, smelled and seen. Vendors seemed more relaxed about attracting customers here and sat or stood in their spaces watching passersby, eating, or chatting with their shop mates.

We were all tired, especially the kids who started to drag, but they all kept on walking. For their size and considering the distance we walked, I was impressed by just how much longevity they had for the day. I thought about it for a moment, then realised that it made perfect sense considering walking was their primary means of getting around when the Lamas weren't taking taxis to traverse greater distances across the city. The way the Lamas' neighbourhood was designed, everything they might need seemed to be within walking distance—recreation, shopping, and sightseeing. Kathmandu was a delightful city for meandering about. If I lived there, I would make it my habit, too.

We found another taxi back—me to the hotel first, and the Lamas back to their home. We were all quiet as the little taxi hummed along dark streets on our side of Kathmandu. The smallest of the children had already fallen asleep, one's head against the window, and the other slouched in a heap in Mari's lap. The movement of the car was putting me to sleep, too.

About 30 minutes later, I was dropped off at the front gate of the hotel. My flight back to Delhi wouldn't be leaving until 2:40 in the afternoon the next day, so plans were made to visit the Lamas again in the morning before making another trek on foot around another area of Kathmandu. I bid everyone goodnight and thanked Mari for another wonderful adventure around her city. I watched as their taxi rumbled off for the short distance home.

The garden was beautiful and quiet as I walked up to the hotel entrance. The gazebo and sweet smell of garden botanicals beckoned, but I wanted to enjoy that balcony again for as long as possible before retiring for the night. I stopped to speak with the familiar lobby concierge about my day. He was clearly amused by the tunic I had on and the colourful *tika* still on my forehead. With bags in my hands, he enquired about the places I saw over the course of the day. Other guests must have been in their rooms for the night or out as there was very little activity other than our conversation and celebratory sounds from around the city. He was a kind gentleman who seemed to take great interest in Westerners. Many, apparently, come for backpacking. I told him that is one thing I wish to do when I come back for a longer stay. "You would love the jungle hills with the temples," he said, pointing north where I had seen the untamed, lush greenery from the roof of The Alliance. "There are monks *and* monkeys there," he added with a chuckle.

I said goodnight and told him I had wine and a balcony awaiting me to quietly celebrate my last night in Kathmandu. I ascended the stairs to a quiet hallway on my floor, with only a couple leaving their room at the opposite end whom I acknowledged as they headed toward me for the stairwell. They were well-dressed, so I guessed that they were about to join festivities in the city somewhere. If I had any more energy, I might have considered doing the same, but it felt right to appreciate the last I'd see of this city at night from my private balcony...until I could see it again.

Farewell to Kathmandu

The next morning, I awoke to another brilliantly sunny day. I had left the blinds open the night before, so my room was filled with brilliant light. I also left windows ajar and could hear voices coming from neighbouring buildings and smell the crisp morning air as it gently lapped its way through the window on the breeze. I slept well and was anxious to greet the day. I had six hours before needing to be at the airport, so I wanted to see whatever else I could of Kathmandu.

Before a shower, I stood at the window, watching flags tickled by the wind, waving their beautiful colours and shapes. In a neighbouring building, a vacuum ran, and indecipherable conversation rose up, as well as the faint sound of autos. It felt like quiet Sunday mornings where early-risers had already set to doing their daily chores, while others in the city might still be sleeping following night festivities. The sights were foreign, but the bustling about of people was very much like mornings at home, and the Anand Lok colony in Delhi, and perhaps just about anywhere else in the world in neighbourhoods like this one.

After showering, dressing, and tidying the room for check-out, I packed my meagre knapsack, readied my photography pack, and consolidated all my purchases into one bag with the hope that three carry-ons would pass through customs and security. As I left my room, I felt content because my visit really was all that I could have asked for and more. Besides the rooftop, that balcony view of the city would be what I would miss the most about my stay at The Alliance. The accommodations were precisely all that I needed, nothing more extravagant than that. The quaint view of the city from the solitary balcony was priceless to me. It was a balcony of one's own to soak up the nuances and details of the city from a broader view. I stepped out on the balcony one last time to see everything I had seen during the night but in the equally beautiful daylight. It was difficult to leave this spot, and I stood there just long enough to sear that time and place into memory, to daydream about later. The day below was calling me, so I said my farewell to the city from this view and was shortly turning the key in its keyhole.

As I finished breakfast and coffee outside with the concierge again, Mari and Tanya showed up to collect me. My bags sat in the lobby as I ate; all that was left to do was pay my hotel bill before heading to the Lamas' home again. As I expected, the final bill was something around $60—a stellar deal for lodging considering all that The Alliance offered and its access to the beauty of surrounding Kathmandu.

I slung my bags over my shoulders to leave and the concierge himself walked me out and bid me farewell like someone might do if I had stayed at their home. It was truly one of the most welcoming hotel experiences I've had, with splendid, comfortable, sufficient accommodations. I don't know that I would have found The Alliance without the Lamas either; rather, I could have ended up somewhere less desirable above the bustle of main roads because that's where a taxi might have suggested easy lodging. The Alliance, though, set out and away from all the noise, was special. I would miss this place.

※ ※ ※

At the Lamas' house, I set my bags down and was again warmly greeted by everyone where I took a seat on the same sofa as before. I was asked about the bag with all my purchased goods to see if that would be enough to get through processing at the airport. Durga wasn't sure the bag I had would be able to sufficiently support everything, so she went to get a cloth handle bag for me to fit everything in. I was worried that I was taking something of theirs just to lug this entire lot back to Delhi, but was told the bag was one of many, sort of how plastic grocery bags are collected and stuffed into another grocery bag for other practical uses. It was awfully kind for them to consider things like this and be so generous. I was still amazed at my good fortune to have connected with this family and enjoy the openness of their hearts and home, something I will never forget.

Durga disappeared after helping me get all my purchases sorted in the new bag for the airport. I sat there and looked out beyond the balcony where we celebrated Bhai Tika just the morning before. There was also the wind again, coming through the open door to the balcony and leaving its cooling presence in the house. My concentration was only broken when Durga came back out with another tray of tea and things to eat. I wasn't expecting another round of food after having just finished breakfast at The Alliance, but this seemed to be how the Nepali people greeted others visiting their homes. She brought out fruit and more *sel roti* I had the first day. I couldn't resist, even after eating just moments before, so I enjoyed what was prepared for me and remained thankful for her kindness and hospitality (and for having some stomach left after my earlier meal). It was all good fuel as Mari, Pranil, Tanya, and

I would all head out for another walkabout. It was also more fuel I needed to get me through the day until I reached Malti's in Delhi later that afternoon.

We took a more pastoral route through Kathmandu than the other days. We first had to walk through the same streets and alleyways as one must—neighbours again attending to their chores and children everywhere playing—before we reached flatter, more wide-open expanses of land. We headed toward a valley where things were greener and the ground looked fertile for agriculture. A long dirt road led us through fields on both sides and fenced properties began to appear. Cattle grazed upon the grass and a few of their heads rose to acknowledge us before bowing down again. Near modest dwellings were small gardens and keeps for smaller livestock. Chickens, as a general observation, always seemed to have free range.

The air began to smell rich of wet soil, the scents of farm animals and agriculture clinging to the damp morning air. As we neared the far side of the valley, we found ourselves in the shade of trees, the air instantly cooler. The dirt road we were on meandered between farmers' homes and made a steady incline, leading us uphill. I got an entirely different view of Kathmandu; it was quiet here, far removed from city streets. I could hear only our footsteps as we tread along the dirt, the brushing of our legs against tall grasses, horses clearing their nostrils, and a rooster crowing.

As we ascended the hill on the other side of the valley, it grew warmer, the sun filling the lowlands with light. We eventually reached more homes—larger and statelier than the ones in the valley—with yards, and some with their own street grocers. I imagined that this was where the wealthier Nepalis lived in Kathmandu—an equivalent of the affluent colony Malti and Monica lived in. We walked along as curious neighbourhood dogs stopped to stare or come up for a sniff of our hands and a nudge with their muzzles. These particular dogs probably belonged to some of the residents as they didn't look like the ordinary street dogs; rather, they appeared well-fed and cared for.

We reached the crest of this hill in front of some houses where a lookout area, designed specifically for pedestrians, curved outward over the valley in a wide, convex formation. We stopped for a while to rest and view the valley. Collectively, the homes looked more packed together, painted natural colours of the valley. The sky didn't have a single cloud and was brilliant blue atop dusty mountain slopes in the distance. In front of those slopes was more distinguishable foliage and wild jungle just on the other side of the city.

Where the tallest peaks of the Himalayas within view of Kathmandu dipped closer to the highest rises of the jungle, I could see snow-capped Mount Ganesh peeking out from behind, just enough to reveal three peaks in an almost molar-like formation. Looking toward the jungle layer, temple tops were nestled between the lush green. I wished that I could have heard the chants of monks coming from the temples, but we were too far away. Next trip, I would need to get closer to those temples and come to know more about them.

We hiked back down into the valley on a long downward stretch that eventually turned from dirt to asphalt, and came upon a slower, shallower flow of the Bagmati River. We would need to cross this waterway to get back to the Lamas' house. Of course, Mari knew the way and we eventually got to a point where a large cement cylinder lay across the water. It sat on short pylons so water could flow beneath it, but I was uncertain as to why such a crossing would be shaped this way. It was not a conventional bridge and I wasn't sure what other purpose it served, but it was the Lamas' known means for crossing when taking this route back home.

We climbed down a short slope of dirt to reach the top surface of the cylinder. It was roughly seven to 10 feet in diameter, so even though we had to be careful with our footing, there was easily enough width to walk cross and feel confident. The Bagmati really wasn't much more than a stream underneath us, but there was garbage in the channel and the water smelled particularly foul, so I wouldn't have wanted to stick even a toe in that water. The length of the crossing was roughly 30 feet, so it wasn't a long stretch to reach the other side.

When we were about halfway across, I noticed a couple of boys playing on the other side who had not yet stepped onto the cylinder to cross. One other boy was in the process of walking his bicycle down the slope on the other side. He looked to be heading in our direction to cross, but I had hoped he'd have the sense to wait until we finished crossing before going any further. I was irritated to see that the kid decided to roll his bike down onto the crossing and proceeded from the opposite direction. At first, I thought we were blocked and we'd have to coerce the kid to retreat. I could recognise the very late realisation on his part of his poor decision, but he couldn't figure out how to back up and off with his bike so we could pass. Instead, he continued toward us. This meant that all of us had to carefully pass around him—basically doing a close-up shuffle around him and his bike—so that no one fell off. Somehow, we all carefully managed to pass him to get to the other side.

When we returned to the Lamas', it was nearing time for me to head to the airport, but the Lamas would not send me off before having another meal and tea. As soon as I sat down on the sofa facing the television—this time with the little ones on the floor in their pajamas giggling at the Nepali cartoons—another platter of food and tea came out. It was lunchtime and I had worked up a new appetite after our walk, so I ate and drank gratefully as I watched telly with the kids.

I finished eating and sat visiting before it was time to go, and Pranil and Tanya came out with unexpected gifts. Tanya handed me a handmade paper bag with rope handles and flower petals revealed in the making of the paper. The petals on the bag looked to be marigold flowers with little bits of their deep yellow colour showing through. In this bag was a tiny, handmade, hardcover journal in crimson red with lighter red leaf prints on the front and back. The paper inside was the same colour as the beige bag and had the same charming coarseness of the letter paper I bought at the stationary store in Durbar Square. I saw these same items while in that store, so I knew that Tanya had secretly bought them while we were there. With this journal came a loose-leaf note from Tanya that said, "Hi!! (Namaste) It was really very nice meeting u. I hope u liked our place (country). And I really enjoyed in funpark and I hope you also enjoyed. So, please do come again to visit Nepal. Always be happy; don't be sad; sad is bad; you know that!! from: -Tanya". At the top of her note, she wrote, "Thank-U for visiting our country". Additionally, Pranil gave me a beautiful, handmade, foldout calendar in a variety of colours, called *Himalayas of the Nepal*. Inside, it detailed the days of each month for the upcoming 2017, next to beautifully illustrated pictures of some of the Himalayan mountains. On the front of the calendar, Pranil had written, "Thank-you for visiting our country."

I was so touched by their thoughtful gifts and notes, on top of the Lama family's extreme generosity of time and hospitality they'd shown me, that it was difficult not to tear up. I didn't though, per Tanya's handwritten advice, but was a happy-sad-happy. Happy for the great experience in Nepal, sad to leave, but also happy knowing that I would soon be returning to India for the last part of my journey.

※ ※ ※

I was told that India's president was coming to Kathamandu that day, arriving before I was to fly out to Delhi. I was signed up for flight change notifications, but I also checked for any delays prior to leaving for the airport. Frankly, I wasn't all that worried about being delayed if that were to happen because Kathmandu is not a bad place to enjoy extra time if one has to for such things as cancellations or flight delays. I'm sure I could have walked around more and seen new things or gone back up to see the stupa again. Any additional time spent with the Lamas would have also been wonderful. I didn't realise how much I would miss them until it was getting close to the time for me to say goodbye—or just bye-for-now—until our next meeting. I really was just a friend of a friend, but the Lama family treated me like their own, and they quickly became an extension of my own family.

We would have to leave even earlier in case of delays due to the president's arrival. Because of security measures, many of the city's taxis and other autos were ordered to stay off the roads, allowing only special fares to be taken to the airport. I thought this was more of a big to-do than necessary but surmised it wouldn't last long as all would return to normal once it was announced (by means I wasn't aware of) that the president had landed and had been escorted to his destination somewhere in Kathmandu. The Lamas, however, were able to arrange for one of the exempt taxis to come to the house where it would take Tanya, Mari, and I to the airport. What their connections were, I did not know.

When the taxi arrived, I said my farewells to the Lama family. I was given another *khata* scarf for blessings on my journey back. The entire Lama family assembled in the living room where I gave hugs and thanked them all for their generosity and kindness during my stay, even though words alone felt insufficient to express the love and gratitude I felt for them. I put my shoes on just outside their door at the landing, gathered my things over my shoulder, and bid them "Namaste" before descending the stairwell. Mari and Tanya followed to join me in the taxi where they would see me off at the airport.

On the way to the airport, we indeed found some of the main streets blocked for the president's arrival, so the driver took back roads I hadn't seen before that led us up through a wide, steep, dirt hill through jungle. Clearly, this car was not made for traversing roads like this—wildly uneven with deep gullies cutting through it from water runoff—so riding it was like riding a mechanical bull in a cage. All the while, the driver appeared perfectly calm and confident he could get us through this. While bracing myself in the tiny car so my head didn't fly through the roof or a window, I had to wonder if the driver was quiet because he was scared himself, or if he truly knew what he was doing. I kept quiet throughout the wild ride, occasionally looking over my shoulder to see Mari and Tanya bouncing on the seat in the back, not looking too pleased themselves. My only hope was that any of these deep gullies we sped over wouldn't swallow us up. I thought about Lois Lane in *Superman* when the earthquake tore the ground open and swallowed her car with her in it before Superman valiantly flew in to save her.

When we weren't taking daring leaps over miniature canyons in this munchkin mobile, this alternative route to the airport was actually a beautiful one. On each side of us was jungle thicket one could hardly see through. I knew monkeys had to be in there but could see none swinging on branches or congregating in treetops. If we had broken down, I wondered if they would have come out of hiding to investigate what the matter was with these humans.

After this long, labouring drive up the dirt road, we made it out and back onto paved roads remarkably close to the entrance for departures at Tribhuvan International Airport. The back road we took was probably the wildest shortcut I've ever taken in a vehicle—especially for its size—even if it felt more like surviving falling down a rabbit hole once we reached civilisation again. Ahead of the airport, there was a notable presence of policemen standing around vigilantly who looked into passing cars as we drove in to the drop-off area. Not many taxis or other autos were on the road, so anyone else who needed to get to the airport must have also taken these designated taxi services ahead of the Indian president's arrival. It was quick getting to my drop point, but I had no idea what the inside of the airport looked like and how the president's arrival affected pre-flight protocol.

Still donning my *khata* scarf, I got out and gathered my things from the boot of the taxi. Mari and Tanya got out as well to wish me farewell. It was a sad departure for me, but I'm too pragmatic for long, drawn-out goodbyes, even when I feel strongly about them on the inside. Two of the kindest, most gentle people I'd ever hope to meet while taking a side trip to a foreign country stood before me—their faces smiling, sweet, and full of genuine nature—while I expressed my deepest gratitude for the experience that would probably not have been so rich had I not met them and braved the city on my own. Mari, Tanya, and the rest of the Lama family were a blessing—perfect stewards of their country and city. I gave Mari and Tanya hugs before nodding in shared acknowledgement and headed into the airport.

I walked inside to throngs of people everywhere; this did not match the lack of vehicles outside. I had two hours to kill before my flight departed, so before I joined the line to get through security, I stopped at an airport shop to buy gifts for Malti, Monica, Raju, and Parkash. Knowing Raju and Parkash were from Nepal, I thought that they, most of all, might appreciate a little something from their country. I had just enough room left in the bag Durga gave me for these purchases, so I settled on some loose tea that came in carved wooden boxes and some sweets.

I had no bags to check-in, so I then went directly to security. When I got to security, there were two lines: one for men and boys, the other for women and girls. I thought this strange at first but then noticed there were only female guards for the women's line. It made sense that they'd assign same genders accordingly given a sensitivity of how men and women are physically checked at security.

Both lines leading up to the carry-on conveyer belts looked horribly long—at least 100 feet each. I was irritable just looking at them but got in line and got my passport ready. The men in front of and up the line from me looked exhausted, many having resigned themselves to sitting on a planter wall to the left while their luggage held their place in line or sat on the floor next to their luggage. This wasn't encouraging. I stepped to one side to see what was happening ahead at the security station: absolutely nothing. The lights were off and the conveyer belt wasn't even running. The farther up the line I looked, the more exasperated the men appeared, many looking around with hopes of spotting a guard that would begin operation of the screening process.

Things looked the same for the women's line, but I noticed that they at least had a female guard up front. The security process hadn't started for them either. I didn't understand the holdup except for supposing that it was somehow due to the Indian president's arrival. At that point, I didn't know if the president had even arrived yet, but the airport staff was taking a long time getting back to routine for all other travellers. The female guard seemed to be occasionally saying something to the ladies in line as if she couldn't do anything until receiving orders, but none looked too pleased.

Our men's line didn't have a guard present to give us updates; the most news we got was from the ladies who stood about 20 feet to our right and shouted updates to us as they travelled by word-of-mouth down the line from their guard. More and more people lined up. There was no airflow, sunlight beamed in hot through the windows, and I eventually set my bags down, including my camera backpack that was making sweat drip down my back. Heat and idling are two things—especially when combined—that make me instantly miserable. My cell signal was too poor to fiddle much on my phone while waiting without killing the battery, so I just checked the time occasionally to make sure I wasn't running late because of this ridiculous holdup. The quick trip to the airport bought me plenty of time for this unexpected wait, so all I had to worry about for the time being was trying to keep cool.

After an hour had passed—right about the time I was getting ready to ask someone to hold my place while I went to ask airport security what gives—a couple of male guards showed up and took their places at the security check. At the same time, the female guard at the women's line began processing the ladies and girls, so their line—though shorter than the men's—got a head start. It took another 15 minutes before there was enough movement in our line for me to move up and scoot my things along the floor with my foot. Once people started to get processed through security, it went quicker than I imagined.

It was another 30 minutes before I faced the guards. My passport, tickets, and belongings were all quickly examined and approved until something in my camera pack alerted the guards after it went through the scanner. What should have been only minutes to get myself through security ended up lasting almost another 15 minutes as the guards insisted on rifling through every possible item stored in this backpack. It wasn't merely a pack holding a camera; it was my entire camera kit that included all my filters, lenses, cleaners, power pack, and other accessories. The guards didn't immediately take everything out themselves; they took the camera out and examined it, but asked that I remove every part and piece that the backpack contained, occasionally re-scanning the pack to figure out by process of elimination what it was the machine was alerting them to.

I started to get angry when they began pulling my filters and lenses out of their separate pouches and cellophane wrappers. I generally don't like strange, careless hands going through sensitive belongings of mine (or any belongings of mine for that matter, but especially the expensive, sensitive stuff). Despite my already-growing embarrassment as now being 'that guy' who was holding up a long line of already-impatient people behind me, I began pulling out every little thing myself and showing the guards that it was all just harmless, innocent camera equipment. The last thing I wanted to be was a pissed off American at airport security in a foreign country, so it was a struggle to contain my anger and impatience. I was not only sweating from the heat but dripping profusely from embarrassment. Finally convinced there no nefarious evidence to be found, they let me through.

I thought that was the worst part of the departure experience, but given the tiny size of Tribhuvan International Airport, it wasn't going to get any more pleasant before boarding the plane.

Because of the Indian president (whom I learned, at that point, had already come and gone), many flights were completely backed up which meant this tiny airport was bursting at the seams with stacked arrivals and departures. I checked my flight status again to find that my flight was now delayed an hour-and-a-half with no indication when boarding would begin. I noticed that they were, however, doing a good job of repetitively announcing when boarding was beginning for other delayed flights, so I just had to keep my flight number in mind and listen close for my new flight time.

In the waiting area where most congregated, people fanned themselves, paced, stood motionless while staring at screens, or were sitting in-place looking pissed. No seats were available in the waiting area when I got there, so I waited on the tiled floor across from a duty-free. There was an empty spot next to a garbage bin that conveniently blocked anyone from brushing into me as they passed. It was a small, welcomed refuge from the flood of people walking in all directions. My back began to sweat again with the camera pack on, so I took it off and crouched down on the floor, eventually collapsing into a cross-legged position of resignation, not really caring how dirty the floor was at that point because I already felt disgusting from sweating all through security. I sat there nibbling on pretzels and taking occasional sips of water as I longed for that damp morning air of the valley I hiked through only hours earlier.

To pass the time, I went through all my purchases again (I don't know why because I did this already, but I guess having a detailed mental inventory of what I was bringing back from Nepal made me feel better and staved off boredom by doing something methodical), and I people-watched. Despite the claustrophobia I felt sitting off to one side of this shoulder-to-shoulder river of people, there were plenty of interesting people to look at—a cornucopia of races, nationalities, and religions; to be expected at an airport next to the Himalayas, nestled between Tibet and India.

Even though I felt like I was forfeiting a VIP spot for squatters, I got up after a while to check the flight screens and meander throughout the corridors leading to and away from the waiting area. The collective sound of crowded voices grew louder as more and more people poured in from security. I walked upstream through this influx to see what security looked like now. There were still two considerable lines but not as long as they were when I was waiting there. Because the main waiting area was now heavily backlogged, people were taking seats on the floor against the sides of the corridors. I knew my original spot would be long gone, so I took a seat against the wall in the corridor to face the window panes that gave at least a decent view of the outside where planes were coming and going. Even if it wasn't time for my flight, I was happy to see activity with arrivals and departures. I sat and read until it was time for me to move in preparation for my flight.

When the blessed hour finally came for pre-boarding, I moved to another corridor of the terminal. The relief of fresh air left me remembering the adventures of the last few days in Kathmandu. I also felt a pang of sadness in realising what little time I had left in Delhi. I busied my thoughts with what I would do with it before flying back to The States. Never again seeing the people I had met also crossed my mind in a strange contemplation; the world and all human population is so vast that this was likely the first and last time I'd see any of them. Strangers in new places always fascinate me; the cosmic recipe that brought us together, paths crossed, for this moment only, and likely never again.

When our plane was finally ready, passengers for the flight lined up eagerly; the more impatient ones hurried their way over with bubbly anticipation. Everyone looked happier and hummed along in lively conversation with travel companions or fellow unknown travellers having shared this same delay. I was in one of the last groups, but seating was assigned, so I was more than happy to watch the majority of passengers board first, knowing I'd have a seat waiting for me about halfway down the aisle.

When it was my group's turn, we were led across the tarmac, hurried along like baggage-toting lemmings to a secondary security check at the bottom of a flight of stairs leading up to the front entrance of the fuselage. I had to wait for a few moments before I ascended, but I just looked around again and took in the last of the Nepal breezes. It was easy to daydream in Kathmandu, even briefly there on that tarmac, with the roaring of plane engines.

It was a full flight back to Delhi, but I can't recall who I sat next to on that flight. I didn't speak to anyone besides the flight attendant when it came time for beverages, so my neighbour must have been just as quiet and contemplative on our return as I was. I thought about the Welch and Scottish couple I sat next to on the flight into Kathmandu and wondered where they were and what adventures that might be having together down there in the vastness of the city nestled in countryside.

Takeoff was glorious and offered clear and brilliant images through the windows to remember Nepal by. Clusters of civilisation turned to green farmland and jungle as we climbed out of the valley, then lush hills dotted with homes, ending with snow-capped mountains of the Himilayas as we veered northwest for Delhi. I was melancholy on that flight back; it is never enough time when visiting someplace new and extraordinary. I did want more time there—badly—but the time I had there was better than none at all and so I appreciated the finite days with infinite gratitude.

※ ※ ※

Delhi looked changed when I returned to it. When it was announced that we were descending, I looked out the windows on both sides and could see nothing but a thick pea soup. I knew Delhi to be polluted, but I had not seen a haze like this one. I hoped that we might cut through this floating bank of muck and moisture, but we never broke free of it the lower we got. Once I heard the landing gear engage beneath us, I thought that surely it would look different on the ground and that I would see the ground and runway right before landing. We descended farther and farther until there was that eerie floating calm in the plane mechanics before landing. When the plane touched down, it was in the same brown mess, no change in air quality. Delhi had grown staler since I left days earlier; I did not look forward to stepping out into this bog of filth. I wondered what the ratio was of actual oxygen to pollutants.

We were over an hour late past my original travel time, so as soon as my cell signal was restored, I checked to see what messages had come in from Parkash because I knew my faithful friend was there waiting for me. Through *WhatsApp*, I saw that he had arrived at the metro and sent photos of the flight screen showing my flight as 'DELAYED', so I was relieved he knew the circumstances before I was able to reach him in a text message. As kind as Parkash was, the dear soul, to retrieve me again from the airport, I felt badly that he had to wait—based on the time stamp of his incoming messages—an hour-and-a-half for me. There was nothing I could do about the delay but was glad that all my belongings were with me so I wouldn't have to create further delay by waiting for luggage at baggage claim.

Soupy Delhi awaited as I sped on foot through the airport to find a jovial Parkash waiting outside. He was in the same spot when he found me upon first arriving almost two weeks earlier. I would have expected him to be a little impatient after such a long wait, but there he was: my joyful, friendly comrade to greet me with a hug. After requisite apologies for the delay, I couldn't help but gush over the beauty of his country and the nature of its people, how they mimicked his own good-hearted, devoted, and welcoming nature. "You come from a gorgeous country of beautiful people," is one of the first things I said. That, of course, was an understatement.

We took the metro back to where Parkash had parked his tuk-tuk on a side street. This was far quicker and easier than driving all the way to the airport and we both enjoyed the relaxation time. It gave us a chance to talk about my trip which, of course, had me yammering on about all I had seen and done and the pleasure of meeting the Lama family. Once I gave a thorough synopsis of the journey, I had to ask about the awful, mucky skies that I came back to. Parkash told me that this happens every year right after Diwali when the normal pollution combines with all the remnant smoke of all the fireworks and smoke from agricultural burnings which take place this time of year—a rather unholy trinity that makes Delhi (and likely a good many other parts of the country) dangerous to be outside in. Passing through the city on the metro rail, I looked down and could see people wearing face masks. Being a tuk-tuk driver exposed to this toxic mess, Parkash had to wear a cover too, using a handkerchief he had tied around his neck that he pulled up and over the lower half of his face while driving.

The ride back to Malti's was depressing in how everything looked with this added pollution. Many people had masks over their noses and mouths. Poor living on the streets—children included—did not have masks and had to endure the rotten air in full effect as they always have, likely not even noticing it the way I did. It was still afternoon, the sun out like a big sphere of liquid amber glowing in the sky, its light so obscured by the pollution that you could look directly at it. The eeriness of it all was that everyone went about their business as normal but wearing these face masks, as if this somehow made it alright or normal.

It was as if the city had been gassed by a foreign enemy while I was gone but no, it was human activity, everyday carbon emissions, celebratory explosives, and agricultural burning. Diwali didn't seem so magical to me anymore after seeing the effect it contributed; I felt guilty for being so dazzled by fireworks the night of Diwali. I was only a visiting spectator of these festivities, but I still felt culpable; there was nothing holy about doing this to the earth, especially in cheering the destructive conditions.

Parkash dropped me off at Malti's. With the next day being my last full day in Delhi, we made plans to visit Chawla Typewriters again in Old Delhi to see if there might have been anything else that came in worth buying and taking back to The States with me. I gathered my things, thanked Parkash for retrieving me again, and watched him rumble off into the thick brown cover of smog before I turned to go in through the gate. A smiling Raju greeted me at the gate after I buzzed to be let in. It was good to be back to my temporary home away from home where I could unload my things, shower, relax, pass out my gifts to Malti, Monica, and Raju, and tell them stories of the time spent in neighbouring Nepal.

Farewell to Delhi

The next morning, I took a final walk through the Anand Lok colony to have breakfast at Diggin. The air quality had improved a little with a crisper morning air that looked paler, mixed with more fog than the previous day's veritable sewer. The sun also shone more brightly with a better chance of breaking through to be enjoyed rather than tolerated. There were still remnants of Diwali: firework ash in small piles in the streets, colourful streamer ribbon littering the kerb-sides and gutters, and lights still strung on houses. The mood in how people moved and conducted themselves, and the usual traffic along August Kranti Marg, however, indicated that festivities were abruptly over and all was back to daily life as usual.

The guards that raised and lowered the same boom gate I would pass through from the sidewalk into the colony recognised me after being absent for a few days and seemed especially delighted to see me again. I wanted to tell them that I wouldn't be seeing them again for a while after that day but kept to my usual, "Namaste; good morning" to which I received their usual reply of, "Good morning, sir!" as they raised the gate for me. They always looked terribly bored, the poor buggers, like the solitary guards that sat out in front of each residence or business, either napping, reading a newspaper, or staring blankly ahead at passersby like idling zombies. Conversation was exciting in comparison.

I walked along my same route through Anand Lok. A woman with two children were in the park; the children running and playing while the woman watched in supervision. A slender man stretched at the exercise station, one leg up on the sit-up bench as he arched himself over in a reach-hold for his foot. The man was in everyday trousers and a button-down shirt—not exactly workout clothing. They were out and about in recreation—play and exercise—even in the poor air quality. Of course, there was my daft self out in it too, but I was only out to get breakfast. The stomach wants what the stomach wants. I suppose, being residents there, mucky days like this are all the same.

Knowing this would be my last full day in India with a vacationer's freedom, I felt the beginnings of longing for my return to cooler temperatures and clean, crisp air of the Pacific Northwest. I felt too, the sharp consciousness that all things— mundane and celebratory—will go on as they have before and after my brief drifting through as an outsider stepping in. I felt lucky to have been welcomed and included the way I had been, living as an honourary citizen.

Breakfast was simple, and I took my time, enjoyed multiple rounds of delicious cold coffee and a yogurt parfait. I sat by the window and read as I occasionally looked out to watch the moisture in the air slowly burn off and let a little more sunshine in, but this only revealed the thicker cover of smog as what it truly was and likely would be throughout the rest of the day. The reality is: it's an incredible country to visit despite abject conditions in parts which will always deliver swift shock and wonder to any Westerner but living in the parts I've seen (I can't speak for the others) for an extended period is not within my tastes. There was a marvellous thought of working for the U.S. Embassy, but upon contemplation, I determined that for me, India would be a country I will enjoy in short spells only when I travel farther during future journeys in the near region.

I returned to my book after pondering this until it was time to leave what had been my morning breakfast haunt. Parkash messaged to say that he was almost there, so I left Diggin and went through a different exit to Anand Lok. This way took me back around to the other end of August Kranti Marg and down sidewalks shaded by trees before reaching the gate at Malti's. I went back in to greet Malti and Monica; they were up and about while Raju was going about daily chores. I sat out in the little patio area and continued to read until Parkash arrived. Scrappy Tom graced me with his presence uttering his male cat meows, and slid in, out, and around my legs before deciding my lap was where he preferred to be. When he got himself comfortable, he continued his low meows and coos as if telling me about all his adventures while I was gone to Nepal. He seemed to just want to talk this time, so I held my book above him to read while occasionally responding with cat chatter of my own.

Just as Scrappy Tom drifted off to sleep with his rumbling purr motor going, I knew Parkash arrived when Raju came to fetch me with his usual short-worded alerts like "Parkash?" Poor Scrappy Tom probably thought he could park himself there on my lap for at least a short napping spell before I had to scoot him off to find another spot. Whenever Raju was around, Scrappy Tom didn't stick around knowing Raju wasn't fond of him, so off Scrappy Tom went into the bushes to nap the day away in peace.

Parkash and I were soon chugging away to Old Delhi again. I

had done just about all the acquiring of things to bring home for myself and others as I wanted to do, but I wanted another try at Chawla Typewriters to see if they might have anything different in stock since my first visit. I had given the little manual Brother typewriter some second thoughts since seeing it, but I was feeling much less adamant about acquiring a typewriter since I was to be going home soon to my bounty of others. I really wanted one from the New or Old Delhi shops for writing work over the course of my stay in Delhi, but now the need was gone. I re-considered the red Brother at Adarsh Typewriters, but 28,000 rupees for one with missing parts was out of the question, I reasoned, and I dismissed the idea entirely.

Once through the maddening wilds of Old Delhi, we were able to park the tuk-tuk on the Chawla Typewriters side of Asaf Ali Road, so there was no leapfrogging across traffic this time. When we got upstairs, the first thing I noticed was that The Heap of Sadness had diminished considerably, so I imagined a dump-run had occurred since my last visit. Where sprawling areas of typewriter scrap was before, boxes and crates replaced it. I still felt something for the poor, old machinery, but having seen the rate of its use in schools and in the streets, I had to again remind myself that the discards had probably served out the full extent of their lives and were happy to be in a typewriter graveyard, finally at rest. As industrious as I find the Indian people to be, I had to believe the scrap wasn't needless waste.

The same gentlemen working during my first visit were there and recognised Parkash and I. Sunil greeted us again and asked if I thought more about the typewriters I inspected before. I told him I'd take another look at the Brother, so he summoned one of his associates to fetch it. I also enquired about any other machines for sale that might have come in since my last visit. Unfortunately, none had, especially due to the Diwali festivities, so I was left with the same options I didn't feel strongly about in the first place. Still, I tried the Brother again and found that my absence did not, in fact, make my heart grow fonder and I rejected it again. I also tried the Olympia Traveller again out of guilt, but even at the reasonable price, I couldn't justify its purchase. I would again be leaving empty-handed. The next time I go abroad, I'll likely bring one of my typewriters.

After Parkash and I left Chawla Typewriters, there was little left to do but go to lunch. We went to another Asian restaurant so I could get my last meal of Indian cuisine. I don't think Parkash ate out as much as I liked to do on my visits to Delhi, so I wanted to treat us but especially as a thank-you to him for all the driving us around that he did. In all the rapid, confusing chaos of Delhi, to have someone like Parkash navigate, translate, and just accompany me was one of the greatest gifts I've been given as a foreign traveller.

Before I would be leaving to go back home, Parkash extended an invite to have me over to his family's new home in another part of Delhi for a home-cooked meal. His brother, Bhoopraj, was in Nepal with their mother, wives, and some of the children, so dinner would be spent with Parkash and Bhoopraj's sister and some of Parkash's nieces and nephews. He was excited to show me his family's new home and I was excited for the honour of spending time with his family again, even if all couldn't be in attendance. One hardly needs to twist my arm to come over for homemade

Indian cuisine either.

After Chawla Typewriters and lunch, Parkash had to get back to some fares he had for the day and other errands before dinner that night. He dropped me off at Malti's where I spent the rest of the afternoon reading and taking it easy after all the travel the day before. Scrappy Tom was pleased that I was back and that I remained seated for a decent amount of time for him to leech my lap warmth and cuddle up for a snooze. I was happy just to spend time with him—the most time I spent with any cat in India up to that point. Despite being feral, and the occasional rough play with my flesh, he really was a sweet cat and helped stave off any homesickness I felt for my own felines. A little heavy in the eyes from reading, I also snuck in a nap so I'd be well-rested for dinner.

❊ ❊ ❊

Parkash came to pick me up around 7:00 that night. Driving through the city at night as a passenger is always a remarkable thing because it's like viewing a documentary of all that is Delhi. It's a contradictory experience in that there is manic repetition, yet there is always something new and strange that demands attention for a stranger to this land. There were the usual fluorescent-lit shops, crowds of people overflowing sidewalks, petrol fumes, and ever-present street dust that wafted by in wakes of air. Beggars worked long into the night at the intersections—children in tattered clothes browned by sweat and dirt; little girls sometimes in dresses that were once nice, but now-soiled made them look like discarded dolls—and the occasional man urinating against a wall. There lingered remnants of Diwali: strung lights and marigold garlands on storefronts and homes, images of *diyas*, and festive banners. I wondered if there was after-Diwali sales specials because throngs of people in the busiest shopping areas reminded me of Black Friday mayhem.

We eventually turned down an alley through multi-storey dwellings, many draped with vertical strings of lights hanging from the rooftops. They were steady or blinking in a sequence like light dripping down. The farther down the alley we drove, the less the street noise I could hear; it was replaced by the sounds of the children playing out in the streets with toys they might have received for Diwali. As we came through, many stopped to wave or stare; a lot of them seemed to recognise Parkash and shouted at him and he responded with what sounded like salutations in Hindi. We stopped in front of a steep, almost 45-degree angle cement incline in front of his garage. It was the oddest little driveway I've ever seen leading into a garage—the incline was just a few feet long at the hypotenuse and too steep, in fact, to drive into the garage on. After I got out, Parkash switched off the engine to the tuk-tuk, then pushed it up this quick incline and into what was a spacious garage.

We ascended a long flight of stairs in a well-lit stairwell until we reached the next level where we removed our shoes at the top before entering. The kitchen and bedrooms were here and so were his nieces and nephews who played while his sister was in the kitchen preparing dinner. Parkash introduced me to everyone again; most of them I had seen on my last visit. Parkash's sister, Jamuna, also popped out of the kitchen for a moment to greet me shyly before returning to food preparation. Parkash took me into what looked like the master bedroom where the king-size bed sat in the centre and the armoire I remember from their last residence stood against the wall. We both took a seat on the bed while the children came in to see their uncle with the same enthusiasm that I remember having whenever my dad would get home from work and I'd want to tell him all about my day. Fluorescent light shone overhead as the kids scurried around and onto the bed to hug their uncle and gather around him and have a look at the guest in their home (that they may or may not have remembered) with little amused faces.

A few moments later, Jamuna brought out chai for Parkash and I before she receded back into the kitchen where I could hear sounds of clamouring dishes, chopping on a cutting board, and the faucet running on and off before the smell of cooking food began to waft from the kitchen. I could smell rice, curry (I guessed dahl), potatoes, and naan. I was excited to be accorded the repeat honour of dining with Parkash's family to eat homemade Indian cuisine. After all the Indian food I had eaten in restaurants both in The States and while in India, it never quite compares to the real thing in an Indian household—or, in this case, a Nepali household. While we waited for dinner to be served, Parkash had the kids practise their English by introducing themselves again, one by one. The youngest and newest of the family was not quite of speaking age yet but was sufficiently mobile to get into mischief. Parkash and I passed her back and forth as she scuttled along on hands and knees on the bed, stopping to laugh or shriek as the other kids playfully encouraged her.

Before long, dishes of food started coming out from the kitchen and were placed on a tray in the centre of the bed. My trained nose knew as everything was exactly what I had smelled during its making. I was asked to serve myself first and quickly made myself a bowl before Parkash helped the kids with their own and then his. I like preparing a pillow of rice upon which I put the dahl, leaving some on the side to scoop up with pieces of naan. Seasoned pieces of skinned potato also go on the side that I eat separately. The kids quieted down as they started eating their helpings next to Parkash and sitting back against the headboard. Soon we were all munching and chewing with delight. Like everyone else, I tried eating mostly with my hands using the naan to scoop up and bring food to my mouth while using a spoon I was given for an occasional assist. Jamuna stayed in the kitchen to eat and would now and then come in to check on portions in the serving dishes or bring fresh naan. Having tasted a little of everything, I had Parkash tell her how delicious I thought it all was and how it was the best way to enjoy my last dinner in India, at least for a while. I felt once again blessed to experience the pairing of excellent food and company in the home of my friend.

Naturally, I was the last to finish eating as I wanted to savour every bite because I knew I wouldn't get the opportunity like this for a while. I could, of course, attempt to recreate it myself, but the result of my efforts to do so would likely fall far short in comparison. The kids, like myself, were sufficiently stuffed and looked quite pleased.

After dinner, Parkash suggested we go to the rooftop where I could see the view of Delhi at night from there. We went up another level where we came out onto a spacious patio where laundry was neatly hung from clotheslines and there were pots and long planters with shrubs and flowering plants that looked meticulously cared for. Parkash said that this was where his mother did gardening. The view from up top was extraordinary. To one side, I could see miles and miles of Delhi all lit up and hear sounds of its city life in the distance. There was a haze in the air that was lit by all the strung lights below. I walked to the edge where there was a barrier around the rooftop and looked down at all the strings of lights hanging from other rooftops to the ground all the way up and down the alleyway. There were still children playing in the street below and made up much of the noise that I could hear within the immediate vicinity.

The opposite view of the city, strikingly, was dark, still, and quiet in which I couldn't detect the faintest of light. I asked Parkash what was over there in that great black void and he said, "That's the jungle." I was immediately enchanted by the fact that he and his family had the convenience of the city in one direction but a great big mystery of untamed land in the other. They were situated between two different worlds: wild known and the wild unknown. I stood there looking in the direction of the jungle and wished that I could have seen the detail of the intricate greenery, but it was yet another mystery of a city I had become familiar with, yet still knew so little about. As it was my last night in Delhi, it was like a subtle invitation to return and discover more.

After taking in rooftop views long enough to remember them, I looked around at the setup of their rooftop space and thought that it would have been one of the most magical places to have a fire pit, lounge chairs, s'mores, wine, and plenty of laughter and storytelling around the fire. It was truly a place for magnificent views and spending quality time with dear ones. It was one of the best of final nights I could possibly spend in a foreign country before journeying back home.

Before going back inside, I noticed little legged things clinging to the walls that housed the stairwell leading to the roof. Once I got close enough, I could see that they were green, big-eyed geckoes that clung to the walls with their adhesive pads. There were a few of them out that were cleverly positioned closest to the sources of light so that they might snatch up the insects attracted to that light. They were the most adorable little things and I realised were the same geckoes I saw under the stairwell light at Malti's. I got close enough to see the detail of their minutely scaly bodies, but once I got too close, they moved to hiding quick as a flash of light. It was amazing how much distance they could cover between blinks of the human eye. I was so amused by this gecko species I had never seen before that I wanted to stay put to witness their activity, but I realised that my presence was depriving them of their evening meal, so I appreciated the bit of them I was able to see before Parkash and I went back inside.

The evening was turning into the late night and there was the long ride back to Malti's where I still had to pack and clean my room. My layover flight to Dubai would be leaving at 10:35 the next morning, so it would have been too much to ask of Parkash to drive me back to Malti's since he was picking me up bright and early for the trip to the airport. Instead, he was kind enough to drive me to the nearest busy intersection where I could order an *Uber* ride. This was the most ideal arrangement considering the time and that Parkash was already home with his family for the night.

It was a short visit at Parkash's new home and with just a few of his family members this time, but to be a guest for any length of time is always an honour. After the hearty meal, I noticed the kids were mellowing down and it seemed bedtime was not far off. Before slipping my shoes back on at the landing, I said goodbye to the kids, wondering how much bigger they might all be the next time I saw them. Jamuna, still tidying up in the kitchen, stepped out to see me off at which point I thanked her for the delicious meal and her hospitality. I parted with "Namaste" before Parkash and I headed downstairs to the tuk-tuk.

I helped Parkash manually back the tuk-tuk out of the garage into the alley that had now grown quiet. The children who were playing there when we arrived must have gone in to eat before preparing for bed like Parkash's nieces and nephews upstairs. Streetlamps lit the way as we drove out to the street. When we got to the intersection Parkash had in mind, I pulled out my phone to book an *Uber* ride through the app. At first, I wasn't getting a sufficient signal. I walked around a little at the corner where we had stopped with the hope of catching a better signal, but I was in a dead zone. Parkash was fiddling with his phone too when he remembered that his came with a hot spot feature, so he turned it on so I could find it on my phone and gave me the password so I could access. It worked. I had plenty of signal now to get a ride booked and a driver headed in my direction. I was panicked before that because I didn't want to inconvenience Parkash any further. I also don't think he would have left until I had secured a ride back. With a driver now on the way with an ETA of roughly 15 minutes, I felt more comfortable, but Parkash still chose to stay until the car arrived.

I only remember precisely where we were because of the *Uber* record which was with a driver named Alok in a Toyota Etios. I had become amused with booking *Uber*s in Delhi because I was usually familiar with the make of vehicle, but never the model when I read what was on its way in the ride confirmation. I suppose I could have just Googled, but I'd usually just wait to see what pulled up. Parkash and I waited at a corner of what was shown as Arora Niwas, A-36, A-Block, Vikaspuri, Delhi which, of course, really means nothing, but it's probably not a spot I'd want to be alone in at night. By the looks of it, Parkash probably knew that and is why he stayed.

At the corner, there was a short block wall that curved around on the innermost side of the sidewalk. In my idling boredom, I walked over to see what was on the other side. The wall barely came up to my waist and there were small trees and shrubs that looked to be struggling to survive in the gravely sand they were growing in. I then caught a whiff of that dirt patch which reeked of urine. I couldn't really see much else but dirt, nor did I care to know what else was down there, but it was basically a human litter box. I looked around and couldn't see anyone living on the streets, but that isn't to say there wasn't. I stepped away, blinking hard at the smell, and walked to the left of the corner where I could see street-side stores illuminated by fluorescent lights—two or three of them—just across a small asphalt lot.

Parkash was leaning against the tuk-tuk as he checked his phone when I walked back over. The intersection was more of a two-way road with offset cross streets under an overpass, so there was the noise of passing vehicles going left and right at ground level and the echoing whoosh sounds of cars and lorries above us. There were some street lights, but it wasn't terribly bright out. I finally had to look up the Toyota Etios (a small, four-door sedan similar to the Yaris) so I could keep my eyes peeled for my ride.

When impatience began to set in (I was more concerned with Parkash feeling that he had to stay than I was with getting myself back; I'd figure it out if the car didn't show), I saw what looked like a little Etios coming from the opposite side of the road from the right. It was going slower than the rest of the vehicles and I saw the driver looking in our general direction, so I waved him over. He passed us, but then I looked down the road to the left and could see that he was doing a U-turn to make it to our side. When he pulled up just before the corner, he rolled down his window, looking confused. Parkash went over to talk to him and must have explained that it was just me as the only fare considering the two of us standing there with a tuk-tuk probably looked strange. After their exchange, I hugged Parkash, thanked him for another lovely visit, and agreed that I'd see him early in the morning for the drive to the airport. I was glad Parkash was now able to get back home to his family and enjoy the rest of his night.

It was another long ride without conversation back to Anand Lok with my head against the window in phases of staring at all that we passed by and occasionally nodding off. The heavy meal—copious amounts of it—put me in a state of just wanting to go straight to bed when I got back, and not worry about cleaning and packing until the morning. Parkash would be picking me up at 7:00 a.m., so I knew I had to at least pack before bed or be mostly packed before I called it a night. Cleaning and tidying up would be best left to do right before departure after getting myself ready in the morning for the long journey home.

I started wondering if Raju had finished my last batch of laundry, but I knew he knew that I would be leaving in the morning, so I decided not to worry about it. What I did worry about (and I only realised this then) was that the poor bugger, or the other lady I would sometimes see providing domestic help, had to hand-wash my underwear before hanging them up from the rooftop for all the colony to see. *Oh Jesus*, I thought, also realising why they had that air-dried roughness not otherwise felt when underwear is dryer-tumbled. I couldn't decide if it was more undignified for whomever washed my underwear or for me. I giggled under my breath in amusement and nodded off again.

When I got back to Malti's, both she and Monica were still up, so I visited briefly with Malti before she was about to head inside for bed. Malti tended to sleep in past the time I'd be leaving for the airport, so we knew we likely wouldn't see one another in the morning. Monica, the night owl, likely wouldn't be up that early either, but she still insisted on seeing me before I left and said to knock as I was heading out so we could exchange a final goodbye.

I had my packing and tidying up to do so we made our final visit short as it was already past 11:00. Before Malti went inside for the night, she gave me a hug and wished me a safe trip back home. Monica went into her apartment shortly after and reminded me to make sure to knock on her door in the morning.

When I went back inside, I noticed that my last batch of laundry had been delivered as it sat there neatly folded on the bed. I smiled and stood there looking around the room imagining all the bustling around, contemplating, and dreaming I had done in that little space over the past two weeks. How had it all come to an end so quickly? I lamented for the time passed but I also felt profoundly changed by it in ways that I knew wouldn't reveal themselves in their fullest until I was back home and immersed in the mundane reality I was relieved of for those two weeks. I was already changed, more enlightened, better educated, and informed in large and small measures after my first two journeys to India. I wondered what new metamorphosis awaited me after living in this country for these two weeks.

Rather than continuing to stand there to reminisce and worry about what obligations awaited me back home, I pulled out my luggage and started to pack everything for the long hours back to The States and set out an outfit to travel in the next day. Packing what I originally brought was the easy part but, as always, figuring out how to fit all the shopping was like Tetris, the challenging part. I usually end up unbagging everything and reconfiguring after taking inventory of it all, determining that the most fragile of things go next to the clothes while things like stacks of paper can go on top. It wasn't just the strategic packing placement of items, but a strange impulse to want to recount each moment had and with whom the experiences were had at the time each thing was bought.

Just as I was finishing up with packing, I heard a familiar voice outside. It was the little tiger himself, Scrappy Tom. I looked over to my right from an already overstuffed suitcase and saw his little meat head staring at me through the screen and uttering his low meows. "I don't think there's enough room left in here for you to come with me, buddy," I said. As soon as I spoke, he spoke louder, so I walked over to greet him at the door. I had never let him in the room during my stay, but since it was my last night, I slid the screen open and invited him in. He sniffed at the entrance for a few seconds before extending his long legs inside and started doing a slow sniff-about, checking under the bed, around the little blue table near the kitchenette, and finally in the bathroom. I left the screen open so he could leave of his own accord while I finished my packing, preparations for the morning, and tidying up.

Scrappy Tom had been a pleasant little companion for me while staying at Malti's, so I thought inviting him in might allow him to sense that I was leaving soon rather than rudely disappear on him the next day. Since this place was an Airbnb, I imagined he'd seen many visitors come and go; maybe some liked him and others not; maybe he had made similar determinations about those visitors. Despite his wild nature, he felt like a chum and I was sad to be leaving him.

As I finished packing, I looked around and noticed that there was no sight of Scrappy Tom. I looked under the bed and in the bathroom but couldn't find him and determined that he had left for the night. I closed and latched the doors and slid the screen shut, thinking that that was perhaps the last I might see of Scrappy Tom on this trip. There was always the possibility of seeing him in the morning after he came back from his nocturnal prowl, but I considered that the last visit and prepared to shower and head to bed.

❊ ❊ ❊

In the morning, I was up early, showered again for good measure because I wouldn't get another in the next 24 hours or so, and did some last-minute cleaning to ensure the room looked better than I found it. The last of things went into luggage and I managed to zip up the suitcases right before Parkash messaged to say that he was 15 minutes out. It allowed me just enough time to set out my luggage and carry-ons and have a seat in the garden one final time.

It was still somewhere between night and day, the air was cooler and a little heavier with morning moisture, and the waking birds were still louder than the few passing autos on August Kranti Marg. Sadly, there was no sign of Scrappy Tom. I imagined he was finishing his night shift and would eventually be home for his daytime nap but likely after I had already gone. Our little visit the night before was memorable enough before he set off into the night to be the wild cat that he is.

Shortly before the 15 minutes had passed before Parkash's arrival, I walked across the courtyard to knock on Monica's door. A moment later, she opened the door, still in her pajamas and a little bleary-eyed, but she greeted me warmly when I said, "Good morning!" as cheerfully as I could, but with a tone of disappointment over my departure. "Parkash is almost here, so I'm off," I added. In a weary morning voice, Monica expressed joy in the company we shared and wished me a safe journey home. "I didn't see Scrappy Tom this morning," I said, "but he did pay me a visit last night by coming in while I packed. Give him some pets for me when you see him next." "Oh, I will," Monica replied, smiling. She looked out into the courtyard behind me and said,

"Yeah, where is that silly boy?"

I heard Parkash's tuk-tuk pull up in front of the driveway and Raju walked over to say, "Parkash" informatively before walking back to the gate to open it. "Well, give me one last hug," Monica said. "I'm going to go back to sleep some more, but we'll keep in touch through *Facebook*, yeah?" "I would love that," I said before waving her goodbye as she shut her door. I walked back over to the patio outside my room to retrieve my luggage, looked around again, and off I went.

I stepped outside the gate to see Parkash waiting outside his tuk-tuk and he walked up to grab my suitcases to load them into the backseat. Parkash and Raju also exchanged greetings and waves before Parkash took my things down the driveway. I wasn't sure how much he would understand, but before Raju closed the gate, I thanked him for all his attentiveness during my stay and shook his hand in gratitude. He shook his head and smiled before saying, "Goodbye" and waved as I headed down the driveway. His simple acknowledgement was good enough for me.

I gave Parkash a big good-morning hug, got in, and we were off. I looked back up at the gate, now closed, and at Malti's house with the 'BHANDARI' plaque by the call box before we started moving and sight of her house slipped by, then disappeared. I sat there, one arm over my stacked luggage on the seat next to me, not exactly sure how I felt about going home. The morning was again murky with a mixture of fog and smoke and the usual carbon emissions, so that had me thinking about the crisp, clean air of the Pacific Northwest and, for a moment, had me feeling slightly more anticipatory, but not entirely without melancholy about returning to all that was familiar.

Instead of taking the metro as we had done to and from the airport for my trip to Kathmandu, Parkash informed me that he would be driving me the distance to the airport parking lot where we would park the tuk-tuk and shuttle in to the terminal by bus as we had done for my arrival. I was warmed by this because it was a little more extra time with my friend before I would be gone again until an unknown time. There was very little speaking though as Parkash and I were still waking up for the day. I snacked on some of the dried fruits and nuts I still had and I looked forward to getting my first coffee of the day once I was checked-in at the airport.

On the ride to the airport, I fished through my carry-on for my passport and sorted through my wallet to see where I was with dollars. I noticed that I still had some rupees left; not an amount worth converting back into dollars, but it was enough to make someone on the streets feel a great deal happier. We were in the general vicinity of Connaught Place, so I told Parkash I'd want to stop soon to give away my remaining rupees. He told me to let him know when to stop. After a few minutes, I saw a poorly-looking old woman sitting on a blanket by herself on the sidewalk outside a roundabout. There was just enough time to pull over in the little traffic there was across the street from her. Parkash waited in the idling tuk-tuk while I dashed out and ran across the street to approach the woman. She looked up and saw me coming, at which point I could see her in more detail. She sat on a modest blanket with just a few small belongings like a knapsack and her sandals positioned to one side. She wore a very ordinary kurti—colourful and perhaps cotton but slightly dirtied from time spent on the streets. She wore a scarf around her shoulders, was thin, dark, and sunken in her wrinkled cheeks, and had greying hair tied in a bun at the back of her head. I wasn't sure if she knew any English, but I stepped onto the sidewalk and slowly approached with the cash in my hand and gave it to her saying, "Here, I thought you might need this." She took it gratefully, extended her other hand out to hold mine like a grandmother might with her grandchild, and softly said, *"Dhanyavaad…dhanyavaad"* with an expression of desperate, elated gratitude. I stepped away, said, "Namaste" with my hands together and waved her goodbye before I turned to dash across the street again. As soon as I was seated in the tuk-tuk, I waved at her once more as Parkash started to pull away. "You did a good thing," Parkash said, looking over his shoulder at me.

When we reached the departures area at Indira Gandhi International Airport, check-in time for my flight had already begun, but my flight for Dubai would not be leaving for another two hours. The airport was just as crowded as always with the comings and goings of the most diverse crowd of people from all over the world. Most airports, of course, are a snapshot of a wide spectrum of people but this South Asian airport, like Tribhuvan International Airport in Kathmandu, is a fascinating, scintillating display of people. For those who had the time to wonder, I was curious what they thought of me as someone clearly from an entirely different part of the world. Ultimately, we're all just one big rushed mix of humans in a vast transient place.

Goodbyes are never easy, especially when you have to say it to a dear friend you know is like an extension of family despite the blur of living your own separate lives halfway across the world. Of course, there's *Facebook* and *WhatsApp*, but nothing compares to the time spent in person where you don't miss any of the nuances in expression, inflections in speech, laughter, and existing in the other's culture while learning significantly from one another. Yet, you both are perfectly ordinary people living each day extraordinarily because of the fine juxtaposition of differences and similarities. The only easy part about saying goodbye to Parkash was that I knew we'd just pick up where we left off the next time we saw one another like we did this time. That's lifelong friendship.

We stood there in the middle of the bustling crowd of people rolling and carrying their luggage here and there and the echoing noise of taxis and vans dropping off passengers, and the hum of foreign languages. I stalled a bit to ramble on about the experiences had and mostly my gratitude for Parkash for helping me make those experiences happen and to enjoy many with him. When I finally lamented over returning to the ordinary, I decided to end on a happier note and say, "This is just bye-for-now, you know" and gave my friend a hug before parting with my luggage into the line for passport verification and then was eventually enveloped by the crowds in the terminal. Once inside, I looked back and saw Parkash still standing there, so we exchanged waves before we were out of one another's sight…until our next meeting.

Once I took a seat at the appropriate gate after check-in, luggage check, and security, I mulled over thoughts with a fresh cup of coffee in-hand. I recounted the entire journey in fine detail, sometimes probably just looking off into space while the seats around me seemed surprisingly fuller every time I happened to look back up out of my reminiscent haze. I would think about this trip, then the two before it, then about how they all fit together. There was so much seen, done, and people met—all within a relatively short distance travelled. I knew with absolute certainty that this would not be the last time I saw India and Nepal; both held many more wonders for me to see and perhaps yet more extraordinary souls who would change my life.

After three trips around the globe within two years, wanderlust was quickly becoming a drug I couldn't withdraw myself from for long. I was glad and felt fortunate that India was the first overseas country I visited, followed by neighbouring Nepal. I was shaken at first, placed entirely out of my comfort zone, but this is what makes a sleeping soul come alive with wonder. When you go to places that make you feel entirely stripped bare of all the familiar comforts you had before you took that leap, you are preparing yourself—consciously or subconsciously—for enlightenment, but only if you make the choice to let it influence you rather than resist it. It is important to remember: while in mysterious places, there is no time like the present. You must appreciate every moment in extraordinary places because how you decide to live those moments will define your regrets and your memories.

Waiting there for my plane, I continued to wonder about the time I had and about the world at-large. Where to next? If one can brave the cultural, environmental, and social differences of India and Nepal and reflect on those experiences fondly and with an eagerness to love more, risk more, and see more of what's outside of my perceived comfort, what further wonders might I experience from the potential wealth of enlightenment still to be discovered?

A betterment of self and an enriched understanding of the world I live in meant getting myself to the next destination I knew nothing about and throwing myself enthusiastically into it. The truth of the matter is: I learned to feel more at home in the most unusual places.

A room to remember.

Scrappy Tom.

Adarsh Typewriters in Connaught Place.

Relics in repose.

Learning to touch type.

Street typist using a Godrej & Boyce typewriter.

Sidewalk along Asaf Ali Road leading to the entrance of Chawla Typewriters.

Entrance to the stairwell leading to Chawla Typewriters.

The Heap of Sadness.

School children.

School children.

A package of marigolds with a nimbu-mirchi totka.

Entrance to the wedding venue.

The beginning of baraat.

Lanterns of baraat.

"My halter is itchy. Is yours?"

Ashish on his carriage.

Caterers-in-waiting.

Caterers-in-waiting.

Awaiting the groom.

Ashish's arrival.

(from left) Meera, friend, Neena, Saumya, and Dia.

Baraati *dancers.*

Photo ops with the groom.

Shruti's procession.

A look worth a thousand words.

Varmala.

A private dinner.

Preparation for Ashish's vows.

Ashish taking vows.

Ashish and Shruti taking vows.

Ashish and Shruti taking vows.

A potter demonstrating his craft.

A Diwali market at night.

(from left) Malti and Sharmeen on the night of Diwali.

(from left) Sharmeen, Raju, and Malti.

Diya and marigolds.

A beautiful puja *display.*

(from left) Monica and Malti.

Diwali delovelies.

A neighbour girl with a sparkler.

Expecto Patronum.

A neighbour's diya *display.*

Diyas.

Street explosives.

Views of Kathmandu from The Alliance Hotel.

Views of Kathmandu from The Alliance Hotel.

Good day for drying laundry.

Nepalis at the neighbourhood bamboo swing.

The neighbourhood bamboo swing.

Pranil reaching for great heights.

A curious little Nepali girl.

A neighbourhood cow, adorned with marigold garlands.

Youth dancing in the streets.

Rebuilding efforts underway.

Entrance to a camp for victims of the 2015 Gorkha earthquake.

A makeshift camp dwelling.

Camp school.

Young ladies who gave me a tour of the camp.

Young football fans.

Temple monkeys.

Enjoying spiritual monkey thoughts.

Monkeys over remnant earthquake wreckage.

A Buddhist monk outside the stupa.

The Bauddha Stupa.

One of the many displays of tealights at the stupa.

Brilliant colour in unusual places.

Beads as "...a reflection of the colourful city itself."

Walking Bauddhanath Sadak/Bauddha-Jorpati Road.

A diverse crowd and collection of shops around the stupa.

One of the many mandala displays outside the Bauddha Stupa.

The Lama family and I.

Earthquake damage in Durbar Square.

Earthquake damage in Durbar Square.

A view of Kathmandu Valley (or Nepal Valley, Nepa Valley).

Acknowledgements

I would like to first and foremost thank my immediate family (especially my mother, Carol Ochs, for taking the time to proofread and edit this book) and my friends and colleagues who expressed continued interest in the book's progress. You encouraged me to keep writing despite the challenges and sacrifices of learning commitment and dedication to my first book.

Thank you to Parveen Kumar for being the first of the Delhi locals I encountered when I set out to explore the city on my own. I was in India for the first time for only a few hours and you made me feel welcome there.

Thank you to Stacy Mann who introduced me to Neena Pawar through *Facebook* which subsequently led to meeting Neena in person. Neena, you were the first person I met in your family and I am grateful for your kindness to include me in family events—birthdays, gatherings, weddings—and making me feel like family. Thank you to Virender Pawar for your intellect, insight, and inclusion. Thank you to Rita Kathju for your thorough critique of this book, your stories, and our discussions both in person and online about a wide variety of topics related to Indian culture. Thank you to Meera Butalia for your kindness and support.

Thank you to Malti and Monica Bhandari for your warmth, welcome, and hospitality. Being a guest at your home for my first Airbnb experience was everything I could have hoped for and more. It was the perfect place for a solitary traveller like myself. I wanted to experience what it was like to live like an honourary citizen and you helped me do that.

I would like to thank the late Martha Gellhorn whose complexity of observation in her book, *Travels with Myself and Another*, and her other works inspired me to be as detailed and honest in my writing. I aspire to continue travelling the world like you, to bear witness to all that I can, and to write (with my typewriters, if possible) about it with as much soul. Your remarkable 20th Century life has greatly influenced mine in the 21st.

Tremendous gratitude goes out to Justin Bullard who introduced me to the Lama family in Kathmandu. Making this connection for me made my short time spent in Nepal an enriching experience by having seen and done more with the Lama family than I would have on my own. Thank you, Justin, for taking the time to read through my account of Kathmandu and for providing thorough, valuable input on the same. One day, we'll travel back to Nepal together.

I will be forever grateful to the Lama family, especially Mari, Tanya, and Pranil, who made my first trip to Nepal extraordinary. I was merely a friend-of-a-friend, but you welcomed me, with *khata* scarf and all, like a member of the family. It was a tremendous honour to be welcomed into your home, included in your festivities, and given tours around Kathmandu—experiences I will never forget.

Many thanks to Bhoopraj Sharma for your kindness and willingness to proofread (and, at times, make vital corrections) parts of *Into the East* while it was still very much in the form of articles. Your input is greatly appreciated.

Last, but not least, I would like to thank Parkash Sharma—to whom this book is dedicated—for being a tremendous part of my experiences in Delhi. You are a frequent presence in this book and the heart of it. You helped make it possible for me to see everyday life in Delhi, away from the tourism, and closer to sights and surroundings that coloured my time spent in a foreign country. I am honoured to have your friendship. *Shukriya.*

Biography

Originally from San Diego, California, Christopher Ochs currently lives in Redmond, Washington with his two cats, Arthur and Gwen. While occupied with full-time work as a senior paralegal and project manager at Microsoft, Christopher is also an antiques enthusiast, crafter, blogger, and traveller. His amassed antique and vintage typewriters are his favourite writing tools with which he composes letters to friends and family and drafts all his article and book manuscripts on.

To create a necessary balance with his work in the Legal industry, Christopher began delving into his creative interests in 2009 and has broadened those interests to include crocheting, knitting, spinning (yarn), weaving, photography, typewriters, and, above all, writing. Christopher periodically posts blog articles about said interests, road trips, current events, and anything else that strikes his fancy. You can visit his blog at http://christopherochs.wordpress.com.

With a strong curiosity for the world around him, Christopher has a special passion for travel writing and journalism. It is in this debut book, *Into the East: Three Journeys Through India & Nepal*, that he wished to blend the two forms of writing that will hopefully be the first of others. Christopher prefers writing non-fiction but one day writing short fiction or novels based on his world travels is not out of the question.

www.ingramcontent.com/pod-product-compliance
Lightning Source LLC
Chambersburg PA
CBHW052052110526
44591CB00013B/2176